UNDER A WATCHFUL EY

UNDER A WATCHFUL EYE

Privacy Rights and Criminal Justice

William P. Bloss

Foreword by Rolando V. del Carmen

PRAEGER
An Imprint of ABC-CLIO, LLC

A B C C L I O

Santa Barbara, California • Denver, Colorado • Oxford, England

Library of Congress Cataloging-in-Publication Data

Bloss, William P. (William Paul)
   Under a watchful eye : privacy rights and criminal justice / William P. Bloss ;
   foreword by Rolando V. del Carmen.
     p. cm.
   Includes bibliographical references and index.
   ISBN 978–0–275–99406–8 (hard copy : alk. paper) — ISBN 978–1–57356–990–3 (ebook)
   1. Criminal justice, Administration of—United States. 2. Privacy, Right of—United States. I. Title.
KF9223.B56   2009
342.7308'58—dc22   2009011681

13 12 11 10 9   1 2 3 4 5

This book is also available on the World Wide Web as an eBook.
Visit www.abc-clio.com for details.

ABC-CLIO, LLC
130 Cremona Drive, P.O. Box 1911
Santa Barbara, California 93116-1911

This book is printed on acid-free paper ∞

Manufactured in the United States of America

CONTENTS

Foreword *by Rolando V. del Carmen*   vii

Acknowledgments   xi

Introduction   xiii

1.   Privacy in Search of Meaning   1

2.   Government Power to Search   15

3.   Investigating Suspects Wherever Found   31

4.   Final Verdict on Defendant Rights   87

5.   Being Watched on the Job   123

6.   Protecting Crime Victims   149

7.   Surveillance of Nontraditional Suspects   159

8.   Navigating the New Privacy Paradigm   185

Notes   195

Select Bibliography   225

Index   239

FOREWORD

The right to privacy is often controversial and highly litigated. That reality will likely intensify in the years to come as courts seek to strike a balance between individual rights and societal preservation in the face of mounting dangers occasioned by domestic crime and the War on Terror. The stakes are high for both parties. The government must maintain peace and order in the face of new dangers bred by ever-changing and sophisticated technology. Those well-meaning and needed efforts, however, are sometimes waged at the expense of individual rights, be that of offenders or innocent members of the public whom the government is sworn to protect. The clash of concerns will continue as a reasonable accommodation is sought between the proper exercise of state power and respect for individual rights.

The right to privacy is best defined as "encompassing various rights recognized to be inherent in [the] concept of ordered liberty, and such right prevents governmental interference in intimate personal relationships or activities, freedoms of individual to make fundamental choices involving himself, his family, and his relationship with others."[1] The more trenchant definition from the same source, however, states that the right to privacy is the right to be "let alone." In criminal justice and in democratic societies, this means individuals are free to do as they wish, particularly in the inner sanctums of their own homes. This denotes being left alone by the government as long as the individual does not intrude into the rights of or endanger others. There are instances, however, when governmental intrusion is justified and necessary because the absence of intervention jeopardizes peace and order to an intolerable extent. In these cases, what standards and guidelines are used by the courts to maintain a fair balance between individual rights and societal preservation? This is an issue with which the courts have wrestled for years and not always with authoritative results.

As this book notes, the right to privacy is not expressly guaranteed in the American Bill of Rights. This was no careless omission by the Framers of the Constitution. Instead, it manifested an awareness among the wise Framers that certain rights needed no guarantees because they were so fundamental as to make their guarantee superfluous. In *Griswold v. Connecticut* (1965), the United States

Supreme Court said that "specific guarantees in the Bill of Rights have penumbras, formed by emanations from those guarantees that help give them life and substance."[2] The Court added that various constitutional rights create zones of privacy, meaning that various provisions in the Bill of Rights assumed the existence of the right to privacy. It concluded by saying, "We deal with a right of privacy older than the Bill of Rights—older than our political parties, older than our school system."[3] In sum, the right to privacy was deemed so fundamental it needed no reiteration even in the Constitution. No right can be more fundamental or as sacred as that.

The right to privacy has been the subject and theme of many law books and journal articles. There is not much in the legal literature, however, that discuss the right to privacy as it specifically relates to criminal justice. This paucity is perhaps best explained by the often-assumed relationship between the right to privacy and the Fourth Amendment prohibition against unreasonable searches and seizures. It is sometimes assumed by legal scholars and litigants that the Fourth Amendment right preempts the right to privacy and thus supersedes its use in criminal justice cases. As this book illustrates, however, although the right to privacy is implicit in Fourth Amendment cases, it encompasses a much broader field than searches and seizures. It includes such concerns as rights of employees, crime victims, and surveillance of "nontraditional suspects." Given its vast and still expanding coverage, the right to privacy will doubtless assume greater urgency in modern society as basic rights are refined by court decisions in the face of evolving technology.

This book addresses issues in privacy rights as they relate to criminal justice. In the words of the author, its purpose is "to examine not only the conceptual but also the practical aspects of the privacy–criminal justice relationship as it considers the operational practices of the three criminal justice subsystems— police, courts, and corrections." It is true, as the author maintains, that "nowhere in the function of government are privacy rights more vulnerable than in the processes of criminal justice." It is time that these important issues be explored within the more narrow confines of criminal justice and as they affect both "consumers" and professionals.

The writer should know whereof he speaks. Professor William P. Bloss is a former law enforcement officer and currently Professor of Criminal Justice at The Citadel in Charleston, South Carolina. He writes on the right to privacy from two perspectives: as a former police officer who often sought to limit that right in the interest of law enforcement and then as an academic who views rights from a more detached, reflective, and analytical tangent. This practitioner-academic background enables him to discuss the subject with a balanced view that is useful for students, law enforcement personnel, and those serving the criminal justice system. Toward the end of the book he states that "a new privacy paradigm has emerged that has changed the balance between police powers and citizen privacy protections." He identifies those as the rapid advances in technology and the events of 9/11. He then concludes that these conditions have "dramatically altered the dynamics between individual privacy rights and criminal justice functions." This is a conclusion worth noting as we face a future where both realities the author identifies will likely be with us for years to come.

The traditional standard academics use to measure whether a book or article is worth writing or reading is whether it represents a lasting contribution to current literature in the discipline. This book certainly does that and in the process enriches an otherwise barren field. Professor Bloss deserves praise for a scholarly work that is analytical, informative, and readable. Hopefully, this book will force the criminal justice community of students and professionals to take a more focused look at an important and still evolving constitutional right that will assume even greater significance as we face technological changes and an uncertain future.

Rolando V. del Carmen
Distinguished Professor of Criminal Justice (Law) and
Regents Professor
College of Criminal Justice
Sam Houston State University

ACKNOWLEDGMENTS

A number of people have been instrumental in bringing this project to fruition and to whom I am indebted. I express my sincere appreciation to the talented staff at ABC-Clio. I am especially grateful to Senior Editor Suzanne Staszak-Silva who patiently and skillfully guided this project, and its author, from inception to completion.

I wish to acknowledge the assistance of the academic community in my professional development. To my mentor and friend Professor Rolando V. del Carmen, who continues to inspire students and colleagues alike, I convey my genuine thanks for your many contributions. I also appreciate The Citadel Foundation's long-standing support of my scholarly endeavors.

It is with deep gratitude and affection that I dedicate this book to those who have been my strength. In loving memory of my parents Charles L. and Mary Alice Bloss, who shaped my life beyond measure. I respectfully express my heartfelt appreciation and trust that the person I have become honors your efforts. Likewise, I voice my admiration and devoted love for my wife, Martha, who provides unwavering support and gives my life meaning. Finally, I profess my adoration for our son, Paul, and canine companions who enrich me in countless ways.

INTRODUCTION

The makers of the Constitution . . . conferred against the Government, the right to be let alone—the most comprehensive of rights and the right most valued by civilized men.
  —Justice Louis Brandeis in *Olmstead v. United States* (1928)[1]

Rudolph Lee pointed a gun at shop owner Ralph Watkinson and ordered him not to move. Lee planned to rob him; however, Watkinson was also armed and the two exchanged gunfire. When the robbery attempt failed, Lee fled the store and was later arrested eight blocks away with a gunshot wound in his chest. In the hospital Lee was identified as the suspected robber. The police asked the court to issue a search warrant authorizing the surgical removal of the bullet. Though Lee opposed the surgery, a Virginia state court issued a warrant authorizing the evidence collection. A unanimous U.S. Supreme Court disagreed and found that the state lacked a compelling need to use such intrusive measures to obtain criminal evidence. Justice William Brennan wrote "a compelled surgical intrusion into an individual's body for evidence, however, implicates expectations of privacy and security of such magnitude that the intrusion may be 'unreasonable' even if likely to produce evidence of a crime."[2]

As this case illustrates, a fundamental right to privacy is deeply rooted in American law and frequently implicated in the administration of criminal justice. Yet, the right to privacy theory existed long before the founding of the United States. Early societies recognized the need for protection against unwanted interference and intrusion. Self-determination became central to liberty and privacy interests and continues to be today. Even though it is an accepted premise that every person wants privacy, pinning down a definition of the concept with any precision has proven difficult. As one writer commented, "Privacy is a concept in disarray. Nobody can articulate what it means."[3] Explaining the meaning of privacy, and its scope, has always been a formidable challenge for jurists and legal experts. Hence, privacy concepts have continued to evolve from early common law to present. This, in part, is because the ideas are conceptually abstract and often do not achieve a clearer meaning until they are converted into written constitutional or statutory rights.

Because of its amorphous nature, there are numerous classification schemes that strive to construct the ideal taxonomy of privacy. What they share in common are characteristics of the human experience that deserve privacy protection such as autonomy, free choice, control over oneself, relationship with others, expression, and movement. Subsumed under these categories are other important self representations such as identity, reputation, and communication. In 1890, Samuel D. Warren and Louis D. Brandeis asserted that privacy is simply the "right to be let alone."[4]

Another obstacle to capturing a clear meaning of privacy is that its interpretation is subjective and depends on the context in which it is framed. The connotation of privacy is subject to political, legal, social, and cultural influences. Its content and importance hinge on the way it is defined and the relative value placed on a right to privacy by a society. Cultural norms governing social interactions, personal relations, and behavioral roles will affect the way privacy is viewed.[5] As a result, the concept of personal privacy varies across nations, cultures, and time periods.

The earliest mention of a privacy right is found among religious scriptures and communal law.[6] In essence, the principle protects members of the community from unwelcome interference or intrusion into their personal affairs. The fundamental ideals of safety, equity, and privacy created a framework for subsequent codified written laws designed to promote individual safeguards and collective peace. Beginning in A.D. 1066, the English common law incorporated principles of human and civil rights, and among those was personal privacy.[7] Since the United States inherited its legal tradition and criminal justice model from the English, it is there one discovers the origins of our legal customs and civil liberties.

PRIVACY RIGHTS IN AMERICAN LAW

The desire to make independent personal decisions, free from government interference, was described as a fundamental right in early English common law. Americans not only adopted the notion but fiercely defend their right to be free from unwarranted official intervention. Even those unfamiliar with the intricacies of law are able to articulate their inviolate right to make their own choices.

The Framers of the Constitution were dedicated to protecting citizens from a domineering federal government.[8] Though disagreement existed among the Constitution's founders, they, nonetheless, purposely placed limitations on the government. The Bill of Rights guaranteed citizens specific safeguards to prevent the government from overextending its authority.

Not all of the intended civil protections, however, were plainly stated in the Amendment's language. For instance, no specific right to privacy was included in the Bill of Rights. Instead, the right was implied as one of several civil liberties. Yet as the title aptly depicts, the Bill of Rights was intended to embody certain inviolate common law principles, including privacy, among the named rights. Principal writers such as James Madison argued that the Bill of Rights should include "certain great rights" to protect citizens from government.[9] In this case, the legal disputes center on the detail since debate about which guarantees should be included, and their meaning, continues today.

Many legal experts agree, however, that in spite of a lack of clarity in the wording, the right to privacy is firmly vested in American civil and criminal law.[10] Clearly, the founders meant to include a right to privacy among American constitutional liberties.[11] Although it took many years for privacy law to develop its own set of principles, as the doctrine evolved the intent of the Framers became evident.

There is an important difference between privacy as a concept versus a right. Daniel J. Solove, Marc Rotenberg, and Paul M. Schwartz find "privacy as a concept involves what privacy entails and how it is to be valued. Privacy as a right involves the extent to which privacy is (and should be) legally protected."[12] Another important feature is the dichotomy between a liberty and a right. The differentiation has been explained as "[liberty] is the absence of restrictions upon what a person wants to do," whereas "rights . . . protect liberty and the authority of government [from intruding] into lives and are the most basic freedoms protected by the U.S. Constitution."[13] There are two significant impediments to a clear understanding of American privacy doctrine. First, its principles commingle and therefore must be understood within the context of a larger body of constitutional rights. Second, the meaning of privacy stems from broad concepts entwined through much of the jurisprudence. Fortunately, as privacy rights are outlined in case and codified law, they become more discernable.

Privacy jurisprudence consists of legal principles and guidelines constructed from American constitutional, statutory, and case law. Early on, courts were not interested in dealing with privacy issues; however, legal practitioners in the 1800s prodded them into eventually wrestling with the concepts. Conversely, protecting criminal defendants had always been a high priority when it came to constitutional safeguards. For the courts, an equitable balance was sought between the need to protect society from criminals and maintaining a rule of law system that respected individual rights. The new American government established a tripart criminal justice apparatus of police, court, and correction units to apprehend, adjudicate, and punish criminal offenders.

The founders of the democracy understood that criminal justice processes, more than any other, could impinge on personal liberties. Therefore, they took steps to ensure that the government's authority to deprive citizens of life, liberty, and property was closely monitored. They included specific measures to protect persons subject to criminal justice processes. Specifically, the Fourth, Fifth, Sixth, and Eighth Amendments outlined criminal defendant safeguards pursuant to the administration of justice. Since privacy rights are an integral part of overarching constitutional protections available to criminal defendants, they coexist with several other rights of the accused.

THE NEXUS BETWEEN PRIVACY AND CRIMINAL JUSTICE

Jack McClellan is a self-professed pedophile who openly espoused his pleasure at watching little girls. On his personal Web site he posted photographs of young girls and described his favorite places to spot them. His Web site came to the attention of parents and officials in Los Angeles, California. The pronouncements so alarmed community members that two Santa Clarita attorneys petitioned the court to issue a restraining order preventing McClellan from going near children. Judge Melvin Sandvig issued an injunction barring McClellan from child contact anywhere in California. The order was enforceable for three years, but subject to periodic court review. One week after the court order was issued, McClellan was arrested by UCLA (University of California, Los Angeles) police for being near a campus child-care center. He was released and rearrested later that day during a television interview about the incident. After spending five days in jail, and having his computer Web site shut down, he was released again, and the Los Angeles city attorney's office dismissed the criminal case. Jack McClellan has never been charged with child molestation, and legal experts noted that in spite of McClellan's troubling behavior, his First Amendment rights allow him to express those views, explaining "preventive detention ... is not part of the law."[14] This incident illustrates the close relationship between constitutional rights and crime-control processes.

Ideally, there is symmetry between citizen privacy rights and the administration of criminal justice. Yet, few could have anticipated the complex contours of this relationship or foreseen the demands of modern crime control. Constitution writers believed that the civil liberties they had instilled would act as an equalizer to protect citizens from government violations, especially during their interaction with the criminal justice system. However, unanticipated influences emerged that dramatically affected the privacy–criminal justice relationship. These include far-reaching globalization effects, technological advancement, and nascent crime and terrorism threats that have impacted crime fighting.

SOCIAL AND POLITICAL INFLUENCES ON CRIMINAL JUSTICE

Interpretation of privacy rights is susceptible to both legal and extralegal influences. These effects shape both the privacy–criminal justice relationship and balance with government crime controls. Factors such as perceived crime threats or societal concerns over social deviance have a bearing on government social control efforts. A survey of American crime and drug control policy, from the mid-1800s to the present, illustrates how crime dynamics, politics, and public opinion affect government responses and judicial decision making.[15] Privacy rights are commonly interpreted in the context of anticrime, drug, organized crime, or terrorism government campaigns. For example, spikes in the violent crime rate and emergence of the new drug culture in the 1960s impacted privacy and search jurisprudence as courts responded to those threats. At the same time, in 1967 the President's Commission on Law Enforcement and Administration of Justice for the first time described American criminal justice as an integrated system consisting of the police, courts, and corrections subsystems.[16] Meanwhile, the civil rights movement received attention from the Supreme Court along with litigant groups such as ethnic minorities, juveniles, criminal defendants, and correctional inmates.

The politics of crime control also affect the status of civil rights.[17] Often, there is an inverse relationship between crime control and individual privacy. The more active criminal justice functionaries are in surveillance, arrest, and prosecution, the greater potential for negative impact on individual privacy rights. Studies on the effects of crime control on citizens and criminal offenders have shown, in many cases, it is detrimental to civil liberties and other aspects of civil life.[18] Yet, there are other factors that influence the crime-fighting functions of criminal justice.

In the contemporary context, dramatic changes have occurred in both the legitimate and criminal worlds. Because of transformations in global technology, commerce, and communication, the interaction among people around the world is significantly different than previously. Criminal justice officials and criminals worldwide have been touched by these changes. Not only are the authorities using more technology to investigate crime and monitor offenders, but globalization effects have also shaped modern crime in profound ways. Criminal actors increasingly communicate, transact business, and coordinate the trafficking of illicit goods using advanced technologies.[19] On the one hand, this has extended their reach, opened fresh criminal markets, and created new disreputable relationships; on the other, it has spawned new types of criminal activity. Contemporary transnational crime and global terrorism have transformed the meaning of crime and criminal evidence, leading criminal justice officials to alter their methods of investigation and prosecution.

As police engage in more complex investigations, particularly involving electronic evidence or transnational illicit activity, their actions have had a different impact on the privacy–criminal justice relationship. In essence, a *new privacy paradigm* has been brought about by changes in crime and technology.

Essentially, new threats and crime-fighting technologies have transformed the role of surveillance in not only preventing crime but how criminal justice officials perceive suspects. But surveillance has played an important role in crime control before. For instance, when the British penologist Jeremy Bentham in 1785 created the wheel-shaped Panopticon prison architecture, it was designed to allow guards to constantly observe the inmates from an elevated walkway above their cells. Yet, the most iconic work warning of a coercive and surveillance-centric government is George Orwell's *Nineteen Eighty-Four, A Novel*, where he described omnipresent government surveillance as "Big Brother is watching you."[20] Though Orwell's imaginative account of government totalitarian control was fictitious, his Big Brother metaphor has become synonymous with constant government monitoring of private activities to detect violators or coerce compliance.

CHANGING PRIVACY BOUNDARIES

In the earliest days of the democracy, privacy protections were largely based on property rights. Those included real property, tangible items, and written documents. In the modern telecommunication age, interpretation of privacy and criminal evidence has changed. Today, evidence includes a range of electronic and communicative information in addition to the traditional forms of physical proof. As more people use digital and wireless communication, these become valuable reservoirs of potential criminal evidence. Just as the Internet and cellular telephony are used for legitimate business, they are also tools utilized by criminals in criminal communications and transactions.

Privacy boundaries continue to be modified as police gain additional surveillance authority to pursue elusive global criminals. In 2007, President George W. Bush signed into law the Protect America Act, which allows government officials to eavesdrop on telephone and electronic oversea communications without a warrant or judicial review in the investigation of terrorism and transnational crime.[21] As new laws give justice officials greater surveillance and search powers, the boundaries of privacy are redrawn. Not only legal authority but surveillance capability has a bearing on the dimension of personal privacy and is contingent upon the sophistication and availability of crime-fighting technology.

TECHNOLOGY AND CRIME FIGHTING

The use of scientific devices and methods in crime investigation has been popularized by the media for many years. Whether it is the exploits of fictitious detectives such as Sherlock Holmes, Agatha Christie's Inspector Hercule Poirot, or the forensic feats of investigators on the television series *CSI,* solving crime is a public fascination.

Though technology has been utilized in criminal investigation for a long time, the nineteenth and twentieth centuries produced a plethora of crime-fighting innovations. Each produced new ways to monitor, investigate, classify, or record suspected criminal activities. By the 1870s, French criminalist

Alphonse Bertillon had devised the anthropometry method of cataloging unique body measurements to identify individual criminals. In 1880, Henry Faulds published a scientific journal article titled "On the Skin-Furrows of the Hand" in which he described the presence of unique ridge patterns on human and primate hands. Though fingerprints were known to the ancient Chinese and Egyptians, Faulds's research provided the impetus for new discoveries in fingerprinting applications for criminal investigations. By 1896 British police inspector Sir Edward Henry had developed a new system for classifying individual fingerprint characteristics.[22]

The 1960s saw the advent of biometric methods that mapped or measured unique physical characteristics to identify or verify persons. These included facial or hand geometry, digital fingerprint identification, eye or vascular mapping, signature or keystroke recognition, and speaker recognition. Within a decade, many of these body mapping and measurement regimes had become automated.[23] In 1985, Leicester University scientist Alec Jeffreys developed the revolutionary DNA fingerprinting process to identify persons using genetic traits found in body fluid or tissue.[24] When the twenty-first century arrived, many of these scientific discoveries were implemented in criminal investigations and surveillance programs.

Criminal justice–related privacy rights primarily safeguarded the dignity of the person's body and protection of property. But as technology advanced, officials were able to electronically trace individuals' movements, monitor their communications, identify them based on physical traits, and scan internal body functions. Hence, personal privacy lines have been changed by government use of advanced surveillance applications. Each of these investigation methods contributes to a loss of individual anonymity and personal control as officials develop comprehensive profiles containing citizen identities, transactions, activities, and movements. Christian Parenti cautioned, "The proliferation of CCTV [closed circuit television] and similar technologies threaten to reshape our culture and public spaces and therefore our very minds in ways that preclude progressive social change, cultural experimentation, and basic liberty."[25]

An experimental technology developed by Lawrence Farwell, named brain fingerprinting, further illustrates the potential for more invasive criminal investigation methods. Researchers conducted a study involving 61 participants who agreed to have their brains scanned using the new functional magnetic resonance imaging technology (fMRI) to detect lies. The subjects agreed to participate in a mock crime, with assurance of pay, if they were able to deceive the brain scan. The researchers found that they could distinguish truth from lie by imaging brain activity with fMRI at a 90 to 93 percent accuracy rate.[26] As this description shows, the extent of privacy protection varies relative to the level of government intrusion and technological capability.

Greater police investigative capacity is just one of the factors that have contributed to the emergence of a new privacy paradigm. Changes in the scope of privacy rights can only be fully understood as a composite of shifting technologies, globalization effects, government surveillance powers, and security threats. New crime and terrorism dangers have played a significant role in repositioning personal privacy borders, even though this transition was under way before the events of September 11, 2001 (9/11 hereafter). Not only did 9/11 accelerate these changes, it redefined national security in the context of a terrorism threat unknown to Americans.

THE 9/11 TERRORIST ATTACKS AND PRIVACY RIGHTS

Not since the Cold War had American national security threats been described in such encompassing terms. Today, both global crime and terrorism clearly fit that description. Few knew about these hazards beforehand, but the 9/11 destruction has since changed much of the world's focus toward the menace of Islamist terrorism. Walter Laqueur warned that a dangerous new brand of Islamist extremism had emerged.[27] He joined others who described an agile, ephemeral, and dedicated group of militants who used suicide bombing as a terrorist tactic. In spite of the warnings, the United States was caught largely off-guard while, as Gerald L. Posner stated, "America slept."[28]

All combined, these circumstances contributed to the transformation of privacy rights and their relationship with the administration of criminal justice. The new privacy paradigm is most evident relative to the use of government surveillance and search in crime control. A shifting landscape of new threats and monitoring gadgets has not only changed surveillance and criminal investigation methods but altered the balance between government powers and civil liberties.

ABOUT THE BOOK

Over the years a body of literature has been written exploring privacy rights from different perspectives. Since privacy principles originate in constitutional law, that is typically the focus of the analyses.[29] However, when a right to privacy is examined in relation to the enforcement of criminal law and functions of criminal justice, it takes on a distinctive meaning. Constitutional maxims and liberties are adapted to a justice context that involves personal liberty, privacy, and possessory interests. The rights are not restricted to government surveillance or search but are joined by other constitutional safeguards available to criminal suspects, defendants, and others. When the Fourth Amendment proclaims a prohibition against unreasonable search and seizure, the Framers' intent extends to a broad protection against government infringements that affect the privacy–criminal justice relationship. Thus, privacy safeguards, which are threaded through American constitutional, case, and statutory law, reach far beyond just the Fourth Amendment. Persons have dimensions of privacy expectation regarding their person, property, liberty, communication, and expression when subject to government control or intrusion. Citizens affected by criminal justice processes can defend their individual privacy by asserting recognized rights or utilizing legal safeguards in each of these areas.

This book takes a panoramic and holistic approach to privacy rights in the administration of criminal justice. It contends that privacy rights and protections are multidimensional, variable, and can be impinged by many official criminal justice functions. The book investigates the privacy–criminal justice relationship using two principal perspectives. First, privacy rights extend to each of the participants in the justice process—criminal offender, criminal justice personnel, and crime victim. Because of each person's legal status or role in the criminal justice system, each has a distinct set of privacy protections in the community, workplace, legal process, or correctional institution.

Second, it holds that a new privacy paradigm has emerged where public attitudes toward privacy, interpretation of security threats by legislators and courts, and protection responsibilities of government have changed. Among these alterations is a post-9/11 threat assessment where government officials have expanded their *net of suspicion* to include nontraditional suspects drawn from a broad cross-section of the public. Though this phenomenon is not unprecedented, these influences have had a profound effect on privacy jurisprudence. Past paradigmatic shifts in privacy interpretation have occurred during periods of rapid change in public threat or technology. In the twentieth century antecedent government policies such as the 1917 prosecutions under the Espionage Act for opposition to World War I, alcohol Prohibition, detention of ethnic Japanese Americans during World War II, or 1960s antidrug and crime campaigns led to official reassessment of personal privacy limits. As Supreme Court Justice Thurgood Marshall cautioned, "Precisely because the need for action against the [drug] scourge is manifest, the need for vigilance against unconstitutional excess is great. History teaches that grave threats to liberty often come in times of urgency, when constitutional rights seem too extravagant to endure."[30]

What Justice Marshall referred to as a time of urgency has arisen more than once in the nation's history. These perceived threats, whether from alcoholic beverage, Communism, organized crime, illicit drug, or global terrorism, have all persuaded citizens, legislators, or courts to reexamine the relationship between individual privacy rights and government powers. For instance, in the landmark decision *Olmstead v. United States* (1928), the Supreme Court ruled that government agents could attach a warrantless wiretap to Roy Olmstead's telephone. Olmstead was being investigated for importing and selling alcohol in violation of the National Prohibition Act. In his famous dissent, Justice Louis Brandeis wrote,

> The makers of the Constitution . . . conferred against the Government, the right to be let alone—the most comprehensive of rights and the right most valued by civilized men. To protect that right, every unjustified intrusion by the Government

upon the privacy of the individual, whatever the means employed, must be deemed a violation of the Fourth Amendment.[31]

The present era is marked by rapid changes in national security threats and technological advances in crime and crime fighting. All exert an influence on a right to privacy in relation to crime control and the functioning of criminal justice. In responding to this fluid and unpredictable environment, court decisions, statutes, and police operational practices have adapted.

The book draws on two principal sources to support its analyses. First, American privacy, search, and seizure laws are used as guideposts. Together, they consist of court decisions, federal and state statutory laws, and legal commentaries that form the body of jurisprudence that explains the surveillance authority of government officials and the dimensions of individual privacy rights. Second, to distinguish valid methods from those that unlawfully impinge on citizen privacy rights, official surveillance, search, and seizure practices are examined.

The book is divided into chapters that provide both a foundation and an in-depth analysis of the relationship between privacy rights and the administration of criminal justice. Chapter 1 surveys the history and principles of privacy law. It explains fundamental legal doctrines and principles used by American courts to interpret individual privacy and formulate guidelines for criminal justice processes. Chapter 2 gives an overview of the general principles of government search and seizure. It outlines the key legal doctrines pertaining to official surveillance, arrest, search, and seizure. Included is a discussion of Fourth Amendment core concepts and law enforcement applications involving warrant search requirements and warrantless exceptions. Chapter 3 examines individual privacy rights in relation to criminal investigation. This detailed analysis contains constitutional guidelines and individual privacy protections regarding the collection of criminal evidence and use of surveillance, search, and seizure in investigation, detention, monitoring, arrest, and interrogation of criminal suspects from suspicion of wrongdoing to grand jury indictment. Chapter 4 reviews defendant privacy rights from postinvestigatory indictment through criminal conviction and sentencing. The appraisal centers on the specific privacy rights of persons adjudicated in the criminal justice process. It explains defendant privacy safeguards as balanced with government justice functions throughout each stage of criminal proceeding, community supervision, and custodial incarceration.

Chapter 5 analyzes the privacy rights of criminal justice personnel regarding employer regulation of workplace conduct and off-duty activities. The topics discussed are workplace search, electronic monitoring, drug testing, compulsory questioning, and freedom of expression, association, religion, and disclosure of personal information. Chapter 6 reviews the privacy rights of crime victims who interact with criminal justice processes. The chapter focuses on protection of crime victim identity, personal records, and private activities. Chapter 7 examines privacy rights and government surveillance of nontraditional suspects. It explains monitoring and data-gathering methods used in public venues, such as schools, airports, and along national borders. Included is a survey of federal privacy and antiterrorism laws concentrating specifically on those that provide citizen safeguards and law enforcement surveillance authority after 9/11. The chapter further describes government surveillance in a new privacy paradigm including the use of emerging computer and biometric investigation technology. Chapter 8 proffers causal explanations for the advent of the new privacy paradigm. Its account attributes the transformation of the privacy–criminal justice relationship to globalization effects, advanced technologies, criminal justice adjustments to nascent crime and terrorism, and the expansive use of surveillance. Finally, it discusses the prospects for future diminution of privacy rights in relation to criminal justice functions, which are increasingly focused on monitoring suspects and offenders.

There should be a word about the terminology used in the book. It purposefully adopts the terms America and Americans to refer to the United States of America and its citizens. The author acknowledges the arguable inaccuracy that suggests those terms correctly denote all persons living in the countries of the Americas in the Western Hemisphere. However, the terms were chosen because they garner a certain familiarity and accepted usage. Since the book restricts its discussion to U.S. jurisprudence and criminal justice functions, the author believes that the terms engender a needed acquaintance with a society dedicated to the preservation of civil liberties and privacy rights. Though the meaning of privacy is both personalized and culturally relative, its usage in this book specifically focuses on American culture and law.

WHY EXAMINE THE PRIVACY–CRIMINAL JUSTICE RELATIONSHIP?

Though perhaps an overused cliché, Patrick Henry's declaration "Give me liberty or give me death" underscores the high value, in American culture, placed on personal freedoms and civil liberties. David Hume said, "Nothing is more obstinate than a faction endowed with a sense of rights."[32] Historically, Americans consider these entitlements nonnegotiable, except under the most extreme circumstances. Packaged within the larger body of rights is an expectation of personal privacy. It is, in essence, a protection against unwanted interference or intrusion that is held to be inviolate in our pluralistic liberal democracy. Jean-Jacques Rousseau explained that there should be a social contract between protectors and the protected.[33] He insisted that it should create a reciprocal relationship between government and the people. When applied to crime control, citizens vest government with the power to enforce criminal laws in exchange for assurances of greater public safety. In the American version, a purposeful balance exists between government crime control powers and civil rights. When vetting this relationship, courts and statutes have formulated constraints on government while establishing express individual rights. These are outlined in constitutional doctrines, laws, and procedural guidelines defining government powers in the administration of criminal justice.

Nowhere in the function of government are privacy rights more vulnerable than in the processes of criminal justice. Persons are subject to intrusions or restrictions as officials conduct surveillance, investigation, and prosecution. Ultimately, these can lead to adjudication, punishment, or imprisonment. Ordinarily, invasion of privacy is viewed strictly as official search and seizure to obtain criminal evidence for prosecution. However, the new privacy paradigm encompasses a more comprehensive type of government surveillance that monitors many facets of person, property, identity, communication, expression, movement, and activity. As a result, official surveillance affects privacy interests in a manner that exceeds the conventional notion of police intrusion.

What is at risk is more than the negative effects of being watched and potential loss of freedom or dignity. The deprivation of liberty due to detention, arrest, or forfeiture of privacy control over identity, person, or property may be the least of the harms to society and its civil liberties. A greater risk is the possibility of a chilling effect on society and its liberties caused by an unconstrained Big Brother.[34]

Given the exponential growth in public use of telecommunications and data storage capability of modern computing systems, more private information is available to commercial and government groups than ever before. Robert O'Harrow, Jr. claims that consumer information has, in many cases, been merged with government data stores leading to a comprehensive database on American citizens.[35] Moreover, increasing use of sophisticated surveillance and biometric measures has gathered more information *of* rather than *about* persons.[36] Together, the bridging of biographical, biometric, and transactional information about persons has given the government the ability to construct a total data composite on any individual of interest. Coupled with modifications in federal surveillance laws and advances in technological capability, criminal justice officials are able to monitor and collect data on a substantial amount of private activities pursuant to criminal investigations.

Therefore, in the fragile balance between government crime control and individual privacy rights, more is at stake than ever. The importance of this book is that it analyzes the powers and constraints on criminal justice officials to intrude into the multidimensional privacy rights of citizens. At a time when Americans are increasingly anxious about global crime and terrorism threats, it has never been more important to map the limits of criminal justice surveillance and control in relation to individual privacy rights.

Greater authority given to criminal justice officials to engage in practices or use methods that impinge on privacy rights comes, in part, from a willingness by society to relinquish some protections in exchange for the belief it will be safer in a dangerous world. For example, in a recent telephone survey, researchers found that 71 percent of Americans favored the use of public space surveillance cameras to aid in crime fighting. The 25 percent of respondents that opposed installation of cameras cited privacy intrusion concerns.[37]

This book examines not only the conceptual but the practical aspects of the privacy–criminal justice relationship as it considers the operational practices of the three criminal justice subsystems—police, courts, and corrections—and their impact on the privacy rights of all those affected by justice processes.

Chapter 1

PRIVACY IN SEARCH OF MEANING

Charles Katz entered a public telephone booth in Los Angeles to call in gambling wagers. He phoned Miami and Boston with betting information. Unbeknown to him, Federal Bureau of Investigation agents had attached an electronic eavesdropping device to the booth. They recorded his conversation, and the evidence was later introduced at his federal interstate gambling trial. Katz was convicted and appealed to the U.S. Supreme Court claiming that the police had conducted an unreasonable warrantless search in violation of his right to privacy. In a landmark decision the Supreme Court agreed. It held in *Katz v. United States* (1967) that officers must have a legal cause to search if a person demonstrates a reasonable "expectation of privacy." Justice John Marshall Harlan II summed it up by stating "the Fourth Amendment protects people, not places."[1]

Long before the *Katz* case, the idea of personal privacy existed. Although dating the origin of the privacy concept is difficult, references are found in ancient scriptures such as the Bible and the Quran. As early as A.D. 1361 in English common law, statutes mentioned a natural right to privacy protection.[2] Even so, the privacy theory has many interpretations and defies easy definition. It is logical to turn to American legal heritage for clues about the meaning of a right to privacy.

ANGLO-AMERICAN HISTORY OF PRIVACY LAW

English Common Law Tradition

The American legal system, and its jurisprudence, is derived from the English common law that dates back to A.D. 1066. Common law is one of the four recognized legal traditions in the world.[3] It originated in England and was transplanted to the colonies between 1066 and 1776. Core tenets of common law come from legal principles that trace their origin to a melding of communal law and cultural customs. Communal law is synonymous with natural law that governs the conduct of all persons and prohibits unnatural acts such as murder, rape, or theft. These proscriptions predate written law, and yet, they are so fundamental that they still exist today. Since the legal system in eleventh century England was primitive, common law depended largely on cultural traditions as a basis for fundamental principles. What emerged was a common law model based on community and family traditions. For instance, an accepted cultural practice was common law marriage. Because of an absence of formal government, and scarce magistrates and clergy in the English countryside, marital arrangements were negotiated between families in compliance with social customs then consummated through public proclamation.

The privacy right idea is inherited from early English common law. However, it took several centuries for the theory to develop into its present form. In the premodern period, English common law combined crimes and noncriminal violations into three categories of trespasses.[4] Together, these included all forms of prohibited conduct believed to threaten community well-being. Basically, there were trespasses against person, property, and business. The most familiar usage of the trespass concept today is the legal protection against unauthorized passage across private land. But under early common law it had a much more encompassing meaning. Over time, two separate tracks emerged creating distinct crimes and torts. Tort law, commonly known in popular nomenclature as civil law in the United States, is predicated on three fundamental premises. First, tort assigns a responsibility to every citizen to refrain from engaging in any act that causes harm. Second, if persons intentionally, recklessly, or negligently harm others, they are accountable for any injury. In tort, injury is used in its broadest sense not just denoting physical hurt but including detriment to property, business practice, personal reputation, and more. Third, if persons are the proximate direct cause of harm, damage, or injury, they are held liable under the law of tort.[5]

In America, modern tort law is used to resolve disputes between individuals or companies, and it prescribes two general types of remedy. Courts can issue injunctive orders commanding a litigant to perform a designated action, such as an order to cease and desist. Or more commonly, the court awards a monetary judgment to the plaintiff or defendant in the case. Tort law was used in English common law to protect a fundamental privacy right and continues to be a remedy in American law involving noncriminal invasion of privacy.[6]

According to William Searle Holdsworth, "British common law recognized a right in tort protecting against one's property, slander of reputation, and intrusion into one's family."[7] In the same vein, John Hamilton Baker insists that common law embodies certain rights of personal choice and liberty.[8] Each of these is a precursor to the modern legal concept of privacy right. Many common law experts agree that the premise of an individual privacy right is vested in the law of torts.

The second common law trespass track is crime. Crimes are forbidden acts that cause damage, injury, or threaten the safety and well-being of society. Though they are derived from original common law, crimes differ from torts in that they endanger the collective society as opposed to harming just one individual or business. Hence, common law traditions integrated customary practices of personal relations and prohibited acts that threaten society. As English common law evolved, the jurisprudence assembled a myriad of legal doctrines and principles. Among these, and central to this discussion, is the fundamental right to privacy.

In common law, the privacy right concept is found in three principal sources—customary practices, written court decisions, and codified statutes. Historically, common law principles were documented in written court decisions. At some point during the 710-year span of English common law, the right to privacy was incorporated. However, to trace its origin to court decisions would be difficult because early cases were not chronicled in a systematic fashion. As a result, a patchwork of concepts, doctrines, and principles have evolved through judicial decisions and legal analysis. Regardless, a right to privacy is considered to be among the most fundamental axioms in common law.

Adopting Privacy Rights in American Law

Early architects of American law understood the importance of privacy protection. However, scholars debate whether the Framers intended to include personal privacy among the original civil rights. Lee Epstein and Thomas G. Walker explain, "Even though most justices agree it exists, they have disagreed over various questions, including from what provision of the Constitution the right to privacy arises and how far it extends."[9] It would be much simpler to verify the existence of a right to privacy if the Constitution writers had unambiguously stated such protection.

Unfortunately, a privacy right is not explicitly mentioned in the nation's founding documents. A review of the Bill of Rights, that is the first 10 amendments to the Constitution, reveals only a tacit reference to personal privacy rights. More than anything, the concept is discovered through inference since an express reference to a privacy right is absent.

However, more than any other place, the right to privacy is embodied in the Fourth Amendment to the Constitution, which states "the right of the people to be secure in their persons, houses, papers, and effects, against unreasonable searches and seizures, shall not violated."[10] In *United States v. Lefkowitz* (1932), the Supreme Court reasoned that the prohibition against unreasonable government search should be "liberally construed to safeguard the right to privacy."[11] But to appreciate the ubiquity of privacy rights in the administration of criminal justice one must also look to safeguards beyond the Fourth Amendment.

Looking to the whole Bill of Rights, vestiges of privacy rights are found in several places. In the First Amendment, the freedoms mentioned are considered inviolate. Hence, the freedoms of speech, religion, and assembly have larger privacy implications involving criminal justice. As an example, the Supreme Court ruled in *Stanley v. Georgia* (1969) that the First Amendment safeguards personal possession of obscene material in the home as a form of lawful expression.[12] Next, the Fifth Amendment contains several privacy right assurances. Most notably are its guarantees of a self-incrimination privilege and due process of law for criminal suspects or defendants. Its proclamation ". . . nor shall [any person] be compelled in any criminal case to be a witness against himself"[13] guarantees a protection against compelled self-incrimination to ensure the privacy of personal statements related to crimes. The due process concept is a hallmark of American criminal procedure and has its origin in the fundamental principle of equity. The Fifth Amendment states that a person shall not be "deprived of life, liberty, or property"[14] without due process of law, which demonstrates the Framers' intent to protect the privacy and property rights of citizens against unlawful government interference. Later in 1868, the Fourteenth Amendment mandated that each state must guarantee Bill of Rights protections for all residents to the extent that "no state shall abridge the privileges or immunities of citizens of the United States; nor shall any state deprive any person of life, liberty, or property."[15]

Many commentators agree that the writers of the Constitution intended for privacy right safeguards to be present in American law. John H. F. Shattuck posits that "although a right to privacy is nowhere expressly contained in the Constitution, personal autonomy and freedom from governmental intrusions are values deeply rooted in American constitutional history."[16] In his legendary dissent in *Olmstead v. United States* (1928), Justice Louis Brandeis expressed concern about government electronic surveillance and characterized personal privacy as "the right to be let alone is the right most valued by civilized men."[17] Almost 40 years later, the Court in *Griswold v. Connecticut* (1965) declared that the Bill of Rights created a zone of privacy where citizens were protected from government intrusion.[18] For some, the right to privacy is viewed as a fundamental liberty. Craig R. Ducat described it as a "set of transcendent values, which were asserted to lie at the core of American life."[19]

The legal privacy debate took on a more recognizable shape by the late nineteenth century. No longer just an obscure common law principle, by the 1880s privacy law began to generate its own working vocabulary. In 1881, Judge Thomas McIntyre Cooley in his prominent book on torts discussed the right to be let alone as an important protection.[20] Though they were influenced by Cooley and others, Samuel D. Warren and Louis D. Brandeis's groundbreaking treatise "The Right to Privacy" became one of the most influential articles of its day in the burgeoning discourse on privacy.[21] Their seminal work conceptualized many of the fundamental principles of modern privacy law.

Moreover, they established two cornerstone premises in privacy jurisprudence. First is the view that privacy was an "inviolate personality," that it is a personal right rather than one derived strictly from property entitlements. Second, they developed a theoretical nexus between personal privacy and the potential threats posed by technology. Responding to concerns about abuses of yellow journalism and the advent of new technologies, they called for the addition of a right to privacy to the corpus of American law. Unlike the technological privacy dangers mentioned today, such as advanced electronic surveillance and communication monitoring, Warren and Brandeis voiced concerns about the use of new photographic techniques. They wrote, "[I]nstantaneous photographs and [the] newspaper enterprise have invaded the sacred precincts of private and domestic life; and numerous mechanical devices threaten to make good the prediction that 'what is whispered in the closet shall be proclaimed from the housetops.'"[22] Interestingly, their premonition about the relationship between privacy protection and technology would later become prophetic. They advocated the use of tort as a remedy for unauthorized privacy intrusions and, more importantly, the creation of a new right to privacy in American law.

The newly minted privacy right concept was soon subjected to close scrutiny by legal scholars and courts that hoped to craft working principles for use in the law. The year after the Warren and Brandeis article was published, Justice Horace Gray discussed a right to privacy in the high Court's decision in *Union Pacific Railway Co. v. Botsford* (1891) commenting "no right is held more sacred, or is more carefully guarded, by the common law, than the right of every individual to the possession and control of his own person, free from all restraint or interference of others, unless by clear and unquestionable authority of law."[23] From here, the legal debate intensified and new privacy models were being conceived.

Conceptual Framework for Defining Privacy

Drawing from legal analysis and a body of court decisions, a majority of commentators maintain that privacy right protections are an intrinsic part of American jurisprudence. Yet, that may be where the agreement ends. Legal scholars have created different frameworks to explain the privacy theory. Its conceptual view comes from three interpretations. First, privacy is described as it relates to alienation where being apart from others is central to the definition.[24] Second, privacy can be interpreted as the control we have over information about ourselves.[25] Third, privacy is construed as a claim of self-determination. Alan F. Westin defined it as "the claim of individuals, groups, or institutions to determine for themselves when, how, and to what extent information about them is communicated to others."[26] For some, privacy is the right to establish one's own social boundaries and to shield personal activities from others. This approach entitles persons to define their own interactions with their surroundings. Conversely, privacy may be simply a move to prevent outside intrusion.

The meaning of personal privacy can defy lucid explanation. David M. O'Brien commented that many definitions of privacy are largely "unfulfilling and inadequate because of vagueness or fallacious logic."[27] Yet, William L. Prosser clarified the concept in tort law using four essential elements:

1. An intrusion upon the plaintiff's seclusion or solitude or into his private affairs;
2. Public disclosure of embarrassing private facts about the plaintiff;
3. Publicity that placed the plaintiff in a false light in the public eye; and
4. Appropriation for the defendant's advantage, of the plaintiff's name or likeness.

Prosser argued that at least one of these characteristics must be present to support a privacy-related claim. His model is considered the definitive authority on privacy applications in tort law. Prosser's framework focused on intrusion, disclosure, false representation, and appropriation of identity as being most violative of personal privacy.[28] The privacy concepts that emerged from common law are not only present in tort but also found in criminal law.

Applying Privacy Rights to Criminal Law

Modern privacy law never strays very far from its common law heritage and is interwoven in tort and criminal law. Many of the common crimes against persons and property involve acts that impinge on privacy interests. These offenses deprive victims of control over their bodies or result in unauthorized disclosure of private matters or unwanted intrusion upon premises.

Prominent among the public protection obligations of government is crime control. The police are responsible for enforcing the statutory criminal laws enacted by state and federal governments. Government enforcement is intended to be carried out in balance with public safety and civil liberty interests. Fearing the past civil liberty abuses committed by their British colonizers, the Framers instilled constitutional safeguards to protect the public from unreasonable or unlawful government enforcement actions.[29] Additionally, they recognized the need to construct criminal procedure guidelines that protected the civil and constitutional rights of the people. The procedure was imbued with many of the equity and due process ideals present in common law. Unlike the British prosecutorial approach, American criminal procedure assigns the burden of proof in criminal proceedings to the government and mandates that any proof of guilt "beyond a reasonable doubt" be based on competent evidence. This requirement obligates the government to use lawful methods to discover, collect, and present criminal evidence in a manner that abides by constitutional provisions and statutory criminal procedure laws. The very nature of these activities can render personal privacy vulnerable to intrusion or violation.

ESTABLISHING A LEGAL PRIVACY STANDARD

Expectation of Privacy Doctrine

Prior to the landmark decision in *Katz v. United States*, the prevailing police surveillance doctrine had been outlined in the influential 1928 case *Olmstead v. United States*.[30] The *Olmstead* case established the early legal guidelines for police electronic eavesdropping. Roy Olmstead was suspected of smuggling alcohol in violation of the National Prohibition Act. As part of their investigation, the police attached a wiretap to Olmstead's outside telephone line and monitored his conversations. The government used his comments as evidence in federal court. Olmstead appealed his conviction to the Supreme Court where he argued that the police intruded on his private telephone conversations without a warrant, thereby violating his Fourth Amendment protection against unreasonable search and seizure. The government countered that since the police did not enter Olmstead's house it was not a Fourth Amendment search. In a five to four decision, the Court sided with the government. It reasoned that the Fourth Amendment applied only to physical premises and material items such as the "person and his house, papers, or effects."[31] Therefore, they found that the government had not physically intruded into those protected areas and thus no search occurred. In essence, *Olmstead* protected places, not persons.

For almost 40 years the *Olmstead* "trespass doctrine" was the standard used to determine the legality of police electronic surveillance. As a result of advances in electronic eavesdropping, in 1967 the Court reversed its interpretation of protected space when it established the expectation of privacy doctrine in *Katz v. United States.*[32] When agents attached a listening device to the outside of Katz's telephone booth, they violated his rights. The Court thereafter extended individual privacy protection to persons. In the *Katz* application, the burden for establishing a legal expectation of privacy shifts from the government to the individual person. Justice Harlan proposed a two-prong formula for determining when an expectation of privacy existed. First, the expectation claimed by the person must be found to be subjectively reasonable. William S. McAninch insists that a finding of expectation of privacy depends on "ascertaining whether reliance on privacy is reasonable or justified."[33] Persons subject to official surveillance, search, or seizure must believe that their activities are protected; thus, the government intrusion is unreasonable. Moreover, they must demonstrate their privacy expectation by taking actions to protect their words or activities from public scrutiny. Hence, if persons knowingly expose their undertakings to public view, they reduce or eliminate any claim to protected privacy. As illustrated in the *Katz* case, after entering the telephone booth Charles Katz closed the door behind him. This simple act is significant because it showed Katz's intention to protect his phone conversation from being overheard. Known as the assumption of risk principle, the strength of a person's claimed expectation of privacy hinges on the extent of exposure of personal items to public view.[34]

In several subsequent cases, the Supreme Court abandoned Harlan's subjectiveness test and replaced it with a lesser standard of mere exposure of private matters to public access or view. For instance, in *California v. Ciraolo* (1986) the Court ruled that the police could use criminal evidence discovered through warrantless aerial surveillance of a residential yard.[35] And in *California v. Greenwood* (1988), authorities were allowed to search curbside trash without a warrant because the owner relinquished his privacy expectation by putting it in a public place.[36]

Second, the Harlan requirement includes an objective reasonableness component. Here, the person's privacy expectation is measured based on whether society is prepared to recognize the claim as reasonable. The courts determine if the citizen's privacy expectation is reasonable under the circumstances in which it is professed.

In sum, the *Katz* expectation of privacy doctrine established a legal standard that measures citizen protection from physical or electronic government intrusion in the absence of a court-issued warrant. If the court determines that a person's expectation is reasonable, the government's warrantless surveillance, search, or seizure will be found unconstitutional. The Court in *Oliver v. United States* (1984) explained, "The test of legitimacy is not whether the individual chooses to conceal assertedly 'private activity.' Rather, the correct inquiry is whether the government's intrusion infringes upon the personal and societal values protected by the Fourth Amendment."[37] These same principles apply to all types of searches and seizures where an individual privacy interest is implicated. However, surveillance, search, or seizure conducted with a court-issued warrant is more authoritative since the government's request is reviewed by a neutral magistrate beforehand.

Creating a Hierarchy of Privacy Expectation

The *Katz* ruling marked a turning point in how American courts interpret privacy in relation to government use of surveillance, search, and seizure in criminal investigations. Though it became the litmus test for determining the constitutionality of government intrusion, subsequent cases created different degrees of privacy protection.[38] A personal expectation of privacy is neither absolute nor all encompassing. Rather, privacy protection is plotted along a continuum where a person's body is more protected than an open field. The critical determination of the reasonableness of one's expectation of privacy is relative to the circumstances and type of government intrusion.

Regarding person searches and seizures, Rolando V. del Carmen describes it as the top 10 degrees of intrusiveness.[39] He ranks the removal of a bullet in the *Winston v. Lee* (1985)[40] case as the most intrusive and roadblocks to control the flow of illegal aliens in *United States v. Martinez-Fuerte* (1976)[41] as the least. His categorization depicts the Court's preference for extending privacy protection to persons over property such as homes, personal possessions, or vehicles.

Essentially, courts construe Fourth Amendment search and seizure protections to be rank ordered. First, a person's body receives greater protection than other categories. Second is a person's home, which is consistent with the common law castle doctrine that guards the dwelling over all other forms of property.[42] Third follows other properties such as personal belongings, noncurtilage residential buildings, commercial buildings, and motor vehicles used as conveyances. Fourth are open fields and abandoned properties, which are generally devoid of privacy protection.

As an illustration of a high-protection circumstance, consider the case of Crystal Ferguson. While she was receiving obstetrical care from the Medical University of South Carolina (MUSC), medical personnel performed a urinalysis test, without her consent, as part of a new drug deterrence policy. After testing positive for cocaine, she was arrested. Ferguson sued the hospital, challenging the drug-testing program on Fourth Amendment grounds.

She argued that since the test results were used as criminal evidence, they were obtained illegally. In a six to three decision in *Ferguson v. City of Charleston* (2001)[43] the Supreme Court agreed holding that a public hospital could not urine test pregnant women for cocaine, without their consent, for the purpose of criminal prosecution.

MUSC officials insisted that the drug-testing policy's primary objective was to identify cocaine-using pregnant women to protect the fetus and encourage the mother to enter drug treatment. It was the deterrent objective that used criminal prosecution that the Court considered most troubling. Justice John Paul Stevens wrote, "...a review of the policy reveals that the purpose actually served by the MUSC searches is ultimately indistinguishable from the general interest in crime control."[44] The Court found that the policy violated Ferguson's Fourth Amendment and privacy right against unreasonable warrantless search.

On one end of the spectrum the courts vigorously protect the inviolability of a person's body, and on the other, they afford law enforcement considerable latitude in surveillance and search of nondwellings and public places. This does not suggest, however, that the police are never permitted to obtain criminal evidence from a person's body. The Supreme Court has authorized such practices under several different circumstances. For instance, in *Schmerber v. California* (1966)[45] the Court ruled that the police could obtain a blood sample from a suspected drunk driver, without a warrant or consent, if the procedure used is reasonable, such as performed in a hospital by medical personnel.

Not all privacy protections involve body intrusion. On many occasions officials conduct surveillance, search, or seizure where they gather criminal evidence from places and things. Therefore, a degree of privacy expectation can be asserted by the owner or possessor of houses, buildings, vehicles, or other properties. The courts, however, consider locations or properties as having a lesser expectation of privacy protection. Although different legal rationales may be used, the courts have also extended privacy protections to personal activities or artifacts such as identity, communication, expression, or association.[46]

IMPLEMENTS OF JUDICIAL ANALYSIS

The Reasonableness Standard

Reasonableness is the most common court standard used to determine the validity of government surveillance, search, and seizure. Though difficult to precisely define, the standard is central to many legal interpretations in criminal and civil law. As testimony to its versatility, the measure was used by the Supreme Court in the renowned 1896 "separate but equal" *Plessy v. Ferguson* racial discrimination case to interpret the Equal Protection Clause of the Fourteenth Amendment.[47] It is found in principles such as reasonable belief, doubt, force, and more.[48] The common denominator among these concepts is the man of ordinary care and prudence element that suggests the application of untrained human reason to make decisions about the appropriateness of official acts.

For example, when the Supreme Court analyzed the sufficiency of probable cause to arrest in *Maryland v. Pringle* (2003), it explained, "[W]e examine the events leading up to the arrest, and then decide whether these historical facts, viewed from the standpoint of an objectively reasonable police officer amount to probable cause."[49] In another case that relied heavily on the reasonableness of a police search, Daniel Murphy was detained at the Portland, Oregon, police station as a suspect in his wife's strangulation murder. Though Murphy was not under arrest, the police collected fingernail scrapings from him without a warrant and over his objection. A crime laboratory found skin tissue, blood, and clothing fibers matching his wife's among the scrapings. The incriminating evidence was used to convict Murphy of murder. In *Cupp v. Murphy* (1973), the Supreme Court held that the police acted properly since a delay might have resulted in the destruction of valuable physical evidence.[50]

The Supreme Court has long held that reasonableness determinations should be based on the stand-alone merits of each case. In *O'Connor v. Ortega* (1987), Justice Sandra Day O'Connor wrote that "the [reasonableness] question must be addressed on a case-by-case basis."[51] Earlier in the landmark police frisk case *Terry v. Ohio* (1968), Chief Justice Earl Warren remarked that ". . . each case of this sort will have to be decided on its own facts."[52]

Inevitably, government search and seizure or citizen privacy challenge in court will be subject to analysis using the reasonableness standard. It has become one of the most favored constitutionality measures, particularly involving criminal justice practices. American courts also use other measures to assess the legitimacy of government invasion of privacy.

Balancing of Competing Interests Test

In privacy cases, courts determine if government intrusions are valid based upon a determination of the reasonableness of their actions. To perform this task, American courts have adopted a "balancing of competing interests" test to weigh citizen privacy interests against government compelling interests, such as public safety. When applying the test, courts first gauge whether the citizen's right to privacy claim is legitimate and reasonable. Second, it balances the individual's privacy expectation with the government's compelling need justification to conduct surveillance, search, or seizure.

In the groundbreaking case *National Treasury Employees Union v. Von Raab* (1989), the Supreme Court held that the U.S. Custom Service's compulsory drug-testing policy for drug interdiction personnel, without warrant or suspicion, was reasonable as a Fourth Amendment search because the government had a compelling need to protect society from the influx of illicit drugs and maintain a drug-free workforce. Justice Anthony Kennedy stated, "[T]he Customs Service is our Nation's first line of defense against one of the greatest problems affecting the health and welfare of our population" and drug impaired officers "might endanger the integrity of our Nation's borders or the life of the citizenry."[53] The Court in *Von Raab* clearly viewed the government's need more compelling than the invasion of privacy claim made by the employee's union. Although American courts utilize a variety of analytical tools to interpret cases, the measures devised for privacy right matters comport with the demands for an equitable balance between government and citizen interests.

Value of Balancing Tests

One of the most important benchmarks in the American legal system is the ubiquitous use of checks and balances. At the macrolevel, the Framers sought parity between the powers of government and the rights of the people. Their intent is evident not only in the interrelations among government branches, but also as a critical consideration in the adjudication process. The founding constitutional principles instilled a purposeful balance between professional jurists and lay jurors, legal adversaries, and citizen participants.

In privacy cases it is crucial that courts respect the balance of interests between government efforts to promote public safety and citizen protection against unreasonable intrusion by well-meaning officials. Although this point has been vigorously debated throughout the twentieth century, post-9/11 events affected this fragile balance more than ever.[54] Nancy Chang insists that American courts have tilted the balance toward the police, allowing them to use more intrusive measures to ostensibly protect society from global crime and terrorism threats.[55] Arguably, government officials conducting surveillance and search have fared better in the courts since 9/11, and yet, jurists continue to rely on the important balancing of competing interests test to authorize many investigation practices. Even before 9/11, perceived threats became the impetus for relaxing government search and seizure constraints. As John B. Mitchell noted, "What we are seeing is the historical tendency to restrict our constitutional rights when our nation comes under stress. Since we are currently experiencing such stress in our war on drugs and crime in general, it is hardly surprising that we would see a broadening of police powers."[56]

In the absence of citizen right to privacy counter claims, courts would be left to determine the legality of official searches entirely on their procedural merits and without any regard for civil liberties. Therefore, in cases involving allegations of government invasion of privacy, the courts interpret whether the citizen's assertion is reasonable and if officials violated a constitutional right by conducting the search or seizure. Whichever party is judged to act most reasonably prevails.

FRAMING MODERN PRIVACY JURISPRUDENCE

Privacy rights have been recognized by common law for centuries. American privacy jurisprudence has been shaped by many interested parties including litigants, legal and criminal justice practitioners, academics, and courts. The law has been framed in the context of our legal and sociocultural tradition. Although citizens may intuitively know they possess privacy rights, the courts are the final arbiters that determine the boundaries of those liberties. This is no simple task as the right to privacy, and its balance with government powers, is constantly affected by legal, technological, and security threat factors in unpredictable environs. The Architects of the Bill of Rights could not have known the rapid advances in technology, nor could modern lawmakers have envisioned the threats posed by events such as the 9/11 attacks.

Together, these considerations have contributed to a post-9/11 privacy paradigm that realigns interpretations of individual privacy rights when balanced against government interests in protecting society from unforeseen threats. What has emerged is a modern privacy jurisprudence that wrestles with the need to remain obedient to the founding constitutional principles, and yet, responsive to the dynamic changes affecting the security of Americans.

The challenge to equitably balance individual privacy interests with those of societal interests in safety and liberty is formidable. Government officials are expected to ensure public safety, while at the same time, vigilantly protect constitutional and civil rights. The obstacles to effectively balancing these interests are substantial in the administration of criminal justice. Criminal justice officials are authorized to use surveillance, search, and seizure to investigate crimes, collect criminal evidence, prosecute offenders, and punish the convicted. However, not every person under surveillance or suspected of criminal activity is charged and convicted in criminal court. These investigative practices contain certain risks where officials may impinge on individual privacy or possessory interests as they seek to prevent and control crime. By their very nature, criminal justice practices and processes can invade individual privacy and constrain liberty. To address these concerns, American courts are constantly interpreting the parameters of criminal justice search and seizure since they pose the greatest threat to personal privacy.

Chapter 2

GOVERNMENT POWER TO SEARCH

Washington, D.C., police received information that Albert Ross was selling narcotics from the trunk of his car. Officers later stopped Ross's car and arrested him for the drug violation. One officer opened the car trunk and found a closed brown paper bag and red zippered pouch. When he looked inside the bag, he discovered glassine bags filled with a white powder, which was later determined to be heroin. An officer drove Ross's car to the police station where officers continued searching the zippered bag, without a warrant, and discovered cash. Ross was convicted of selling narcotics, and he appealed.

The Supreme Court in *United States v. Ross* (1982) ruled

> the scope of the warrantless search authorized . . . is no broader and no narrower than a magistrate could legitimately authorize by a warrant. If probable cause justifies the search of a lawfully stopped vehicle, it justifies the search of every part of the vehicle and its contents that may conceal the object of the search.[1]

Justice John Paul Stevens commented, "An individual's expectation of privacy in a vehicle and its contents may not survive if probable cause is given to believe that the vehicle is transporting contraband. Certainly the privacy interests in a car's trunk or glove compartment may be no less than those in a movable container."[2]

This case illustrates the intricacies of Fourth Amendment search and seizure law. Moreover, it shows how government searches can raise important privacy issues. Though the jurisprudence originates from just one constitutional amendment, it has produced a voluminous amount of court decisions, doctrines, and principles that guide the police in the proper use of surveillance, search, and seizure. Privacy principles closely intersect with those of the Fourth Amendment. Claims of government invasion of privacy commonly stem from official searches and seizures.

Modern search and seizure law is constantly changing as courts strive to balance individual privacy protections with government authority to investigate crimes. The responsibility lies with the judiciary to provide relevant and timely guidance to officials conducting searches. Early on it was apparent to jurists that the original tenets of the Fourth Amendment required interpretation in the context of extant society. As societal norms, laws, and technologies change, the courts evaluate search and seizure methods to ensure that they comport not only with the immutable values of the Constitution but also provide practical tools for government officials to use. To accomplish these dual objectives, the courts formulate legal concepts, such as reasonable suspicion, for officers to apply in the field. Both the courts and police recognize the inherent fluidity of search and seizure rules since they are subject to continuous reinterpretation. Although courts adhere to the obligatory stare decisis rule, which requires them to abide by prior court decision precedent, changing fact situations enable them to analyze search and seizure principles in light of the circumstances. The result is a dynamic process where the law undergoes regular reevaluation. Fortunately, everyone uses the same fundamental search and seizure operating principles. These provide an analytical framework for judicial officers when balancing privacy rights and government intrusion powers.

PRIVACY RIGHTS AND THE FOURTH AMENDMENT

Realizing the importance of privacy protections in the enforcement of criminal law, the writers of the Bill of Rights drafted an amendment to act as the gatekeeper of citizen rights to prevent unreasonable government intrusion. In 1791, they wrote the Fourth Amendment to the Constitution with the express purpose of shielding the public from unwarranted searches by enforcement agents. The Amendment states,

> The right of the people to be secure in their persons, houses, papers, and effects, against unreasonable searches and seizures, shall not be violated, and no Warrants shall issue, but upon probable cause, supported by Oath or affirmation, and particularly describing the place to be searched and the persons or things to be seized.[3]

The Fourth Amendment is the authoritative standard used to interpret the legality of police search and seizure. However, since the Amendment's founding, American courts have modified several of its fundamental principles. These include the interpretation of most aspects of the warrant and probable cause requirements.[4] Privacy law also views the Fourth Amendment as the principal constitutional guardian protecting citizens from unreasonable government surveillance, search, or seizure.[5]

Authors of the Fourth Amendment could not anticipate all of the changes in social norm, law, technology, crime, and criminal justice destined to follow in the years after they drafted the original precepts. Remarkably, however, the original constitutional documents have not only proven to be amenable to interpretation but flexible in meeting the changing social and legal environment.[6]

In one significant case, the police use of modern surveillance technology illustrates the adaptability of Fourth Amendment principles. Suspecting that Danny Kyllo was growing marijuana inside his home, federal drug agents used an infrared thermal imaging device from across the street to scan the house for heat signatures. Their device detected hot spot areas around the perimeter of the garage, which suggested the use of indoor growing lights. The officers assumed since they did not enter Kyllo's home to gather infrared evidence that no warrant was necessary. They combined the thermal imaging results with informant information to obtain a court-issued search warrant. When they searched Kyllo's home, they discovered more than 100 marijuana plants. Kyllo appealed his drug conviction, arguing that the use of the thermal imaging device constituted a police warrantless search that violated his expectation of privacy. In 2001, the Supreme Court agreed. It ruled in *Kyllo v. United States:*

> [At] the very core of the Fourth Amendment stands the right of a man to retreat into his own home and there be free from unreasonable governmental intrusions. We think that obtaining by sense-enhancement technology any information regarding the interior of the home that could not otherwise have been obtained without physical intrusion into a constitutionally protected area constitutes a search, at least where the technology in question is not in general use . . . .[7]

FOURTH AMENDMENT CORE PRINCIPLES

Fourth Amendment authors imbued the document with certain essential provisions. James R. Acker and David C. Brody commented, "They [Framers] used just 53 words to enshrine in the Bill of Rights the precious freedoms guaranteed by this provision [Fourth Amendment]."[8] The writers purposely established a dichotomy between official intrusion, named a search, and the possessory interests of citizens, labeled a seizure. In *Texas v. Brown* (1983), Justice Stevens explained, "Although our Fourth Amendment cases sometimes refer indiscriminately to searches and seizures, there are

important differences between the two . . . The Amendment protects . . . —
the interest in retaining possession of property and the interest in maintaining personal privacy. A seizure threatens the former, a search the latter."[9]
Individually, both notions are of critical importance in the relationship
between official search and seizure and the privacy rights of citizens.

The Fourth Amendment established key principles that have not only
defined government search and seizure but provided a framework to analyze
the dimensions of personal privacy. In essence, the Amendment's language supplied the seed for privacy jurisprudence. First, it spoke directly to the need to
strike a balance between government search powers and citizen safeguards in
stating "The right of the people to be secure . . . against unreasonable searches
and seizures."[10] Second, the wording suggests that most, if not all, government
searches and seizures would make use of a court-ordered warrant when it mentioned "no Warrant shall issue, but upon probable cause, supported by Oath or
affirmation."[11] Craig R. Ducat insists "it is clear that the general rule with
regard to the conduct of searches and seizures is that they are to be executed
pursuant to a warrant."[12] The Supreme Court explained this preference in
Terry v. Ohio (1968) asserting "that the police must, whenever practicable,
obtain advance judicial approval of searches and seizures."[13] Third, it added
the phrase ". . . and particularly describing the place to be searched and the persons or things to be seized,"[14] which is commonly known as the particularity
requirement. It obligates government officials to precisely describe the person,
place, or thing they wish to search when requesting a search warrant.[15] Courts
have long rejected police fishing expeditions and compel not only probable
cause but a detailed account of the person or item targeted by the search.
As Justice Potter Stewart in *United States v. Rabinowitz* (1950) wrote, "The
Fourth Amendment was in large part a general reaction to the general warrants
and warrantless searches that had so alienated the colonists and help speed the
movement for independence."[16]

WARRANT REQUIREMENTS FOR SEARCH AND SEIZURE

Warrants authorizing government officials to conduct search, arrest, or
seizure must be issued by a court of competent jurisdiction signed by a neutral
and detached magistrate.[17] Court-ordered search and seizure warrants allow
the greatest amount of official intrusion. In fact, this legal process clothes officers with the full authority of the court, thereby enabling authorities to make
forcible entry and to engage in extensive search and seizure as authorized.
This can significantly impinge on a person's privacy, liberty, and property
interests as law enforcement officials are permitted to thoroughly search and
seize persons, places, and things under the provisions of the warrant.

Due to the need to protect constitutional and privacy rights, the courts have outlined specific procedures for the application, issuance, and execution of search and seizure warrants. There are several stages in the process beginning with the completion of the search affidavit by government officials describing in detail, and with particularity, their probable cause, object of the search, criminal or regulatory violation, and suspected criminal offenders.

Probable Cause

Law enforcement officials are responsible for explaining the probable cause used to justify their requested search. Yet, a precise definition of probable cause can be elusive. According to Henry Black, "Probable cause exists where the facts and circumstances would warrant a person of reasonable caution to believe that an offense was or is being committed."[18] Since probable cause is conceptual, like many other ideas found in privacy and search jurisprudence, the courts have been left to interpret its meaning in both warrant and warrantless circumstances.[19] They have formulated two primary doctrines to address the development and sufficiency of probable cause used in search warrant affidavits. Essentially, courts have held that the information used to construct probable cause can originate from two sources. First, probable cause facts or claims made by a police officer are considered inherently credible by the courts. Therefore, if undercover police officers buy illicit drugs from a street dealer, they can use those facts as probable cause to make an arrest or request a warrant. Second, if the police are relying on information provided by a third party, they must provide a probable cause explanation using complete and corroborating evidence based on a totality of circumstances measure.[20]

Totality of Circumstances Standard

In the *Illinois v. Gates* (1983) case, police near Chicago received an anonymous letter providing a detailed description of the marijuana trafficking operation of Sue and Lance Gates. The writer explained the Gates' method of purchasing the drug in Florida and returning to Illinois in a car filled with $100,000 of marijuana for local resale. Investigators partially verified the information and obtained a search warrant for the Gates' home. The search yielded 350 pounds of marijuana, and the Gateses were convicted of drug trafficking. They appealed challenging the sufficiency of the probable cause used to obtain the search warrant. They argued that the police did not comply with the existing *Aguilar-Spinelli* two-prong requirement. Under that rule, probable cause information derived from a third-party informant must be credible, reliable, and have a basis of knowledge about the reported facts used in a search warrant affidavit.[21] Since the informant was anonymous, the police were unable to satisfy these requirements.

The *Gates* decision revised the *Aguilar-Spinelli* rule replacing it with a "totality of circumstances" standard. Justice William Rehnquist wrote, "[W]e conclude that it is wiser to abandon the 'two-prong' test established by our decision in *Aguilar* and *Spinelli*. In its place we reaffirm the totality-of-circumstances analysis that traditionally has informed probable cause determinations."[22]

In addition to the probable cause statement, the warrant application must contain detailed information about the person, place, or thing to be searched and the criminal evidence sought. Once the search warrant affidavit is reviewed by a neutral magistrate, the court may issue a signed warrant authorizing police to search for the items named in the warrant and seize the same as criminal evidence.

Execution of Search Warrants

Several constitutional and statutory provisions must also be abided by in the execution of the warrant. The warrant may be restricted by statutory time limits, such as the number of days it is valid before expiration, time of day, as in special nighttime provision, and the announcement requirement.

For instance, in *Wilson v. Arkansas* (1995) the Supreme Court found that "[common law] recognized a law enforcement officer's authority to break open the doors of a dwelling, but generally indicated that he first ought to announce his presence and authority."[23] Under typical circumstances law enforcement officers are expected to announce their presence and intent to carry out the search warrant before making entry or searching. However, there are circumstances that allow for a no-knock warrant, typically in drug searches. The Supreme Court has not mandated how long officers must delay entry following their announcement. For example, the Court in *United States v. Banks* (2003) held that no fixed time should be imposed; rather, the reasonableness of the wait depends on the circumstances and if an exigency, that is emergency, exists.[24]

Generally, the scope of the search is governed by its focus. Rolando V. del Carmen explains "it is unreasonable for a police officer to look for an elephant in a matchbox."[25] The object of the search, which is particularly described in the affidavit and warrant, controls where the officer can look. Obviously, small items such as illegal drugs provide the greatest search latitude. This is generally true because many statutes make it illegal to possess any usable amount of a drug substance.[26] Such small quantities can be hidden virtually anywhere; therefore, the police are permitted to search wherever it could likely be stored. Clearly, officials are expected to narrowly restrict their search to the object authorized in the warrant.[27] However, given that officers have a lawful presence when executing a search warrant, they may also seize unnamed evidence if it is discovered in plain view and within the scope of the search.[28] Finally, officials executing search warrants are required to provide a copy of the warrant and inventory of items seized to the person in possession of the searched premises.

When it comes to government search and seizure, many legal experts and courts agree that the implicit intent of the Fourth Amendment is to require a warrant for official intrusions.[29] However, there are two principal categories of government search and seizure authority—warrant and warrantless. Over the years, likely every facet of each type has been interpreted by the courts. Yet, by the twentieth century American courts demonstrated an increasing receptivity for warrantless searches. They have carved out a growing number of exceptions to the original warrant and probable cause requirements, thereby expanding search, arrest, and seizure to circumstances unforeseen to the authors of the Fourth Amendment. What has followed is a host of warrant exceptions that provide government officials many opportunities to engage in surveillance, search, and seizure without a court-ordered warrant.

EMERGENCE OF WARRANTLESS SEARCH AND SEIZURE

As early as 1925 the Supreme Court responded to the practical challenges of emerging technology by creating a warrant exception for automobiles. These types of modifications have generated a considerable body of search and seizure law that has become an extension of privacy rights of persons subject to governmental intrusion.

Doctrinal Exceptions to the Warrant Requirement

Once intractable, the Fourth Amendment bi-part provisions have been subject to significant interpretation since first written. Although probable cause continues to be central to Fourth Amendment jurisprudence, it has been supplanted by several exceptions that allow officials to engage in search and seizure using lesser standards. Three specific classes of exceptions have had a profound effect on the meaning of probable cause.

Administrative Search and Inspection Standard

In the 1960s, the high Court developed guidelines governing administrative searches and regulatory inspections conducted by government officials.

In several cases the courts established requirements such as probable cause in an administrative or statutory context, search warrants for code inspections, or allowed warrantless searches in closely regulated industries.

The seminal case of *Camara v. Municipal Court* (1967) produced an analytical framework for the code inspection of residences thus providing guidance in subsequent administrative search cases.[30] Roland Camara refused to allow San Francisco housing officials to conduct a warrantless inspection of the building where he was residing. His refusal resulted in a criminal conviction for housing code violations, and he appealed. The Supreme Court held that in the absence of the resident's consent, inspectors must obtain a court-ordered warrant to conduct an administrative search. Although the warrant must be based on probable cause, the Court ruled that officials could rely on factors such as the "passage of time, nature of the building, or condition of the area."[31] The Court's analysis included a finding that a valid public interest in preventing dangerous conditions, less intrusive noncriminal search, and lack of effective methods of conducting administrative searches could be used to allow specific administrative searches. The *Camara* case is significant because it used several lines of legal reasoning that produced doctrine allowing for an administrative search exception to the warrant and probable cause requirements, warrantless regulatory searches, and spawned search exception principles such as the "special needs beyond law enforcement."[32]

Subsequent cases widened the net on government administrative searches, giving officials greater latitude in conducting inspections or regulating industries. Like *Camara,* the Court in *See v. City of Seattle* (1967) extended the consent or warrant protection to commercial buildings. Again, it ruled that officials can inspect a commercial building on less than probable cause if they show it belongs to a class of structures subject to code inspection.[33]

However, in a series of later cases the courts went further, allowing officials to also conduct warrantless administrative searches in closely regulated industries. In *Colonnade Catering Corp. v. United States* (1970), the Supreme Court reasoned that federal Treasury agents, using valid statutes governing a closely regulated industry, were permitted to conduct a warrantless search of a liquor storage area.[34] Similarly, the Court in *United States v. Biswell* (1972) ruled that federal agents were permitted to conduct warrantless regulatory inspections of a firearms dealer.[35] The Court clearly distinguished the type of warrantless administrative searches and inspections allowed in closely regulated industries from non-regulated-type inspections that may require a warrant.[36] Moreover, the courts had sharply contrasted administrative searches or inspections and searches intended to discover criminal evidence.

However, in a significant departure, the Supreme Court in *New York v. Burger* (1987) blurred the lines between administrative and criminal searches.[37] New York City police officers conducted a random administrative inspection of Joseph Burger's junkyard business as authorized by state and municipal statute. When Burger informed them that no inventory records for the business were available, the officers conducted a search of the premises, finding stolen vehicles and auto parts. Though the officers acknowledged they had no prior suspicion, probable cause, or warrant, Burger was arrested and convicted. The *Burger* Court reasoned that the government had a substantial interest in regulating the junkyard industry and held that the search and seizure was reasonable under the administrative search exception relating to a closely regulated industry. The Court concluded that the search was consistent with the *Colonnade-Biswell* doctrine permitting warrantless regulatory inspections; therefore, the criminal evidence was lawfully obtained when discovered during a statutorily mandated inspection.

The *Burger* decision is noteworthy because its reasoning substantially deviated from case precedent when it stated "the discovery of evidence of crimes in the course of an otherwise proper administrative inspection does not render that search illegal or the administrative scheme suspect."[38] Essentially, the Court created another exception to the Fourth Amendment provisions for criminal searches under the auspices of administrative inspections.

Stop and Frisk Search Standard

In the landmark *Terry v. Ohio* decision, the Supreme Court established an alternative to the venerable probable cause requirement. It created a "reasonable suspicion" standard to authorize warrantless stop and frisk of suspected armed persons.

Cleveland police detective Martin McFadden observed two suspicious men walking repeatedly past downtown storefronts. With each pass, one would pause and gaze in the store windows and then rejoin the other around the corner in an alley. After numerous trips, they were met by a third man who stopped to confer with them. Detective McFadden was convinced the men were casing the stores in preparation for a robbery. He approached the three, identified himself as a police officer, and patted down John Terry. McFadden discovered a handgun in his coat, and the subsequent frisk of the others turned up another concealed pistol. Both of the armed men were convicted of possessing an illegal weapon and sentenced to prison. Terry challenged his conviction on the grounds that the detective's search and seizure were an unreasonable violation of his Fourth Amendment rights. He contended that the officer did not have probable cause to detain him or conduct the weapon search and seizure.

Chief Justice Earl Warren characterized the officer's actions as a "serious intrusion upon the sanctity of the person, which may inflict great indignity and arouse strong resentment, and it's not to be taken lightly."[39] Yet, the Court recognized the need to allow police officers to disarm potentially dangerous persons during a street encounter. It reasoned that the officer's decision to frisk Terry for a weapon stemmed from an articulated reasonable suspicion that the suspect was armed and dangerous. Warren wrote,

> At the time he seized petitioner [Terry] and searched him for weapons, Officer McFadden had reasonable grounds to believe that [Terry] was armed and dangerous, and it was necessary for the protection of himself and others to take swift measures to discover the true facts and neutralize the threat of harm if it materialized.[40]

The Court's monumental decision in *Terry* instantly affected the boundaries of police search. Under these circumstances officers are authorized to conduct an outer clothing pat-down search of the person. If a weapon-like object is encountered through touch, the officer is allowed to investigate further to determine if the item is a weapon. If actual arms are discovered, an arrest may follow and the limited search is considered a lawful police detention and intrusion.

But the Court did not stop mollifying the probable cause standard with the *Terry* case. In the 1980s, it issued other decisions that created substitute standards that became rationale for searches in carefully tailored circumstances where probable cause was no longer required.

Special Needs beyond Law Enforcement Standard

Often, criminal justice–related privacy jurisprudence originates in civil or administrative cases. As revealed in the *Terry* decision, the courts recognize that government officials need to conduct searches where there are insufficient grounds for probable cause or in noncriminal settings. In an effort to address irregular situations, the high Court instituted the "special needs beyond law enforcement" exception (hereafter special needs) to authorize administrative, regulatory, or noncriminal government searches using traditional police-type search and seizure practices.[41] Historically, the demarcation was between nonprosecutorial searches, where government officials sought to ensure regulatory compliance, and law enforcement searches for criminal evidence.[42] As the Court commented in several special needs cases, it is a search authority "divorced from the State's general interest in law enforcement."[43] Yet in spite of its claim that the diminished special needs standard should be applied strictly to noncriminal administrative searches, the Court has allowed the government to prosecute persons using criminal evidence obtained through this class of search. Not only do these exceptions expand government search powers beyond the realm of the original Fourth Amendment, but they increase the potential for privacy invasion.

In essence, the Supreme Court sought to remove procedural obstacles that had prevented government officials from conducting searches for reasons other than to gather criminal evidence. It found that the warrant and probable cause requirements of the Fourth Amendment were so restrictive as to be impractical in some situations.[44] In several cases the Court addressed these constraints stating "the burden of obtaining a warrant is likely to frustrate the governmental purpose behind the search."[45] Therefore, the Court created the special needs exception to allow a range of administrative-type searches.

Consider the *New Jersey v. T.L.O.* (1985) case where the new standard was applied to administrative searches conducted by public school officials.[46] Here, a student identified by the pseudonym T.L.O., along with another youth, was suspected of smoking cigarettes in the high school restroom. Though one student admitted to the violation, T.L.O. denied smoking on campus. When the assistant principal searched her purse, he found cigarettes, rolling papers, marijuana, and a written list of students owing T.L.O. money for marijuana purchases. T.L.O. was prosecuted for delinquent acts stemming from the marijuana found in her purse. She challenged her prosecution on the grounds that school administrators conducted an unreasonable search and seizure without warrant or probable cause.

The Supreme Court held that "the balance between the school child's legitimate expectations of privacy and the school's equally legitimate needs to maintain an environment in which learning can take place"[47] tilts toward public school officials. Further, the Court concluded that public school officials should be permitted to conduct searches to promote safety and the educational objectives of the institution.

This case is significant because it permits criminal evidence searches using an administrative search rationale. Hence, while use of the special needs doctrine in *New Jersey v. T.L.O.* was intended to help school officials maintain a controlled learning environment, it has been utilized to authorize warrantless searches and seizures based on reasonable grounds. In fact, many of the warrantless government searches in administrative settings rely on the special needs standard instead of Fourth Amendment warrant and probable cause requirements.[48] In many ways, the special needs exception has become a substitute for the Fourth Amendment and is used as a second tier search justification even less rigorous than the reasonable suspicion *Terry* standard.

Together, these exceptions and their progeny have substantial privacy implications since government officials can conduct searches using less than

Fourth Amendment requirements. Joining the probable cause exceptions is a group of warrantless searches.

Specific Exceptions to the Warrant Requirement

Each is considered an exception to the Fourth Amendment warrant requirement under specific circumstances.

Consent to Search Exception

One of the most common warrantless search methods used by the police is consent. Law enforcement officers can request verbal or written consent to search items within a person's control. However, courts have ruled that the police must comply with certain requirements for the consensual search to be considered reasonable and valid. First, consent must be given voluntarily, without police deception or coercion, by the person lawfully authorized to give search permission.[49] The right to provide search consent is given to the person with the greatest expectation of privacy over the object of the search.

As an illustration, if two persons share a residential apartment with each having a private bedroom, a roommate is authorized to give police consent to search only his or her own personal space and the common areas. Third-party consent is invalid here because it is given by someone without the greatest expectation of privacy over that place.[50] Some variations to this principle exist with spousal and parent-child living arrangements; however, the expectation of privacy doctrine remains the standard used by the courts. Additionally, the general scope of the search is controlled by the conditions of the consent in terms of location or extent of search.[51]

Search Incident to a Lawful Arrest and Inventory Exception

A second category of warrantless search is known as search incident to a lawful arrest. The exception includes search of persons after arrest, search within their immediate reach, and inventory of items under their control. A twofold rationale is used to conduct inventory-type searches. First, the searches are intended to enhance officer safety by allowing the officers to disarm arrestees. Second, they are to protect criminal evidence from loss or destruction.

Police officer postarrest search is limited to the body exterior, clothing, and within the suspect's immediate reach in the location of the arrest. The Court in *Chimel v. California* (1969) explained,

> When an arrest is made, it is reasonable for the arresting officer to search the
> person arrested in order to remove any weapons that the latter might seek to

use in order to resist arrest or affect his escape. In addition, it is entirely reasonable for the arresting officer to search for and seize any evidence on the arrestee's person in order to prevent its concealment or destruction. . . . There is ample justification, therefore, for a search of the arrestee's person and the area "within his immediate control."[52]

To be valid, the search must also immediately follow the arrest unless there are reasonable grounds for delay. If the search is postponed, the courts prefer the use of a warrant unless the officer can provide a reasonable justification for the noncontemporaneous search.[53]

A parallel idea is the principle of inventory. Here, officials are permitted to survey, document, or collect possessions within the control of an arrestee. Generally, possessed items are on the arrestee's person, in a carried package, or in his motor vehicle. The process of inventory also extends to custodial institutions where incarcerated persons must relinquish their personal effects upon entering the facility. Their belongings are catalogued and stored during the time of detention.

The rationale for inventory is first to protect the personal property of the arrestee and, second, to shield the officer from allegations of theft. As noted in the *Chimel* doctrine, the police are authorized to search both arrestees and the area within their immediate reach for criminal evidence. The same logic extends to the arrestee's motor vehicle if it is seized after a lawful arrest. If the driver is arrested and the police impound the vehicle, they are permitted to conduct an inventory of accessible items in the passenger compartment and trunk. If officers are unable to gain access to locked compartments, they are prohibited from using force to gain entry for the purpose of inventory. Any contraband or criminal evidence discovered during a valid inventory can be used in trial. Basically, vehicle inventories are authorized in three circumstances—abandoned, illegally parked, or driver arrest—if the police tow or impound the vehicle.[54] Together, postarrest searches and inventories are authorized warrantless search procedures designed to ensure officer safety or protect the citizen's personal belongings after arrest or impoundment.

Exigent Circumstance Exception

Police may be faced with an emergency situation where they have to act decisively to protect evidence or capture a suspect. Such circumstances could force an officer to conduct a spontaneous warrantless search that produces criminal evidence. Since the courts recognize these urgencies occur, they created the exigent circumstances rule that "permits police to make warrantless entry to effect an arrest when exigencies of the situation make that course imperative."[55]

One type of exigency is a hot or fresh pursuit where police are chasing a dangerous suspect and must make a warrantless arrest to prevent escape.[56] For example, in the *Warden v. Hayden* (1967) case,

> The police were informed that an armed robbery had taken place, and that the suspect had entered 2111 Cocoa Lane less than five minutes before they reached it. They acted reasonably when they entered the house and began to search for a man of the description they had been given and for weapons which he had used in the robbery or might use against them. The Fourth Amendment does not require police officers to delay in the course of an investigation if to do so would gravely endanger their lives or the lives of others . . . and only a thorough search of the house for persons and weapons could have insured that Hayden was the only man present and that the police had control of all weapons which could be used against them or to affect an escape.[57]

In *Warden,* the Court ruled that the police arrest of Bennie Hayden and warrantless search and seizure of weapons in the house were reasonable under the Fourth Amendment. It held ". . . the seizures occurred prior to or immediately contemporaneous with Hayden's arrest."[58]

Situational exigencies also apply to the protection of evidence. Yet, the courts have clearly held that there must be an imminent "indication that the evidence would be lost, destroyed, or removed during the time required to obtain a search warrant" to support a warrantless search and seizure.[59]

In *Mincey v. Arizona* (1978), an undercover police officer was killed during a narcotics raid at Rufus Mincey's apartment. The police immediately secured the apartment and designated it as a murder scene. They conducted an extensive search and collected numerous pieces of criminal evidence. Their decision to not obtain a search warrant was based on the murder scene exception that had been adopted by the Arizona Supreme Court, which classified it as an exigency-type exception to the warrant requirement. The U.S. Supreme Court in *Mincey* rejected this argument and ruled that only when criminal evidence is at imminent risk of loss or destruction is a warrantless exigency search reasonable.[60]

Similarly, in *Cupp v. Murphy* (1973), the Court authorized the warrantless seizure of fingernail scraping evidence, without consent or following an arrest, because there was insufficient time to obtain a warrant and such delay would result in the loss of critical evidence.[61] Thus, for a police search or seizure to satisfy the exigency test, an emergency situation must exist where imminent dangerous threat, risk of escape, or destruction of criminal evidence compel them to make a warrantless search and seizure.

Motor Vehicle Exception

Soon after the beginning of the twentieth century, motor vehicles became a popular mode of transportation. As more persons owned and operated vehicles, the likelihood they would become a target of police searches increased.[62] The Supreme Court in *Carroll v. United States* established the automobile exception finding that the vehicle's mobility created an exigent circumstance that risked the loss of criminal evidence if police were required to obtain a warrant before conducting a search.[63] Acker and Brody explain the exception as follows:

> The warrant requirement has been relaxed for car searches for two principal reasons. First, the inherent mobility of a car is said to create an exigency that obviates the need for a warrant . . . The second reason . . . is the diminished expectation of privacy that people presumably have in autos and their contents.[64]

If police officers develop probable cause to stop a motor vehicle and can establish further that criminal evidence is present, they may conduct a thorough warrantless search of the automobile, its contents, occupants, and their personal belongings if any may contain the object of the search. Though a warrantless search, the scope is the same as that authorized by a warrant.[65]

Plain View Exception

Technically, plain view is not an exception to the warrant requirement since it is not the product of a police search. Rather than a search, plain view deals with the seizure of criminal evidence. Justice Stevens in *Horton v. California* (1990) explained, "If an article is already in plain view, neither its observation nor its seizure would involve any invasion of privacy. A seizure of the article, however, would obviously invade the owner's possessory interest."[66] Basically, the doctrine states that the police must visibly observe criminal evidence, without making any additional intrusion, to seize it. Under plain view, two criteria must be satisfied. First, officers must legally be in a position to see the evidence. To fulfill this requirement their presence has to be lawful and provide them a vantage point to observe the criminal evidence without conducting a search. Second, the evidence must be immediately apparent to the officer that the item is seizable.

> [Horton] was convicted of the armed robbery of Erwin Wallaker, the treasurer of the San Jose Coin Club [and appealed]. Pursuant to the warrant, Sergeant LaRault searched [Horton's] residence, but he did not find the stolen property.

During the course of the search, however, he discovered the [illegal] weapons in plain view and seized them. Thus, the seized evidence was not discovered inadvertently.[67]

The right of the police to lawfully seize visible evidence does not require that they discover it inadvertently but only that they have probable cause, lawful presence, and recognize the evidence as something illegal, such as contraband, instrumentality of crime, or fruits of crime.[68] The Court in *Horton* held that the discovery of the firearm evidence, in plain view in Terry Horton's residence, was reasonable since he was legally executing a search warrant. Additionally, the police may use mechanical devices such as a flashlight to gaze into a dark car or binoculars to observe from a distance as long as they comply with the conditions of the plain view doctrine.[69]

FOURTH AMENDMENT CONTOURS AND PRIVACY INTERESTS

For over 200 years the Fourth Amendment has provided the courts and law enforcement a constitutional framework for searches and seizures. More than just a practical guide for proper government conduct, the Amendment is all that stands between a person's privacy and possessory interests and government intrusions. In doing so, it continues to safeguard constitutional privacy rights and acts as the definitive standard bearer for lawful search and seizure.

Chapter 3

INVESTIGATING SUSPECTS
WHEREVER FOUND

On November 5, 2003, Gary Leon Ridgway, dubbed the Green River Killer, pled guilty to the murder of 48 Seattle-area women. He confessed to a killing spree that spanned from 1982 to 1998. Investigators collected physical evidence from each crime scene and victim over the 16 years and submitted it to the Washington State Crime Lab for analysis. Though the police considered Ridgway a suspect almost immediately, they were unable to link him to the murders. In 1984, Ridgway even consented to a police polygraph test and passed. Later, in 1987 investigators obtained a search warrant and collected saliva samples from Ridgway, as well as other evidence from his house and truck. They seized hundreds of evidentiary items, and again, all of the crime scene comparisons were inconclusive. Officials simply had insufficient evidence to charge Ridgway even though they were convinced he was responsible for the worst case of serial murder in U.S. history.

Detective Tom Jensen relentlessly pursued every lead in the Green River cases for years. In 2001, he learned of new DNA testing and decided to resubmit a sample of Ridgway's saliva for comparison with semen evidence collected from three of the victims. This time the lab reported a conclusive DNA match. The forensic findings revived the 19-year murder investigation, and detectives resubmitted hair, paint, and other samples. Because of advances in science, lab tests were much more accurate than in 1987, and now with regularity they found positive comparisons between crime scene samples and those obtained from Ridgway. On December 5, 2001, Gary Ridgway was arrested and charged with four counts of Aggravated Murder in the First Degree. After exhaustively reviewing each unsolved case, detectives uncovered additional evidence that linked Ridgway to dozens of the killings. In April 2003, more murder charges were brought against him. Now faced with the death penalty, Ridgway agreed to a plea bargain in exchange for a life imprisonment sentence. As part of the plea deal, he confessed to 48 of the Green River murders and over a period of weeks provided investigators with the horrific details of his killings.[1]

As the Green River case shows, criminal investigations involve different methods to discover, collect, and analyze evidence for prosecution. Since investigations entail gathering physical and communicative evidence, the manner in which it is obtained affects the constitutional and privacy interests of the person and their communications and possessions. No longer are suspect privacy safeguards restricted to just the search and seizure of objects. Because of the threat to privacy posed by questionable police searches, the courts have created rules that prevent the government from gaining an unconstitutional advantage as a result of such practices. These guidelines require the police to follow prescribed procedures when using surveillance, search, interrogation, or seizure to acquire any type of criminal evidence against a suspect.

PRIVACY INTEREST AND EVIDENCE COLLECTION

The primary objective of criminal investigations is to solve crimes; however, most often officers must gather criminal evidence to achieve that goal. This involves independent search and seizure processes to get the information necessary to prove the suspect's guilt.

Use of Evidence to Convict Defendants

Evidence is used in criminal proceedings for its probative value, which is "... having the effect of proof; tending to prove, or actually proving."[2] The renowned legal scholar William Blackstone described evidence as "that which demonstrates, makes clear or ascertains the truth of the very fact or point in issue, either on the one side or the other."[3] In criminal proceedings, evidence must satisfy a multipart standard to withstand challenges in trial. Although the overarching objective of evidence is to demonstrate proof, it must also be deemed relevant, reliable, competent, and material to the case for the court to allow it to be used to convict a person of a criminal offense. Together, these measures require that any evidentiary item presented as proof of guilt must be believable, accurate, trustworthy, and directly related to the case at hand.[4] In the adversarial legal model, the trial interaction between prosecutor and defense attorney is oppositional with each challenging the credibility of the criminal evidence presented by the other. The legal tactic is known as impeachment where the opposing attorneys strive to persuade the court that the evidence presented is inaccurate, prejudicial, or untrustworthy. Theoretically, the credibility of any type of evidence can be attacked in court. However, impeachment is commonly used to question the character or testimonial content of a witness. According to the Federal Rules of Evidence, "The credibility of a witness may be attacked by any party, including the party calling the witness."[5]

Categories of Evidence

Criminal evidence is broadly classified as either direct or indirect. Indirect evidence is also known under the label circumstantial, which suggests that it shows proof through inference, as opposed to, being more straightforward in its ability to demonstrate guilt. One of the most highly publicized prosecutions that depended solely on circumstantial evidence was the 1995 O. J. Simpson murder trial in Los Angeles, California.[6] Simpson, a celebrity and former professional football star, was charged with two counts of intentional murder in the brutal stabbing death of Nicole Brown Simpson, his ex-wife, and her friend Ronald Goldman in Los Angeles.

When notified of the murders, Los Angeles Police Department (LAPD) officers immediately went to O. J. Simpson's Los Angeles residence where they conducted an exigency search. There they collected several evidentiary items including gloves and a knit cap. Police forensic technicians also worked for hours processing the crime scene at Nicole Brown Simpson's home. It contained a large amount of physical evidence, including blood drops and a bloody shoeprint, they believed belonged to O. J. Simpson. They also found traces of the victim's blood in O. J.'s automobile, house, and on the gloves they seized. Though they had no direct evidence, such as a confession or eyewitness, they collected a wealth of circumstantial physical evidence that was used as exhibits in Simpson's trial, among which were forensic laboratory results that showed a positive DNA match with both O. J. Simpson and the victim's blood collected by investigators. As Vincent Bugliosi characterized the DNA evidence,

> to distill this case down to its irreducible minimum (and temporarily ignoring all the other evidence pointing inexorably to Simpson's guilt), if your blood is found at the murder scene, as Simpson's was conclusively proved to be by DNA tests, that's really the end of the ball game. There is nothing more to say.[7]

The strength of the prosecution's case was the DNA typing comparison of blood found in O. J. Simpson's house, car, and the murder scene. O. J.'s lawyers challenged every piece of evidence introduced by the prosecution. Using expert witnesses and strategic cross-examination, they attacked the credibility of the evidence, the method of police collection and handling, and the veracity of the police investigators. After months of trial and only four hours of deliberation, the jury acquitted O. J. Simpson of both murders.[8]

The Simpson case illustrates first the importance of the credibility of evidence used in criminal proceedings. Second, it demonstrates how circumstantial evidence can be vulnerable to challenge because it relies on inference, and the reasoning of the judge or jury, rather than having a more factual basis like direct evidence. Third, the case shows the significance of the trustworthiness of both the evidence and the officers collecting it.

Though direct evidence may also be challenged, it can be very persuasive because it attempts to prove or disprove a fact in the case. Three types of direct evidence are used in criminal proceedings. The first is a statement or testimonial evidence supplied by the defendant, such as a confession, admission, or incriminating comment. The second is physical evidence such as illegal contraband seized while in the defendant's possession. The third is eyewitness testimony provided by a witness who has personal knowledge of the involvement of the accused in the crime. Subsumed under each general classification are several categories.

Types of Seizable Evidence

Direct and indirect evidence comprise the body of articles and information that are presented in criminal proceedings as testimony or exhibits. Testimony is a statement made under oath at trial. This can come from a witness, police officer, or defendant. Since defendants are protected by the Fifth Amendment self-incrimination privilege, they cannot be compelled to testify. Next, exhibits include physical items such as crime scene articles, documents, photographs, or scientific evidence.

Together, testimonial and physical evidence are classified as contraband, fruits of crime, instruments of crime, or evidentiary items. Contraband refers to any article or item that is prohibited by law, for example, objects such as illicit drugs, stolen property, illegal weapons, or prohibited materials. The term fruit is used to denote an article that is derived from or a product of a crime or search. Here, fruits of crime refer to "material objects acquired by means and in consequence of the commission of crime."[9] Instruments, also known as instrumentality, of crime are objects used in the commission of a crime. These refer to dangerous weapons, burglar tools, counterfeit products, or even a cyber hacker's computer software if these items are used to perpetrate a crime. Finally, evidentiary items entail articles that are utilized as criminal evidence by the police or prosecution, for instance, scientific evidence collected from a suspect or found at a crime scene. Among the evidentiary materials are human body fluids, human or animal tissues, fingerprints, drugs and toxins, hairs and fibers, firearms and ballistic materials, tool marks, casts of footprints or tire tracks, dental bite marks, explosive or flammable liquids, illicit drug precursors, handwriting samples, or documentary materials.[10] These articles are collected by law enforcement officers during warrant or warrantless searches. They are submitted as exhibits in criminal prosecutions either in their natural state or after forensic laboratory testing.

Criminal evidence is known by several different names depending on where it is found. For example, latent evidence is discovered at a crime scene. The term refers to its hidden nature suggesting that it may be present only in small trace amounts and thus difficult to find. Some types of latent evidence must be sent to a crime laboratory for scientific analysis or comparison. This is necessary to identify or match the latent sample to a suspect.

Crime labs compare evidence to an "exemplar," or comparison sample, to determine if they have the same origin. This is used with fingerprint, DNA, firearm ballistic, or handwriting evidence where investigators want to prove that the latent sample is connected to the suspect. An exemplar sample can be discovered during a field investigation or obtained directly from the criminal suspect. For example, police officers may find a gun, used in a shooting, abandoned in an open field or in a suspect's house. Once seized, the firearm will be taken to the crime lab to compare the bullet removed from the victim with an exemplar sample fired from the suspect gun by forensic technicians. When microscopically compared, a criminalist can determine if the two bullets originated from the same gun. If matched, the latent-exemplar comparison evidence will be presented in court as an exhibit to prove the defendant's guilt.

The second method is to gather an exemplar directly from the criminal suspect. Unless the suspect consents, a court-ordered search warrant is required because of the level of privacy intrusion. The only exception is if an exigency precludes obtaining a warrant. In the case of biological evidence such as fingerprint, body fluid, or hair, the suspect will be required to provide a sample for comparison.

Physical evidence, and the procedures used to collect and manage it, is an integral part of solving crimes. However, they affect the constitutional and privacy rights of persons subject to investigation, arrest, or prosecution.

Investigative Practices and Constitutional Safeguards

The probity of evidence, the person collecting, and the legality of the search and seizure are crucial to the integrity of the process and protection of individual privacy rights. Law enforcement officers play an indispensable role in building cases against criminal suspects. They are expected to abide by widely accepted procedures in compiling information for the prosecutor. The manner in which evidence is searched, seized, and handled is critical in protecting the privacy interests of the suspect.

For instance, consider the situation of the LAPD's Rampart Division corruption scandal that resulted in the dismissal of 171 criminal cases and $70 million in victim lawsuit settlements.[11] Officer Rafael Pérez and other members of the Community Resources against Street Hoodlum's antigang unit were responsible for a host of civil right violations involving false criminal accusations and fabricated evidence. The officers planted phony evidence on suspects, altered police reports, and committed perjury. Among the charges was a 1996 incident involving Rampart Sergeants Edward Ortiz and Brian Liddy, Officer Paul Harper, and suspected gang member Allan Lobos. "The criminal complaint against the three officers charged that Liddy 'or an unidentified co-conspirator rubbed the gun in Allan Lobos' fingers,' that Ortiz 'falsified statements in the sergeants log' and that Harper 'knowingly relied on the false report in preparation for filing the probable cause determination.'"[12] Other officers were involved in the wrongdoing. Perhaps the most egregious offender, however, was Officer Rafael Pérez who admitted to stealing eight pounds of cocaine from the police evidence locker and using it to frame gang members in false drug cases. But the most serious allegation involved Officer Pérez and his partner, Nino Durden, who were accused of shooting unarmed Javier Francisco Ovando and then planting a gun on him to cover it up.[13]

Unfortunately, the Rampart abuses are not isolated. Other documented incidences of police violation of constitutional rights have occurred including those involving illegally obtained confessions. In the famed Chicago Area Two interrogation probe, investigators revealed that Chicago Police Department officers, under the command of Jon Burge, used tactics such as beating, burning, and electric shock to obtain coerced confessions from dozens of suspects as far back as the 1980s. Following an internal investigation begun in the mid-1990s, numerous wrongful convictions stemming from the forced confessions were overturned.[14]

These cases show only a portion of the police misconduct problem.[15] Yet, they raise serious privacy right concerns stemming from the fraudulent collection and use of evidence by police officers. Criminal evidence is instrumental to the outcome of a prosecution where the case may hinge on the credibility of the exhibits against the accused. In order for seized evidence to be admissible in a criminal trial, it must be obtained legally.

EXCLUSIONARY RULE

As early as 1914 the Supreme Court addressed the issue of using illegally searched evidence in criminal prosecutions. In *Weeks v. United States* (1914), the Court held that criminal evidence searched and seized in violation of the

Fourth Amendment must be suppressed and is inadmissible in trial under the "exclusionary rule." Justice William Day explained, "The tendency of those who execute the criminal laws of the country to obtain conviction by means of unlawful seizures . . . should find no sanction in the judgments of the courts."[16] Later in *Mapp v. Ohio* (1961) the Court extended the federal rule to state cases prohibiting the admissibility of criminal evidence that was unlawfully searched and seized. There Justice Tom Clark wrote, " . . . the [Fourth and Fifth] Amendments 'apply to all invasions on the part of the government . . . [into] the sanctity of a man's home and the privacies of life . . . the essence of the offence . . . is the invasion of his indefeasible right of personal security, personal liberty, and private property.' "[17]

Fruits of the Poisonous Tree Doctrine

To address the matter of secondary illegal evidence, the Court established the "fruits of the poisonous tree" doctrine. It holds that any searched and seized evidence, which is connected to an invalid search preceding it, becomes tainted and is also inadmissible.[18] As an illustration, police officers unlawfully stop a motor vehicle and search the passenger compartment where they discover illegal drugs. Based on that evidence, they arrest the driver and, upon conducting a postarrest inventory of the car, they find stolen property in the trunk. The illegally obtained drugs will be excluded by the courts pursuant to the exclusionary rule. And since the stolen property was found only as a result of an unlawful search and arrest, it too will be inadmissible because of the fruits of the poisonous tree doctrine. The exclusionary rule and its progeny, however, are not absolute, and the courts have created several exceptions to the doctrines.

Exceptions to the Exclusionary and Fruits of the Poisonous Tree Doctrines

Given the uncertain course police investigations may take, federal courts recognize that unconditionally excluding all evidence determined to violate the Fourth Amendment is unrealistic. Therefore, the Supreme Court has created four exceptions that may allow, on a case basis, improperly searched evidence to be used in trial. The courts have endorsed the good faith, inevitable discovery, purged taint, and independent source exceptions to the exclusionary or fruits of the poisonous tree rules.

Although not accepted by some state courts, the good faith exception allows the use of evidence if the police conduct an invalid search based upon a reasonable belief that their actions were lawful, such as relying on defective court papers or erroneous information.[19] Second, the inevitable discovery exception states that if a police search would have ultimately discovered the evidence without outside assistance, such as a coerced confession, the items found are admissible.[20] The third exception is the purged taint rule. It applies in situations where the police conduct an unreasonable search and later obtain voluntary information from an arrested person leading them to the evidence.[21] A fourth recognized exception is independent source. This application requires that the police demonstrate that they obtained evidence as a result of information completely detached from their Fourth Amendment violation.

In *Murray v. United States* (1988), federal agents entered a warehouse without a warrant and observed a large quantity of marijuana. Without mentioning their discovery, they obtained a search warrant for the same location and returned to seize the evidence. The Court remanded the case to the trial court stating

> ...Knowledge that the marijuana was in the warehouse was assuredly acquired at the time of the unlawful entry. But it was also acquired at the time of entry pursuant to the warrant, and if that later acquisition was not the result of the earlier entry there is no reason why the independent source doctrine should not apply.[22]

Suppressed Evidence and the *Miranda* Rule

Privacy safeguards also extend to evidence derived from incriminating gestures or statements made by persons in custody. In the landmark *Miranda v. Arizona* (1966) decision, the Supreme Court established a bright-line rule requiring the police to inform arrestees of their Fifth and Sixth Amendment rights to remain silent and request legal counsel prior to interrogation. The procedure is required in all police custodial interrogations. Suspects have the right to refuse to answer questions, if the answers could produce incriminating evidence, or they may invoke their right to legal counsel, which forces the termination of police questioning. Although the *Miranda* requirement has multiple dimensions, its primary focus is on testimonial evidence, such as admission or confession, obtained in violation of the defendant's Fifth Amendment self-incrimination privilege.[23] The relationship between the *Miranda* warning and acquisition of tainted evidence is important to examine.

In *United States v. Patane* (2004), the Court explained the distinction between protected statements and physical evidence subject to the exclusionary rule. Samuel Patane was arrested for harassment and released subject to a restraining order prohibiting him from contacting his ex-girlfriend. While out on bond, Patane telephoned his former girlfriend in violation of the court order. During the investigation police received information that Patane, a convicted felon, was illegally in possession of a handgun. When they went to his home to arrest him, they tried to advise Patane of his *Miranda* rights but he obstructed their attempts to explain the warning. During unwarned questioning after arrest, Patane told the officers where the pistol was located. He was convicted on the weapons charge and appealed arguing that the handgun evidence should be suppressed by the exclusionary rule since it was a fruit of an illegal search. The Supreme Court disagreed, finding that since Patane provided a voluntary statement, albeit unprotected by the *Miranda* warning, the exclusionary rule does not require the evidence to be suppressed because it was not discovered as a result of an unreasonable police search.[24]

Unequivocally forbidding the use of illegally searched and seized evidence, under the exclusionary rule, is the most rigid evidentiary restriction in the world. Justice Antonin Scalia, in his dissent in *Roper v. Simmons* (2005), commented, "The Court-pronounced exclusionary rule ... is unique to American jurisprudence."[25] The primary goal of the rules is to be a deterrent against unlawful police searches. At the same time, they protect the Fourth Amendment and privacy rights of persons who may be unfairly disadvantaged by the introduction of improperly obtained evidence. American police are expected to abide by specific guidelines and use legal practices when investigating crimes whether in public or private places.

POLICE INVESTIGATIONS AND PRIVACY INTERESTS

Criminal Investigations in Public and Private Space

One of George Orwell's contributions to the popular lexicon is the idea of Big Brother government monitoring citizens to ensure compliance with official regulations.[26] The reasonableness of a person's expectation of privacy depends, in part, on whether criminal investigations are conducted or laws enforced in a public or private domain. Clearly, police officers have greater latitude to investigate crimes in a public space than they do in a private home. Therefore, when people voluntarily enter public places, whether it is a street, building, or common space, they reduce their level of privacy expectation and ability to challenge some police intrusions.

Regulating Behavior in Public Space

The intersection between privacy rights and broader constitutional protections, such as liberty or expression, in the public sphere can be difficult to parse. Obviously, governments can regulate behaviors that threaten public safety and peace. As Sue Titus Reid explained, "All crimes might be considered offenses against the peace of the king or the state, but common law and modern statutes use 'offenses against the public peace and order' to refer to those offenses that are punishable primarily because they invade society's peace and tranquility."[27]

Although persons have no expectation of privacy claim regarding their physical appearance exposed to public view, it is well established in common law that they do have a privacy interest in their identity.[28] They also have a liberty interest in free movement in public places and a right not to be unlawfully encumbered by government officials. And yet, the authorities can control public activities to promote the greater interest of society. In furtherance of those goals, laws and courts place limits on certain behaviors and modes of expression in public places.

Consider the fashion laws in Lynwood, Illinois. Community leaders there enacted an ordinance that restricts the wearing of saggy pants if they expose more than three inches of underwear in public. Town Mayor Eugene Williams said, "[P]eople who wear those pants look as though they have no regard for anything."[29] Williams insists he wants to improve the community's image and attract more businesses. He claims that young males exposing their underwear sullies the town's image and hinders prospects for economic growth. Violators will be subject to a $25 fine if caught by the police.[30] This law illustrates a local government's ability to regulate public behaviors or expressions. Critics could certainly cite the right to be let alone privacy theory in arguing that such laws unduly restrict expression. Some forms of First Amendment expression are also subject to government regulations.

In general, five categories of speech are not protected by the First Amendment and can be controlled—obscenity, fighting words, inciting threats or unlawful conduct, defamation, and public nuisances.[31] Regarding free speech, the Supreme Court noted in *Speiser v. Randall* (1958) "the line between speech unconditionally guaranteed and speech which may be regulated, suppressed, or punished is finely drawn."[32] In *Schenck v. United States* (1919), Justice Oliver Wendell Holmes wrote, "The most stringent protection of free speech would not protect a man in falsely shouting 'fire' in a crowded theater, causing panic . . . The question in every case is whether the words . . . create a clear and present danger . . . ."[33] Not all public displays of expression, however, are restricted by laws. Some may be considered offensive, but the courts have ruled that certain public words or symbolic expressions are protected. For instance, the Supreme Court ruled that statutes cannot restrain vulgar words that do not incite public disorder or displays of flag or cross burning.[34]

When individuals expose their persona or property to public view, they have a diminished privacy protection against others, including government officials, observing their activities. Conversely, persons placed in the private sphere, such as pertaining to their bodies or located in their homes, have an increased expectation of privacy regarding government invasion. When police question, investigate, search, or seize, privacy rights are measured in the context not only of reasonable expectation but also relative to the location or object targeted.

Pedestrian Contact Investigations

Police officers regularly observe and converse with citizens in public space. Law enforcement best practices suggest that an officer's visible public presence yields several benefits. Among those are improved police-community relations, fear-of-crime reduction, crime deterrence, crime reduction, and increased criminal apprehensions.[35] Although police research has produced mixed findings on the precise crime-reduction effects of police officer visibility, it clearly heightens the prospects of officer-citizen contact.[36] That, in itself, can improve relations and enhance police efficacy. In fact, some of the most fundamental principles of the community-oriented policing model, adopted by most American police agencies, are predicated upon police-citizen interaction.[37] When authorities merely approach or contact citizens in public space, that in and of itself does not raise constitutional concerns or necessarily threaten privacy interests. However, when police officers engage in authoritative actions that stop, detain, search, or seize individuals, these actions have important legal ramifications.

A police officer's authority to question, stop, or detain individuals in public places is an indispensable field investigation tool in crime fighting. Such procedures produce valuable information and have proven to be instrumental in furthering criminal investigations and developing probable cause for lawful searches and seizures. Whether responding to a complaint, informant tip, or acting on an officer's observation, police commonly confront persons to ask for identification or question for information. People have both privacy and liberty interests regarding freedom of movement on private property or in authorized public places.

Yet, police officers are also allowed to stop, question, and even frisk persons if they have reasonable suspicion, are investigating crime, or ensuring safety. Antithetically, if a lost person stops a stranger on the street to ask for directions, no constitutional interests are affected because the questioner is not a government official and lacks the authority to restrict the stranger from leaving or to compel him to answer questions. However, these same acts performed by a police officer, in an official capacity, have important privacy implications for the person stopped.

Officer-Citizen Contact

An antecedent to an officer's official stop is simply contacting a person in a public place. By itself the act is benign and can be a nonintrusive element of reasonable inquiry or preliminary investigation. But such overtures can uncover a furtive response or behavior that prompts the officer to investigate further, leading to more restrictive actions. In a legal context, identifying clear demarcations between an officer's approach, stop, and search can be difficult. Thus, on several occasions the Supreme Court has been asked to clarify the difference between mere questioning, authoritative stop, and seizure. For instance, in *United States v. Mendenhall* (1980), officers approached the suspect in an airport terminal, identified themselves as federal agents, and asked to see Sylvia Mendenhall's identification and airline ticket. She claimed that the agents made an unlawful seizure since they lacked any reasonable suspicion. The Court held that their approach did not constitute a seizure. Essentially, the *Mendenhall* Court reaffirmed a police officer's authority to approach and question people in public places as long as their actions are not coercive or too restrictive.[38]

Similarly, in *Florida v. Bostick* (1991), the high Court supported police suspicionless questioning of bus passengers in a public place. Before its departure, Miami police officers boarded a bus, bound for Atlanta, to question passengers as part of a drug enforcement initiative. They approached passenger Terrance Bostick and asked to see his identification and bus ticket. After reviewing the documents, they asked if he would consent to a search of his personal bag. Although they informed Bostick he could refuse, he agreed and they found cocaine. Justice Sandra Day O'Connor commented,

> Our cases make it clear that a seizure does not occur simply because a police officer approaches an individual and asks a few questions. So long as a reasonable person would feel free 'to disregard the police and go about his business,' the encounter is consensual and no reasonable suspicion is required.[39]

Officer Questioning

Obviously, police officers regularly approach people to verify identity, gather information, or investigate suspicious activity. What logically follows is collecting information that may lead to further inquiry, search, or reveal criminal evidence. Just as the *Miranda* doctrine protects persons in custody from being compelled to answer questions, people subject to police inquiries in the field also have the option of refusing to answer in some situations. Generally, persons cannot be required to answer questions during a mere field questioning as an extension of a stop. However, exceptions exist where statutes require information from crime witnesses, motorists to produce a driver's license upon demand, or in situations where compulsory identification is required. In *Hiibel v. Sixth Judicial District Court of Nevada* (2004), the Supreme Court addressed the latter. A Nevada sheriff's deputy arrested Larry Hiibel for violation of a stop and identify state law requiring "... any person [subject to a *Terry* stop] so detained shall identify himself, but may not be compelled to answer any other inquiry of any peace officer."[40] The deputy was investigating a reported assault and encountered a pickup truck on a rural road fitting the description of the suspects' vehicle. When the deputy approached the driver, he asked for identification. The man appeared intoxicated, refused to answer or provide identification, and goaded the deputy into arresting him.

In upholding the Nevada law, the Court held that it violated neither the Fourth Amendment as an unreasonable seizure nor Fifth Amendment privilege against self-incrimination. It reasoned that the "request for identity has an immediate relation to the purpose, rationale, and practical demands of a *Terry* stop" and that "the request for identification was reasonably related in scope to the circumstances which justified the stop."[41] Although the *Hiibel* Court narrowly focused on the constitutionality of the Nevada statute, the case is significant because it clarified the relationship between a reasonable *Terry* stop and the police questions that are a natural part of such investigations. Thus far, the Court has not established a bright-line rule bestowing a blanket constitutional or privacy protection that would allow persons to refuse to answer police questions. In the context of a *Terry* stop, which by its nature progresses beyond a mere approach, statutes may require persons to provide identification, but they cannot compel them to make incriminating statements.

Official Stop and Detention

Using this multistage process—approach, stop, question, and search, it has been established that police officers can approach and question people in public places without the practice illegally invading privacy or restraining their movement as long as the person is not coerced by the authorities. The second stage is stopping a person in public. This connotes a temporary detention or restricting voluntary movement. That action has greater privacy implications because the individual is not free to leave until officers complete their inquiry or frisk.

Police officers can stop and temporarily detain persons during field investigations if they have reasonable suspicion to believe that the individual is armed or crime is afoot.[42] The constituent elements of reasonable suspicion can emanate from the police officer's experience, contextual circumstances, or a detainee's behavior. On the one hand, individuals are constitutionally protected against unreasonable police detention or seizure; and on the other, authorities have the power to lawfully restrict a person's movement for a brief period with legal cause.

The Supreme Court explained whether a police officer's effort to stop someone constitutes a seizure in *California v. Hodari D* (1991). Two Oakland, California, plain-clothes officers on patrol noticed several youth congregated around a car. When the teens saw the police approaching, they ran in separate directions and the car sped away. Officer Jerry Pertoso chased Hodari Dulan on foot and just before catching him, the youth discarded an object. The officer handcuffed him and recovered the article later determined to be crack cocaine. Hodari was convicted of drug possession, and he appealed on the grounds that the cocaine was the fruit of an illegal seizure and should be suppressed under the exclusionary rule. The Court majority disagreed. Justice Scalia wrote, "In sum, assuming that [Officer] Pertoso's pursuit in the present case constituted a 'show of authority' enjoining Hodari to halt, since Hodari did not comply with that injunction he was not seized until he was tackled. The cocaine abandoned while he was running was in this case not the fruit of the seizure . . . ."[43] In *Hodari D.,* the Court ruled that the illegal drugs were voluntarily abandoned by the suspect; hence, he relinquished all expectation of privacy and the officer could recover the evidence. Since the officer saw Hodari toss the object away, he could place the drugs in the teen's possession prior to its recovery. Therefore, the discovery was not the result of a search in connection with Hodari being handcuffed.

Terry Frisk Search

The terms stop and frisk are frequently combined in a manner that suggests they are a single process. More accurately, stop, question, and frisk are separate official acts. From a privacy perspective, three separate stages are actually involved. The initial step is when officers use their legal authority to stop a person. Next, they may question the person detained. Last, if officers have sufficient reasonable suspicion, they can conduct a pat-down search, known in legal parlance as a frisk. Under the *Terry* doctrine, stop and frisk is a bifurcated process. Rolando V. del Carmen comments, "Although the term stop and frisk is often spoken as though one continuous act were involved, it is actually two separate acts, each having its own requirements for legality."[44]

If a field contact rises to the level of a *Terry* stop, the last stage of the encounter is a frisk search. The procedure involves a greater degree of intrusion than the preceding stage. Here, the legal impetus for commencing a frisk is if the officer has reasonable suspicion to believe the person detained is armed. Its intrusiveness depends on an incremental justification at each level of the search. If the approach and temporary detention are lawful, then the officer can proceed to search the outer body and clothing using plain touch. If an object's contour, when felt with the hand, suggests that what lies beneath in the pocket or clothing is a weapon, the officer can proceed with the search. Under those circumstances, if an illegal gun or knife is discovered, the officer has probable cause to make a lawful arrest. If the stop and frisk procedures are properly applied and results in the suspect's arrest, an inventory search can follow and any criminal evidence found may be used.

As explained in *Minnesota v. Dickerson* (1993), the Supreme Court reiterated that the justification for a *Terry* frisk is construed very narrowly to allow a search for weapons based only on the need to immediately disarm a suspect. To be admissible, any other type of criminal evidence seized pursuant to *Terry* must be discovered through plain hand touch and immediately apparent that the object felt is contraband other than a prohibited weapon. In *Dickerson,* an officer conducting a pat-down frisk felt an object through the outside of the suspect's pocket that, based on his experience, he concluded was rock cocaine, not a weapon. He proceeded to search inside the pocket, discovered the drugs, and arrested Timothy Dickerson. On appeal, the Court found that the evidence was inadmissible because the scope of the officer's search exceeded the *Terry* limitation.[45]

Police-citizen encounters occur in different public settings. Though many of the constitutional principles and practices used in pedestrian encounters apply to motor vehicle contacts, the conveyances themselves have a lesser privacy expectation than persons.

Motor Vehicles and Police Traffic Encounters

Police Traffic Encounters

Given the common use of motor vehicles for transportation and commerce, every state has enacted extensive traffic laws to promote the safe operation of vehicles. Laws impose requirements for licensing, mechanical condition, and operation of motor vehicles on public roadways. Together, these laws provide considerable enforcement opportunities for authorities to regulate the public use of motor vehicles. Not to mention, law enforcement officers frequently use motor vehicle stops as a pretext for investigating other suspicious activities.[46] Even though the Supreme Court created a warrant exception for motor vehicles, it has not abandoned all constitutional protections in vehicle-related circumstances. The courts have essentially extended the principles used in pedestrian privacy and search jurisprudence to motorists.

In every sense, however, a vehicle stop is considered a seizure that invokes Fourth Amendment protections. As such, officials must have either probable cause or reasonable suspicion to lawfully search and seize motorists and their vehicles. The Supreme Court in *Delaware v. Prouse* (1979) rejected the use of evidence obtained as a result of a roving patrol stop to check for driver's license and registration because the officers lacked probable cause or reasonable suspicion to initiate the vehicle's seizure.[47]

Conversely, if the police have probable cause indicating a traffic violation has been committed, they are authorized to make a stop. As Justice Scalia commented in *Whren v. United States* (1996), "As a general matter, the decision to stop an automobile is reasonable where the police have probable cause to believe that a traffic violation has occurred."[48] In this case, Washington, D.C., plain-clothes vice officers, patrolling in a high drug-traffic area, observed a truck make an extreme U-turn, turn without a signal, and travel at an unreasonable speed. When they caught up to the truck at a red light, one officer approached the driver, commanding him to park the vehicle at which point he observed passenger Michael Whren holding two bags of crack cocaine. Whren was arrested for drug possession. After conviction, he appealed arguing that the traffic stop was unreasonable because it was only a pretext for a drug search. A unanimous Supreme Court disagreed.[49]

As a general rule relying on the totality of circumstances, the Supreme Court has held that reasonable suspicion is an appropriate legal standard to justify vehicle stops, as well.[50] The federal Court of Appeals in *United States v. Hunnicutt* (1998) explained the justification as "[a]n initial traffic stop is valid under the Fourth Amendment not only if based on an observed traffic violation, but also if the officer has a reasonable articulable suspicion that a traffic or equipment violation has occurred . . . ."[51]

Like other aspects of public life, a person's expectation of privacy is diminished when traveling in a motor vehicle in public places. Here, people are not afforded the constitutional privacy protection available for a person's body or dwelling. The Supreme Court in *United States v. Knotts* (1984) reasoned that "[a] person traveling in an automobile on public thoroughfares has no reasonable expectation of privacy in his movements from one place to another."[52] Moreover, the courts view vehicle or traffic stops as less intrusive than some other types of search and seizure.[53] And since obtaining a driver's license is a privilege, as opposed to a constitutionally guaranteed right, the license holder must comply with the statutory conditions placed on the permit. Although expectation privacy is reduced, motorists retain a modicum of constitutional and privacy protections when it comes to enforcement actions taken by police officers.

Just as officers contact pedestrians and may be justified in questioning, detaining, or frisking them, they may utilize the same investigative tools with motorists or passengers. There are also three circumstances in which the motor vehicle itself stores or transports contraband or evidence and acts as a provable element in the commission of a crime. Offenses involving driving under the influence of alcohol or drugs (DUI), vehicular homicide, and motor vehicle theft/larceny treat the motor vehicle as a requisite element of the crime. In other words, the police and prosecution must show that a motor vehicle was involved in the physical act of committing these crimes. Here, the vehicle functions as an instrument or fruit of crime, depending on the offense. As the offense title denotes, DUI requires the driving or operation of the motor vehicle thereby making the conveyance a necessary instrument of the crime. Likewise, proving a vehicular homicide offense necessitates showing that the vehicle was the proximate cause of a traffic death. From a different perspective, motor vehicles are also implicated as a fruit of crime in offenses involving stolen vehicles. If a person is charged with possessing a stolen car, the vehicle becomes a critical element in proving the crime.

There are other criminal offenses, such as motor vehicle burglary, arson, and vandalism, where the auto may be important to a criminal investigation or a provable element in an offense. However, since the courts view motor vehicles and their use as a special privacy situation, the expectation of owner, possessor, driver, or passenger is dramatically reduced. Although motor vehicle compartments can store evidentiary items, the automobile by itself can be a repository of criminal evidence. In the *Cardwell v. Lewis* (1974) case, police seized the defendant's car from a public parking lot and collected paint and tire tread samples to compare to crime scene evidence. The Supreme Court commented, "With the 'search' limited to the examination of the tire on the wheel and the taking of paint scraping from the exterior of the vehicle left in the public parking lot, we fail to comprehend what expectation of privacy was infringed."[54] In spite of the frequency of motor vehicle and motorist involvement in police investigations, one of the most common encounters affecting constitutional interests is the prevention and investigation of DUI.

Driving under the Influence of Alcohol or Drug

Driving under the influence of alcohol or drug laws typically define a motor vehicle as an automobile, truck, watercraft, airplane, or other motorized conveyance. This class of offenses criminalizes operating the motor vehicle if the driver's intoxication impairs his or her function. Intoxication is outlined in statutory law based upon designated blood alcohol or drug level criteria. In these instances the motor vehicle operation, the driver, and the substance intoxication content are all elements of the offense that must be proven in trial to obtain a conviction.

In two substantial areas, police have been allowed to infringe on motorist privacy and liberty interests when enforcing DUI laws. DUI investigations involve several progressive steps as officers first must develop reasonable suspicion or probable cause to stop and temporarily detain the driver. This occurs when the officer observes the motorist violate a traffic law or display manifestations of intoxication during a sobriety checkpoint or traffic stop. Roadside sobriety tests are designed to assist police in making a determination of driver intoxication. Since alcohol and drug impairment exhibit physical indicia, such as slurred speech or staggering, officers use them as signs of intoxication. Police officers may ask the driver to perform standard maneuvers to detect symptoms of impairment.[55] By consenting to participate in the tests, drivers forfeit their privacy expectation, which allows the officer to use the observations in establishing probable cause for arrest. Law enforcement officers can utilize both sobriety tests and portable breath-alcohol content measuring instruments to determine the driver's presumed intoxication level. The handheld Breathalyzer™ or Passive Alcohol Sensor™ devices detect the presence of alcohol on the driver's breath. They collect either directly exhaled or ambient breath from the driver or automobile compartment and provide the officer with an instrumentation display of the blood alcohol level.[56]

Regarding field sobriety tests, many police agencies rely on the Standardized Field Sobriety Tests model that consists of a battery of three measures to assess physical coordination or psychomotor indicia of intoxication. It uses the Horizontal Gaze Nystagmus Test, Walk and Turn Test, and One-Leg Stand Test to assess the eye trembling and balance coordination of suspected drunk drivers.[57] The Supreme Court has not directly addressed the constitutionality of each field sobriety test; therefore, there continues to be debate regarding the legality of some procedures and devices used to determine a presumption of intoxication in the field.[58] However, the Court has established a line of cases giving the police considerable Fourth Amendment leeway in DUI enforcement.

The Supreme Court found that measures to determine driving sobriety were generally permissible, given their minimally intrusive nature, when balanced against the interests of society.[59] Since such tests are not communicative, and the driver is only under investigation at that point, no constitutional Fifth

Amendment self-incrimination protection is available in these circumstances. Likewise, if the driver has not been arrested, no *Miranda* warning is required. Although results of the field sobriety test may be used to formulate probable cause to arrest, and as circumstantial evidence in trial, they fail to be grounds for a privacy violation claim.[60] In essence, drivers have no expectation of privacy over observed physical traits or exhaled breath smelled by a police officer pursuant to a DUI investigation in the field. And by consenting to take field sobriety performance tests or contribute their breath for portable analysis, they have relinquished any privacy claim over the collected evidence. However, the driver may refuse to take the test, but the officer can use any observed driving behavior, driver physical trait, or presumptive blood alcohol content instrument results to construct probable cause for arrest and as evidence in trial.[61] As insurance attorney Michele Fields explains, "You have no privacy interest in the way [your breath] smell[s] . . . there is no Fourth Amendment protection."[62]

After an arrest a breath, urine, or blood sample is collected for testing. Since states require the test to determine intoxication level, driver refusal to provide a sample results in automatic DUI charges and the possibility of license suspension in many states.[63] Given that states compel suspected drunk drivers to supply breath or body fluid specimens, the Supreme Court in *Schmerber v. California* (1966) considered whether the nonconsensual warrantless seizure violated the Fourth Amendment.

In this seminal 1966 case, the Court held that the police can have medical personnel draw blood from a person arrested for drunk driving without consent or warrant to secure evidence of intoxication. The high Court reasoned that seizing the body fluid evidence was reasonable as an exigency because to delay would risk loss of critical evidence.[64] The forcible removal of blood from an arrestee is extremely intrusive, yet, because of the ephemeral nature of the evidence, the Court authorized that level of privacy invasion. *Schmerber* became not only the test case but is the benchmark regarding seizure of body fluids using exigency as an exception to the warrant requirement.

Warrantless Motor Vehicle Search and Seizure

Search and seizure jurisprudence related to motor vehicles and their occupants is voluminous. Privacy right doctrine has also been applied by the courts to this specialized setting with increasing regularity. If authorities have a court-issued arrest or search warrant for motor vehicles or their occupants, they may execute them in the same fashion as in a nonvehicle situation.

The courts have established three legal standards that permit officials to stop motor vehicles without a warrant—probable cause, reasonable suspicion, or tailored roadblocks. In some circumstances, the police officers' legal position is strengthened in the traffic context because they may have formulated reasonable suspicion or probable cause prior to stopping the vehicle. Furthermore, search and seizure rules are more relaxed in the motor vehicle setting because of the atmosphere of exigency surrounding the mobility of people and evidence.

When it comes to balancing civil rights and police powers, American courts view police-citizen traffic interaction from two perspectives. First, movable vehicles present an exigent circumstance that jeopardizes the seizure of criminal evidence. Second, police-citizen traffic encounters are dangerous as officers have an elevated risk of injury or death.[65] Some research refutes the actual hazard posed by routine traffic contacts, instead finding that death and injury occur infrequently.[66] Nevertheless, the perception of officer risk prevails in many courts that have granted greater latitude in searching vehicles and occupants. Due to safety concerns, courts allow police officers, without individualized suspicion, to order drivers and passengers out of vehicles during a lawful traffic stop.[67] Consistent with *Terry* stop and frisk, if officers can articulate reasonable suspicion that a vehicle occupant may be carrying a dangerous weapon, they are permitted to conduct a pat-down search. Additionally, under the *Chimel* doctrine, the officer may search the passenger compartment of the vehicle within the person's reach for threatening weapons.[68]

If police officers legally stop a motor vehicle, they are in a position to exercise a complete range of search and seizure powers already allowed in non-traffic situations. In vehicle stops, if the initial police contact is based on one of the three legitimate standards, officers have standing and can legally use their natural senses to detect criminal evidence or elements of criminality that would prompt further investigation.[69] In this context, the plain view doctrine allows officers to look in the vehicle and even use a mechanical device such as a flashlight to enhance their sight to discover contraband.[70] The Supreme Court addressed this issue in *New York v. Class* (1986) where a police officer stopped a car for a traffic violation. After the driver exited the car, the officer moved papers on the dashboard that, in violation of state law, obstructed the Vehicle Identification Number (VIN) placard. While inside the vehicle, the officer observed a handgun on the floor and arrested Benigno Class for illegal weapon possession. Although the Court concluded that the officer reaching into the car technically constitutes a Fourth Amendment search, moving the papers to see the VIN was not, and the driver had no reasonable expectation of privacy violated.[71]

Even though the natural senses doctrine, such as plain view sight, touch, or smell, was designed for situations where officers discover illegal items without conducting an intrusive search, one case allowed a drug dog sniff of a vehicle to formulate probable cause. The Court in *Illinois v. Caballes* (2005) was asked to decide "whether the Fourth Amendment requires reasonable, articulable suspicion to justify using a drug-detection dog to sniff a vehicle during a legitimate traffic stop."[72] In ruling that it did not, the Court explained,

> The legitimate expectation that information about perfectly lawful activity will remain private is categorically distinguishable from respondent's hopes or expectations concerning the nondetection of contraband in the trunk of his car. A dog sniff conducted during a concededly lawful traffic stop that reveals no information other than the location of a substance that no individual has any right to possess does not violate the Fourth Amendment.[73]

Here, Roy Caballes was stopped for speeding by an Illinois state trooper. A second trooper joined the stop with his drug interdiction dog, which sniffed the car's exterior while the violator was being ticketed. The dog alerted to the trunk of the car, and the officers conducted a search that produced marijuana. Caballes was arrested and convicted of drug charges, which were upheld on appeal.[74] This case shows that individual expectation of privacy is reduced even further concerning contraband stored in vehicles located in public places and subject to law enforcement sweeps using dogs. In *Caballes,* the driver's drugs were not immune from detection even though the police had no individualized suspicion or probable cause until the dog's reaction to the scent of the contraband. Hence, once police formulate valid probable cause, they can initiate searches and seizures during traffic stops in various circumstances.

The Supreme Court has long considered motor vehicle stops Fourth Amendment seizures. Ordinarily, however, they concluded that the driver was the only person seized in the process since they are in control of the vehicle.

In 2007, the Court was asked to clarify whether a passenger was also seized, as the driver, by a police vehicle stop. California deputy sheriffs on patrol noticed a suspicious expired license plate on a parked vehicle. Later they encountered the same car on the road displaying a temporary permit. They stopped the car and during a review of the driver's license, one deputy recognized the passenger as a wanted parole violator. He verified that passenger Bruce Brendlin had an outstanding arrest warrant for parole violation. Brendlin was arrested and searched, leading to the discovery of drug paraphernalia. A pat-down search of driver Karen Simeroth also uncovered a syringe and suspected marijuana that resulted in her arrest. The subsequent vehicle search produced equipment used to manufacture methamphetamine.

Brendlin was convicted of manufacturing illegal drugs, and he appealed arguing that the evidence obtained through searches of his person and the vehicle were fruits of an unconstitutional seizure. In *Brendlin v. California* (2007), Justice David Souter wrote,

> When a police officer makes a traffic stop, the driver of the car is seized within the meaning of the Fourth Amendment. We hold that a passenger is seized as well and so may challenge the constitutionality of the stop . . . Brendlin was seized from the moment Simeroth's car came to a halt on the side of the road, and it was an error [by the lower court] to deny his suppression motion on the ground that seizure occurred only at the formal arrest.[75]

Two general circumstances trigger authorization for police officers to conduct warrantless searches of motor vehicles, its contents, or occupants. First, law enforcement officers can search a motor vehicle if given voluntary consent by the person with the greatest expectation of privacy over the vehicle.[76] Second, if officers formulate legitimate probable cause, they are permitted to arrest the driver, occupant, and search the vehicle. Though privacy expectations are reduced and warrant exceptions abound in this environment, occupants retain constitutional protections and the police are obliged to comply with court-stipulated procedures. Yet, once officers develop probable cause, they are empowered to arrest, search, and seize persons and criminal evidence. The *Carroll* doctrine provided the foundation for warrantless search of automobiles. As stated in *Carroll* and its progeny, if officers have valid probable cause to search the vehicle without a warrant, the scope of the search can be as extensive as though they had a court-issued warrant. But police do not have to restrict their search just to the passenger compartment, belongings of the driver, or items in plain view. The Supreme Court has authorized the search of containers throughout the vehicle and the possessions of passengers.[77]

Another aspect of vehicle search and seizure has produced a string of cases distinguishing driver versus occupant arrest. Police officers encounter a variety of situations where they are authorized to arrest vehicle drivers or passengers. Some circumstances provide the official with predetermined probable cause, as in the case of an outstanding arrest warrant for an occupant. On other occasions, officers formulate individualized probable cause that a vehicle occupant is a criminal suspect based on information they receive or collect. Many arrests stem from law violation or possession of criminal evidence by a vehicle driver or passenger. On occasion, authorities uncover criminal evidence following a legitimate vehicle stop and develop probable cause during questioning or investigation. This situation may lead to the discovery of instruments of crime, fruits of crime, or contraband in the vehicle or occupant's possession.[78]

The Court in *Maryland v. Pringle* (2003) upheld the arrest of all of the passengers after the discovery of bags of cocaine during a consent search of the vehicle. Since no one confessed to owning the drugs, Baltimore County officers arrested each passenger under the theory that each was in constructive possession of the contraband. Joseph Pringle later admitted that the drugs belonged to him unbeknown to the other passengers. The other occupants were released, Pringle was convicted, and he appealed. The Supreme Court held,

> We think it an entirely reasonable inference from these facts that any or all three of the occupants had knowledge of, and exercised dominion and control over, the cocaine. Thus a reasonable officer could conclude that there was probable cause to believe Pringle committed the crime of possession of cocaine, either solely or jointly.[79]

Although these arrest scenarios involve felonious contraband possession, in one case the Court upheld a driver's arrest for a misdemeanor traffic code violation that provided for no jail punishment. Gail Atwater was observed by a Lago Vista police officer driving without a seatbelt. Neither she nor her two children were wearing the belts, in violation of Texas traffic law. The officer stopped Atwater and arrested her, as allowed by state law. She was processed at the nearby jail and released on bond by a magistrate. She later paid the traffic fine but filed a federal civil rights lawsuit challenging the constitutionality of the arrest, claiming it violated her Fourth Amendment right against unreasonable search and seizure. In a five to four decision, the Supreme Court disagreed. Justice Souter's opinion stated, "If an officer has probable cause to believe that an individual has committed even a very minor criminal offense in his presence, he may, without violating the Fourth Amendment, arrest the offender."[80]

Another situation where motorists are stopped is police roadblocks. Fixed checkpoints are a method used to efficiently screen vehicles or drivers for traffic law compliance or criminal investigations. The Supreme Court has authorized the use of police checkpoints without individualized suspicion in several circumstances.

Police Checkpoints and Roadblocks

Roadblocks constitute an authoritative stop that has privacy and liberty interest implications. Though often allowable, the Court has not supported usage of checkpoints in every situation. As noted in *Michigan Department of State Police v. Sitz* (1990), sobriety checkpoints are regularly used to prevent and investigate drunk driving. The Court balanced the government interest in controlling intoxicated driving with the Fourth Amendment and privacy interests of motorists. It concluded that the sobriety checkpoint was minimally intrusive, of a short duration, and on the whole the seizure promoted the greater safety interests of society. Consistent with its rejection of roving patrols seen in *Delaware v. Prouse,* however, the Court in *Sitz* held that police agencies must devise a sound procedure that provides for stopping all motorists to avoid being capricious.[81]

Before *Prouse,* the Court ruled in several cases that roving patrol stops or vehicle searches for illegal aliens at permanent checkpoints required probable cause to be legal.[82] However, in the 1976 case *United States v. Martinez-Fuerte,* the high Court held that stationary roadblocks used to detect illegal aliens away from the border were permissible, without individualized suspicion, if vehicle occupants were only briefly questioned. Here, the Court restated its disapproval of discretionary stops, akin to roving patrol types, and instructed that illegal alien roadblocks should only stop cars passing through the designated checkpoint. However, they could be referred to a secondary inspection area if more than brief questioning was required.[83]

When it came to roadblocks designed to stop motorists for the detection of illegal drugs or other crimes, the Court departed from its previous rulings in border and sobriety cases. City police in Indianapolis, Indiana, established vehicle checkpoints that included the use of drug dogs to interdict illicit drugs. Justice O'Connor, in *City of Indianapolis v. Edmond* (2000), commented, "...we [have not] indicated approval of a checkpoint program whose primary purpose was to detect evidence of ordinary criminal wrongdoing."[84] Absent an exigency or "appropriately tailored roadblock set up to thwart an imminent terrorist attack or to catch a dangerous criminal who is likely to flee by way of a particular route," the Court found general crime control checkpoints violated the Fourth Amendment.[85]

On Saturday morning Joseph Pytel was riding a bicycle home from his U.S. Postal Service job. On the way he was struck by a car and killed near Lombard, Illinois. The driver of the car failed to stop, and local police had few leads. Lombard police set up a checkpoint on the same road the following Saturday to distribute flyers and solicit information about the hit-and-run. Among those stopped was Robert Lidster. After he drove away from the checkpoint, his minivan swerved, narrowly missing an officer standing in the center lane. The officer ordered Lidster to pull over and produce his driver's license and proof of insurance. While inspecting Lidster's papers, the officer smelled a strong odor of alcohol on his breath and, upon questioning, noticed the driver's slurred speech. Lidster was given a field sobriety test, which he failed, and was arrested for DUI. Following his conviction, Lidster appealed, arguing that the roadblock was unconstitutional.

Unlike its ruling in *Edmond* that involved a general interest in crime control, the Supreme Court in *Illinois v. Lidster* (2004) held that the checkpoint designed to gather information about a fatality accident was reasonable and did not violate the Fourth Amendment or liberty interest given its purpose and minimal interference. The Court found "[the] stop's primary law enforcement purpose was *not* to determine whether a vehicle's occupants were committing a crime, but to ask vehicle occupants, as members of the public, for their help in providing information about a crime in all likelihood committed by others."[86] Individual privacy rights are considerably diminished by the nature of police motor vehicle roadblocks. Courts have permitted police agencies to use these methods as long as their procedure is standardized, nondiscriminatory, and not a fishing expedition for ordinary crimes. Although the courts have extended *Terry* stop and frisk principles to motorists, they have tailored some applications to comport with the characteristics of motor vehicles and their occupants.

Just as the courts have accorded motor vehicles a special status under the Fourth Amendment, they have taken a similar approach to border situations where search and seizure rules are relaxed resulting in a diminished expectation of privacy. By entering the United States at border points of entry, entrants give authorities implied consent to search their belongings, and in some cases their person, to detect contraband and ensure compliance with federal laws.

Border Stop, Search, and Seizure

Border stops and searches are viewed as an extraordinary legal circumstance where officials are authorized to screen, without individualized suspicion, persons and property entering the country. This is no small task given the number of legal international visitors and returning U.S. citizen or resident travelers processed by authorities each year. In 2006, 51.1 million international visitors came through U.S. border checkpoints, and government officials estimate a 21 percent increase over the next five years,[87] not to mention returning citizens or the approximately 11.5 to 12 million illegal migrants that authorities search only when they are stopped or apprehended.[88]

In border situations, the courts have not abandoned the Fourth Amendment, only adapted it to that context. Extremely intrusive searches, such as body cavity, require probable cause or warrant justification. However, in *United States v. Mendenhall* and *Florida v. Bostick,* police in public venues, such as airports or bus stations, were allowed to approach and question travelers without reasonable suspicion.[89] Though not at a border check-point, it was in a similar setting where the Supreme Court in *United States v. Sokolow* (1989) authorized police to rely on drug courier profile facts to formulate reasonable suspicion necessary to stop Andrew Sokolow and his companion traveling from Honolulu to Miami. Using the totality of circumstances information of cash payment for airline ticket, traveling under an alias name, nervous demeanor, abbreviated stay at destination, and no checked luggage, federal drug agents had Sokolow's bag sniffed by a drug dog after he was detained at the airport. Cocaine was detected and he was arrested.

These principles are amplified in border situations where it is expected that authorities will stop every person seeking entry. The Supreme Court in *United States v. Ramsey* (1977) explained, "[S]earches made at the border, pursuant to the long-standing right of the sovereign to protect itself by stopping and examining persons and property crossing into this country, are reasonable simply by virtue of the fact that they occur at the border."[90]

As in other contexts, the courts have held that the privacy expectation available to persons supersedes that given to vehicles and property in border searches. In *United States v. Montoya de Hernandez* (1985) U.S. Customs agents suspected that a traveler was transporting illicit drugs in her alimentary canal. The practice of using human "mules" who swallow drug-filled balloons as a means of smuggling drugs is a favorite of Latin American traffickers. Rosa Montoya de Hernandez was detained at the Los Angeles airport after arriving on a flight from Colombia, a known drug-source country. She was carrying a large sum of cash, evasive when asked about her purpose for entering the United States, and agents observed her distended abdomen. She was detained and given a choice of submitting to an x-ray or waiting to pass the suspected drugs. After being held 16 hours, she was examined by a physician pursuant to a search warrant who discovered cocaine drug balloons. Later, she passed a total of 88 such balloons. Montoya de Hernandez was convicted of trafficking cocaine, and she appealed on the grounds that her detention was unconstitutional since federal agents held her for a prolonged period awaiting a warrant. Justice William Rehnquist reasoned, ". . . here the seizure of respondent took place at the international border . . . Routine searches of the persons and effects of entrants are not subject to any requirement of reasonable suspicion, probable cause, or warrant . . . . Under these circumstances, we conclude that the detention in this case was not unreasonably long."[91] Stopping vehicles at border checkpoints is a common practice for law enforcement agents. Consistent with their view in other border situations, courts allow officials to make such stops without individualized suspicion.

The Supreme Court in *United States v. Flores-Montano* (2004) commented, "but the reasons that might support a requirement of some level of suspicion in the case of highly intrusive searches of the person—dignity and privacy interests of the person being searched—simply do not carry over to vehicles."[92] In this case border agents made a routine checkpoint stop of a vehicle, and when tapping on the gas tank, noticed it sounded suspiciously solid. They disassembled the tank and discovered marijuana, arrested Manuel Flores-Montano, and he appealed. The Court upheld the suspicionless search as reasonable since it occurred at the border.[93]

Conversely when police engage in roving patrol stops in the interior away from a border zone, the courts require reasonable suspicion or probable cause for searches and seizures. Consistently, the courts have voiced their disapproval of suspicionless roving patrol stops. Fourth Amendment rule modifications evident in the border setting cease to apply elsewhere. In two cases, the Supreme Court held agents, making ostensibly border-type stops miles inside the interior, to the same search standards established for nonborder situations. Border patrol agents stopped a car far from the border and conducted a warrantless search without probable cause. They discovered marijuana and arrested the driver. The Court ruled the search and seizure unconstitutional and restated that routine vehicle searches require probable cause to be legal.[94] In *United States v. Brignoni-Ponce,* the Court rejected a roving patrol stop that officers acknowledged lacked individualized suspicion and instead was based solely on the Mexican appearance of the occupants. During the stop, agent interviews determined that the passengers were illegal immigrants, and they arrested the driver for smuggling. The Court reasoned that such roving stops must stem from reasonable suspicion or probable cause to be valid.[95]

In sum, persons entering the United States through border checkpoints provide implied consent to stop, question, and search simply by requesting entry. Courts view border areas using modified Fourth Amendment provisions because of government's compelling interest in protecting the country from crime threats and illegal trafficking. Unless officials engage in intrusive searches, individualized suspicion, probable cause, or warrant are not required. Persons entering border zones have a diminished expectation of privacy and are subject to warrantless suspicionless search.

Technology-Assisted Search in Public Places

As a general rule, persons have little expectation of privacy over their physical appearance, public activities, personal possessions, or vehicle exterior if exposed to public view. Increasingly, closed circuit television

(CCTV) and video cameras mounted in police patrol vehicles record police-citizen encounters in public space.[96] The courts permit police to use technological devices to track, photograph, and videotape people in public places.[97]

In *United States v. Knotts* (1983), the high Court ruled police could use a beeper to track suspects on public thoroughfares.[98] However, they prohibited the warrantless use of beepers and thermal imaging (infrared) devices to seize evidence in private residences because those locations carry a much greater expectation of privacy than public arenas.[99] The Court has acknowledged that technology affects the fragile balance between privacy and police surveillance activities. In *Kyllo v. United States* (2001), the Supreme Court commented, "[I]t would be foolish to contend that the degree of privacy secured to citizens by the Fourth Amendment has been entirely unaffected by the advance of technology . . . [Yet] to withdraw protection of this minimum expectation [of the home] would be to permit police technology to erode the privacy guaranteed by the Fourth Amendment."[100]

Not always is it simple to separate public from private areas. For example, in *California v. Ciraolo* (1986), the Supreme Court authorized the use of aerial observations and photographs of marijuana plants, growing in a backyard, to obtain a search warrant. In this case, officers in an airplane made several low-altitude passes over the backyard of Dante Ciraolo's residence where they observed the illegal plants. Ciraolo had erected a tall fence to shield the yard and marijuana from public view. Moreover, residential yards are ordinarily considered a curtilage, that is, an extension of the dwelling for Fourth Amendment purposes. In spite of the elevated expectation of privacy over the yard, the Court found that the police observations "took place within a publicly navigable airspace in a physically nonintrusive manner" and therefore were considered reasonable.[101]

An emerging but unsettled area of law involves police detention to collect evidence exemplars for identification or forensic comparison. These investigative methods raise a number of privacy right issues due to the intrusive nature, potential for coercion, and absence of individualized suspicion.

Police Detention for Identification Purposes

Although the preponderance of police warrantless detentions entail mere questioning or are justified as a *Terry* stop, some situations allow persons to be restrained temporarily for identification purposes. Although the Supreme Court has not directly ruled on the permissibility of police pedestrian or traffic detention to collect physical evidence, it has decided cases with similar circumstances.

For instance, the facts in *Davis v. Mississippi* (1969) show that the police detained and fingerprinted a group of 24 youth during a rape investigation. Among those was John Davis whose fingerprints matched those taken from the crime scene window where the assailant entered the victim's home. The evidence was presented at his trial; after conviction he appealed, arguing that the fingerprints were illegally seized since the police had no probable cause. The Court agreed holding that the fingerprint evidence should have been excluded.[102] Yet, as Yale Kamisar et al. explain, ". . . [the *Davis* Court] intimated that a detention for such a purpose might sometimes be permissible on evidence falling short of the traditional probable cause needed for an arrest."[103] And later in *Hayes v. Florida* (1985), the Court proffered a parallel reasoning as again Kamisar et al. state, "[the *Hayes* Court] reserved the possibility, as it had in *Davis,* that 'a brief detention in the field for the purpose of fingerprinting, where there is only reasonable suspicion not amounting to probable cause' might pass constitutional muster."[104] The *Hayes* Court held that the detention and transport to the police station for fingerprinting were unreasonable because the police lacked probable cause, consent, or warrant.

The Supreme Court allows carefully tailored roadblocks to be used in searching for dangerous criminals or fugitives. However, in Daytona Beach, Florida, police are gathering DNA exemplar samples from motorists on traffic stops and suspects arrested in prostitution sting operations as part of an area serial murder investigation. Officers are taking oral swabs of profile-specific persons during routine traffic stops and suspects arrested by undercover investigators posing as prostitutes. The samples are collected to find a match for the predator who has killed four women execution-style. Police Chief Mike Chitwood said, "[G]enetically we know who he is. And sooner or later, we will match the DNA to the physical person and bring closure to everything that is going on."[105]

Although the Daytona Beach traffic swabs are collected with driver consent, the possible coercive atmosphere of a traffic stop could raise concerns about the voluntariness of the consent. As Samuel Walker and Michael Harrington comment,

> Law enforcement officers have a legal right to ask for a voluntary DNA sample. Such requests are analogous to "consent searches" in the context of motor vehicle stops. In both situations, a citizen has a legal right to refuse to grant consent. But as the racial profiling controversy has revealed, there are potential problems in making such requests. In addition to questions of voluntariness and whether it is a knowing waiver of one's rights, there is the question of whether the police are making such requests in an evenhanded and non-discriminatory fashion.[106]

In 2002, Baton Rouge, Louisiana, police conducted a voluntary DNA drag-net asking more than 1,200 local men to provide a DNA sample as part of a serial rapist-murder investigation. Shannon Kohler refused, so the police obtained a search warrant to seize the DNA evidence. Police named Kohler as a suspect in the local media while investigators based their probable cause for the warrant on anonymous tips and a similarity with Federal Bureau of Investigation (FBI) offender profile characteristics. Kohler was later cleared as a suspect in the case, and he filed a civil rights suit in federal court for Fourth Amendment and privacy violations.

In 2006, the federal Fifth Circuit Court of Appeals in *Kohler v. Englade* ruled that the warrant and subsequent DNA search were unreasonable because the police lacked sufficient probable cause. They found the facts police used to support their probable cause were overly vague and generalized rendering it invalid.[107] This case demonstrates that in spite of the appeal of DNA profiling to solve crimes, obtaining samples from persons involuntarily has profound privacy implications, causing some courts to require investiga-tors to adhere to Fourth Amendment requirements.

Courts have not clarified the circumstances where the police may collect identification exemplars during a detention. However, existing cases show they must have something more than mere reasonable suspicion if the person is detained or subject to providing evidentiary samples in the absence of a prob-able cause arrest and related to a legitimate pretrial identification procedure.[108]

Police use various methods to search and seize evidence that leads to a law-ful arrest. The validity of these practices turns on their adherence to Fourth Amendment and privacy guidelines. However, once an arrest is made, courts view constitutional and privacy rights in a different light.

Privacy Rights after Arrest and Criminal Charge

Privacy, Arrest, and Postarrest Search

Governments have executive branch authority to enforce enacted laws. Moreover, they have an obligation to take lawful measures to ensure public safety. The police are the instrument used to accomplish both of these objec-tives. In the criminal justice apparatus, their functional role is apprehending suspected criminal offenders. In 2006, American police arrested over 14 mil-lion persons for nontraffic violent or property crimes.[109] The arrest event triggers a number of mechanisms in the justice process. Obviously, police arrest has an immediate and profound impact on the liberty interests of the accused. And arrest activates constitutional protections not available during prearrest investigations, such as a right to an attorney, to name only one.

If the police transfer the arrestee's case to the prosecutor for criminal charges or send him or her to jail, additional constitutional safeguards are invoked. Hence, privacy rights are framed in a different context after arrest than when the person is free to go. Once persons are subject to authoritative arrest, police are allowed to search them and their immediate surroundings with greater intrusion than a cursory stop and frisk.

When police stop people or vehicles, some courts have ruled it constitutes a seizure. An arrest, however, is a specific type of seizure that consists of certain legal elements that must be satisfied. American courts have explained that an arrest contains four essential elements—authority to arrest, intention to arrest, restraint of the person through actual control, and arrestee understanding that he or she is under arrest.[110] One of the elements needed to establish an arrest is the authoritative act of taking control of the person by a law enforcement officer. Control connotes that a "reasonable person would have believed that he was not free to leave."[111] Restraint, brought about by a show of authority, must also include an element of force as the Court commented in *California v. Hodari D.,* "[A]n arrest requires either physical force or, where that is absent, submission to the assertion of authority."[112] When police officers identify themselves, demonstrate their intention to make an arrest through words or actions, and take physical seizure, they have complied with the requirements necessary to consummate a lawful arrest. From that point, the arrestee is in the custody of the police. The custodial circumstance bestows certain authority to restrain and intrude upon the officer but also carries legal liabilities for the protection and constitutional treatment of the arrestee.[113] Officers typically search persons in custody and their immediate surroundings, including vehicle or packages, after an arrest has been made.

Postarrest inventory search, also known as search incident to a lawful arrest, is a familiar police practice designed to protect the belongings of arrestees, discover contraband or evidence in their possession, and protect officer safety. It can result in the discovery of illegal drugs, weapons, fraudulent papers, or other seizable items. Courts have ruled that the search must be closely related to the authorizing arrest. That is, the postarrest search must be "contemporaneous with the arrest and is confined to the immediate vicinity."[114] In the *Chimel* doctrine, vicinity also includes the area within the person's immediate control or reach. Furthermore, it can entail criminal evidence found inside a motor vehicle if the person in custody was an occupant when arrested. The Supreme Court in *New York v. Belton* (1981) held "when a policeman has made a lawful custodial arrest of the occupant of an automobile, he may, as a contemporaneous incident of that arrest, search the passenger compartment of that automobile."[115] In *Belton,* the Court explained that the scope of a vehicle's interior spanned to any accessible area or item, such as compartments, containers, or packages where evidence could reasonably be stored.[116]

In another case, a patrol officer checked the license plates of a car and discovered they had been issued to another vehicle. Before the officer could stop the vehicle, the driver pulled into a parking lot, parked, and walked away from the car. The officer approached Marcus Thornton, the driver, informed him the license plates were displayed illegally, and asked if he had any illicit drugs in his possession. Thornton admitted having drugs and produced marijuana and crack cocaine from his pocket. He was arrested, placed in the police patrol car, and then the officer searched the passenger compartment, finding a handgun. Thornton was convicted of federal drug and weapon charges, and he appealed arguing that the postarrest search was unlawful because it extended beyond his immediate control. The Court in *Thornton v. United States* (2004) disagreed holding "so long as an arrestee is the sort of 'recent occupant' of a vehicle . . . officers may search that vehicle incident to the arrest."[117]

Arrest-Related Exigencies

Courts have given considerable deference to police officer safety. In fact, they have on occasion retreated from their adherence to common law privacy right traditions in cases where officers may be in potential danger. Ordinarily, citizens have an elevated expectation of privacy in their homes that is surpassed only by the sanctity of the body. However, the Court has allowed law enforcement officers to make warrantless protective sweeps of an arrestee's home to ensure that other dangerous suspects are not present elsewhere in the house.

Officers executed an armed robbery arrest warrant at Jerome Buie's house. When they entered the house, he was found hiding in the basement. He surrendered, was arrested, then an officer searched the remainder of the basement where he saw in plain view clothes that matched those worn by the suspected robbers. Buie was convicted and appealed on the grounds that the unconstitutional search uncovered incriminating evidence that was used in his conviction. In upholding the search, Justice Byron White in *Maryland v. Buie* (1990) wrote, ". . . a protective sweep, aimed at protecting the arresting officers, if justified by the circumstances [and articulable facts], is nevertheless not a full search of the premises, but may extend only to a cursory inspection of those spaces where a person may be found [and] no longer than is necessary to dispel the reasonable suspicion of danger."[118]

The courts are not only concerned about protecting police officers but also criminal evidence. Ordinarily, this risk is viewed as an exigent circumstance where the police are permitted to conduct warrantless search or seizure to safeguard evidence from loss.

In *Illinois v. McArthur* (2001), police were called to the Charles McArthur residence regarding a domestic dispute. They waited as Mrs. McArthur entered the home to collect her belongings. Upon her return, she informed the officers that her husband had marijuana hidden inside. The officers asked for permission to search the premises, but Mr. McArthur refused. One officer left to obtain a search warrant while the other kept McArthur on the porch. When the police executed the warrant, they found illegal drugs. Upon his conviction, McArthur appealed, arguing that the porch seizure was unreasonable under the Fourth Amendment. In the ruling, Justice Stephen Breyer wrote, "We conclude that the restriction at issue was reasonable . . . the police made [a] reasonable effort to reconcile their law enforcement needs with the demands of personal privacy . . . this brief seizure of the premises was permissible."[119] Not all postarrest searches are considered exigencies. Most standard arrests are followed by a limited full body inventory search.

Invasive Postarrest Searches

Postarrest searches are designed to ensure that the person in custody does not have hidden weapons or contraband. The inventory entails a minimal intrusion search of the person and immediate surroundings. The privacy invasion permitted in *Schmerber v. California,* that is, to obtain a blood sample for alcohol intoxication testing without consent, is clearly an exception in typical arrest situations. The *Schmerber* Court authorized the drawing of blood because it viewed the circumstances as exigent.[120] Conversely as the high Court explained in *Winston v. Lee* (1985), authorities are not permitted to invade the arrestee's body, such as to collect bullet evidence, without a compelling need authorized by a warrant.[121] Even in jails or prisons, officials wanting to conduct inmate strip or body cavity searches must either have individualized suspicion that contraband is secreted in the body, specific justification such as contact with persons from outside the facility, segregated high-risk inmates, or a search warrant to justify an intrusion of that dimension.[122]

Thus far, the Supreme Court has not established a bright-line rule that clearly outlines the limits of strip or body cavity searches following a lawful arrest. With individualized reasonable suspicion or probable cause, officers are permitted to conduct strip and visual body searches after an arrest. Intrusive manual body cavity searches, however, require a search warrant in the absence of a compelling exigency. Even then, the parameters lack clarity and many courts rely on two leading Supreme Court cases to guide their reasoning with this level of intrusion. *Schmerber,* which permitted an instant bodily intrusion, and *Bell v. Wolfish* (1979), where the Court held that officials were allowed to conduct strip or visual body cavity inspections after pretrial detainees had visitor contact while housed in a jail.[123]

In a 2005 case, New York City police officers stationed on a rooftop observed Azim Hall make a cocaine sale. Hall was arrested and at the police station Officer Frederick Spiegel ordered him to remove his clothes and squat to visually look for hidden drugs on his body. Based on his experience as a narcotics officer, Spiegel knew that it was a common practice among drug peddlers to hide drugs on or in their bodies. Upon visual inspection, the officer observed a string dangling from Hall's rectum and asked him to remove it. Hall refused so the officer pulled the string, revealing a plastic bag filled with crack cocaine. Hall was convicted of selling illicit drugs, and he moved to suppress the evidence. The trial court suppressed the evidence and after two appellate reviews, the New York appeals court agreed ruling the police had conducted an unreasonable body cavity search without a warrant and in violation of the defendant's Fourth Amendment rights. The New York Appellate Court reasoned,

> Pursuant to the Fourth Amendment . . . and based on the difference in the degree of intrusiveness between visual and manual body cavity searches, a visual body cavity search could be justified by a reasonable suspicion that the arrestee was concealing a weapon or contraband. However, probable cause and a search warrant were required prior to a manual body cavity search unless an emergency situation existed . . . no exigent circumstances, such as the imminent destruction of the drugs, were established; thus, a search warrant was required.[124]

People arrested have privacy interests regarding their person and possessions, which are balanced with law enforcement interests in safety and protection of criminal evidence. Officers are permitted to conduct a full body search of a person following a lawful arrest. Normally, a permissible search is restricted to outer body, clothing, and within immediate reach to inventory belongings and detect criminal evidence. Unless officials have individualized reasonable suspicion that evidence is concealed on or in the arrestee's body, they are not permitted to conduct strip, visual body cavity, or manual body cavity searches as part of a postarrest procedure. Many courts have held that only a search warrant can authorize an intrusive search that violates the sanctity of the arrested person's body. Even though arrestees have a diminished expectation of privacy, searches that intrude beyond a cursory body inventory will likely violate their constitutional privacy rights. Authorities must have specific justification or a warrant to conduct postarrest invasive searches.

In sum, people lawfully arrested have minimal expectation of privacy over their physical appearance or behavior. Such characteristics may be observed, recorded, documented, and used as evidence in criminal proceedings. Physical attributes and behaviors are neither self-incriminating nor protected by the Fourth or Fifth Amendment if nonverbal and voluntarily exposed to officials.

POSTARREST CONSTITUTIONAL PROTECTIONS

Every arrest incident does not automatically close a criminal investigation. Police are responsible for developing prosecutable cases against the accused based on credible evidence. Tangible evidentiary objects are only one category of evidence used in criminal investigations. Investigators also rely on witness testimony and suspect identification to corroborate physical evidence or presumptive factual guilt.

Pretrial Identification

Evidence gathered from witnesses can be very persuasive and strengthen a case. Pretrial identification of the suspect is performed by witnesses, who may include victims, eyewitnesses, bystanders, or criminal accomplices. Identification evidence can be credible and probative although often more susceptible to challenge in court due to the veracity of the witness. Witnesses provide pretrial identification of the criminal suspect in four ways—showup, sketch, photographic array, and lineup. Each of these types relies on eyewitness identification based on physical likeness. A showup consists of a face-to-face confrontation between the eyewitness and the suspect. This typically occurs in the field when officers show only the suspect to the witness for identification contemporaneous to an arrest. This procedure has been challenged in the courts due to the absence of comparison suspects and its highly suggestive nature.[125]

For years eyewitness identification has been criticized for being inaccurate and unreliable. According to Margery Malkin Koosed, "of forty cases of innocent people who were convicted of serious crimes and served time in prison, five on death row, [the study found] that 90 percent involved eyewitness identification evidence in which one or more eyewitnesses falsely identified the person."[126]

Identification legal challenges commonly stem from claims of due process right violations.[127] The high Court has held that such claims should be considered in the totality of the circumstances.[128] In one significant case, the

Supreme Court used an exigency rationale to permit the use of showup identification evidence. Mrs. Behrendt was hospitalized with multiple stab wounds
following an attack that also left her husband dead. The police apprehended
Theodore Stovall the day after the killing. Due to her life-threatening injuries,
investigators felt it was immediately necessary to allow Mrs. Behrendt to look
at Stovall to confirm they had arrested the actual killer. Officers arranged with
her surgeon to bring Stovall to Behrendt's hospital room for a suspect
showup. When they arrived with Stovall, the only black man in the room,
Mrs. Behrendt positively identified him as her attacker. She also later repeated
her hospital room identification of Stovall in court testimony. Stovall was
convicted and appealed on the grounds that the showup identification was
unduly suggestive in violation of his Fifth and Fourteenth due process rights.
The Court in *Stovall v. Denno* (1967) rejected his argument and Justice
William Brennan wrote,

> Faced with the responsibility of identifying the attacker, with the need for
> immediate action and with the knowledge that Mrs. Behrendt could not visit
> the jail, the police followed the only feasible procedure and took Stovall to the
> hospital room. Under these circumstances, the usual police station line-up,
> which Stovall now argues he should have had, was out of the question.[129]

Investigators also use sketch drawings of alleged perpetrators when they
have neither a photograph nor the suspect in custody. Either an artist's cari-
cature or image produced by computer identification software is used. These
illustrations provide a likeness for comparison to offender mug-shot photographs or distribution to patrol officers to watch for the wanted suspect.
In both applications they are viewed as an investigative tool and do not
infringe on the privacy rights of the suspect since they act as a probable cause
element or antecedent to in-person identification.

Another type of pretrial identification is a photographic array, also known
as a pack or spread. To avoid making the procedure improperly suggestive,
investigators present a group of photographs to the eyewitness that shows
several persons who are as similar as possible in appearance. For example,
an unreasonable photographic spread would entail one photograph that
was clearly different from the others, such as, one color picture among five
black and white prints, or only one Caucasian male photo displayed in a
group of several pictures of African Americans. The courts have not settled
on a required number of pictures that must be used in a photographic array;
however, they typically range from five to eight photographs displayed side-
by-side.[130] Barring any other elements in a totality of circumstances analysis,
using only one photo rather than a group for identification would likely be
rejected by the courts because of its suggestibility.[131]

The last identification method is the lineup. Its widespread use by police has generated a number of court decisions due to the number of constitutional protections implicated. Many of the cases cite a right to counsel during identification processes. Though it applies to any witness-suspect confrontation, the counsel guarantee is activated by an issuance of a formal charge. Basically, once suspects are officially charged with an offense, they have a right to the presence of their attorney during pretrial identification.[132]

In this procedure the criminal suspect is joined by a group of other persons, bearing a physical resemblance, and viewed by a witness with the aim of identifying the alleged perpetrator. As with the photographic spread procedure, police efforts to avoid emphasizing one member of the lineup or creating a situation that is overly suggestive is important to the constitutionality of the process. Lineups are typically staged at the police station; however, the legal considerations and procedures would apply the same regardless of where officials conduct the pretrial identification.

Since identifications are based on physical appearance or characteristic, these methods do not evoke self-incrimination safeguards. Even though suspects are in custody, nothing they are asked to display or demonstrate involves communicative incriminating evidence. Thus, the pretrial identification process is immune to *Miranda* since the arrestee is not compelled to make incriminating statements.

During pretrial procedures, however, the arrestee can be required to provide gesture or physical exemplars, such as showing a tattoo or mark, as part of the identification process. Officers conducting lineups may direct the arrestee to perform particular acts as long as they are germane to the case, reasonable, and minimally intrusive. The lineup suspect has neither an expectation of privacy nor self-incrimination privilege right to refuse since such routines are authorized as part of the pretrial identification process.

Based on its relevancy to each case, officials can require the lineup suspect to provide a voice exemplar by speaking specific words or phrases to assist the witness with identification.[133] In the same vein, handwriting samples can be demanded of the arrestee or defendant for comparison purposes.[134] And courts have permitted the police to obtain or use without consent photograph, video, fingerprint, distinctive physical feature, hair, and clothing exemplars in the identification context.[135]

Cliff Roberson explains,

There is no right to counsel at a pretrial confrontation for the purposes of taking handwriting exemplars, blood or other body fluids, or fingerprints . . . the taking of bodily fluids, however, normally requires a warrant to enter a person's body unless there are exigent circumstances . . . the taking of voice recordings and handwriting samples does not violate a person's reasonable expectation of privacy . . . .[136]

Barring an intrusive seizure of body fluids, other than the blood draw authorized by *Schmerber,* collection of identification exemplars does not violate the custodial person's expectation of privacy. The Court in *United States v. Dionisio* (1973) summarized, "No person can have a reasonable expectation that others will not know the sound of his voice, any more than he can reasonably expect that his face will be a mystery to the world."[137]

During postarrest investigations, authorities may compel arrestees to provide exemplars that do not unreasonably invade the body. Those can be used to assist witnesses in identifying perpetrators and as probative evidence in formal charging or trial. Persons subject to pretrial identification have no reasonable expectation of privacy over physical characteristics available to the public. In spite of the known flaws of eyewitness identification, courts allow the use of pretrial identification in criminal prosecutions because it is unprotected as nontestimonial evidence. Conversely, testimonial evidence, particularly that which is compelled, is constitutionally protected, and the Supreme Court has provided specific guidelines for police investigations.

Collecting Arrestee Biometric Samples

Courts may authorize highly intrusive searches to collect exemplar evidence from criminal suspects. If police officials obtain a judicial search warrant, they can forcibly take biometric or bodily evidence from the person in custody. This may include hair, tissue, body fluid, and DNA. Standardized collection and preservation practices are well established for handling these types of forensic evidence.[138] Warrant-authorized body evidence search and seizure are governed by the same rules that apply to the execution of other warrants, although evidentiary searches may have conditions imposed by the courts in some jurisdictions.

The authorities may also seize physical identification information from arrested persons without a warrant or the need for additional individualized suspicion. After lawful arrest, officials can take photographs, fingerprints, and in some jurisdictions, collect DNA samples from people arrested.[139] With the possible exception of DNA fingerprinting since the matter is unsettled in the courts, these identification procedures are not considered Fourth Amendment searches because of the practical needs of law enforcement to identify arrestees plus they occur after a probable cause-based arrest. Given the increasing use of genetic fingerprinting in criminal justice, DNA collections and databases have been challenged in court in recent years. Yet, they have withstood Fourth Amendment scrutiny, especially if the DNA sample collection involves postindictment and conviction testing. One federal Circuit court mentioned "DNA testing has changed the criminal justice system. All 50 states and the federal government have enacted DNA collection and database statutes."[140] On the other hand, the permissibility of pretrial and preindictment DNA collection varies across jurisdictions and offenses. Although the Supreme Court has not directly addressed this issue, some legal experts suggest the collection of DNA from arrestees is not constitutionally prohibited. David Kaye comments,

> These dicta [*Davis v. Mississippi*] suggest that the Supreme Court would uphold compulsory acquisition of biometric data from a person when the process is not physically or mentally invasive, when the data are useful primarily to link individuals, and when data are valid, reliable, and effective for this purpose. In these circumstances, harms to individuals and the benefits of judicial review are minor; hence, the balance between individual privacy and government interests points to the reasonableness of the collection and use of the identifying data without a judicial warrant.[141]

Biometric identifiers, that is, measurable physiological or behavioral traits, can be collected using manual or automated methods. Once gathered, these data can be stored, disseminated to other agencies, or used as exemplars. Technology such as the Automated Fingerprint Identification System allows law enforcement to quickly scan digital fingerprint images for classification and identification storage. Similarly, the FBI maintains the Combined DNA Index System to electronically share offender DNA profiles among police agencies. Again, the arrestee has little constitutional privacy protection that prevents collection of such catalogued information. The same line of legal reasoning applies here regarding diminished expectation of privacy during the pretrial identification and booking processes. However, the only caveat involves the broad permissibility of DNA fingerprinting, which continues to be challenged in courts from arrest to postconviction.

Collecting Body Fluids without a Warrant

Prior to the advent of DNA fingerprinting, the Supreme Court addressed the issue of intrusive warrantless extractions of body fluids from arrestees. Although the Court's analyses in two cases were based on due process challenges, their reasoning was consistent with Fourth Amendment protections and privacy interests over a person's body. In 1952, the Court in *Rochin v. California* established the "shocks the conscience" standard to measure the gravity of police intrusions into the body of a person in custody to obtain criminal evidence. Based on information that Richard Rochin was selling narcotics, deputy sheriffs went to the suspect's home to investigate and found the front door open. They went in the residence and forcibly entered Rochin's bedroom where he was sitting near a bedside table. When the suspect saw the officers, he grabbed two capsules from the table and swallowed them during the ensuing struggle. Unable to seize the evidence, the deputies arrested Rochin, transported him to a hospital in handcuffs, and directed a physician to pump his stomach to retrieve the evidence. The suspect's stomach contents contained the two capsules later found to be morphine. Rochin was convicted on drug charges and appealed, claiming the arrest and forcible evidence extraction violated his due process rights. The Court agreed and overturned the conviction. Justice Felix Frankfurter commented,

> This is conduct that shocks the conscience. Illegally breaking into the privacy of the petitioner [Rochin], the struggle to open his mouth and remove what was there, the forcible extraction of his stomach's contents—this course of proceeding by agents of government to obtain evidence is bound to offend even hardened sensibilities.[142]

Three years later the high Court ruled on another case involving the drawing of blood to acquire evidence. In *Breithaupt v. Abram* (1957), the Court upheld the manslaughter conviction of a drunk driver involved in a fatal automobile crash. Police directed a technician to draw blood from the unconscious driver to test for alcohol content. Tests showed the motorist was intoxicated, and the evidence was used to obtain a manslaughter conviction. Upon appeal the Court held that the blood sample was "taken under the protective eye of a physician . . . [and the] interests of society in the scientific determination of intoxication, one of the great causes of the mortal hazards of the road, [outweighed] so slight of an intrusion [into the body]."[143]

Later in 1966, the Supreme Court in *Schmerber v. California* authorized the warrantless drawing of blood from a drunk driving suspect without his consent. In this case the Court relied on an exigency exception to justify the bodily intrusion finding "the officer . . . might reasonably have believed that he was confronted with an emergency, in which the delay necessary to obtain a warrant, under the circumstances, threatened the destruction of evidence."[144]

Even though the courts unequivocally prefer law enforcement officers to obtain a judicial warrant, when feasible, they have authorized the warrantless collection of blood for intoxication testing. Other bodily invasions to obtain evidence must be justified by a compelling government need, as held in *Winston v. Lee* for surgical removal of a bullet, in a manner that does not violate *Rochin's* shock the conscience principle.[145] In this context, arrestees retain their substantial expectation of privacy over their bodies; however, authorities may use medical procedures to seize evidence contained in the arrestee's body with a warrant or valid exceptions allowed by the courts.

A person in custody has no constitutional self-incrimination protection over physical traits, behaviors, or biological samples; however, testimonial and communicative statements are protected by the Fifth Amendment and assured through *Miranda* guidelines. When the Supreme Court established the bright-line rule mandating the *Miranda* warning for all police custodial interrogations, the protection was thought to be impenetrable. Yet since 1966, its tenets have been thoroughly scrutinized by the courts, and in several incidences, the original *Miranda* applications have been modified.

Privacy Rights and Testimonial Evidence

It is an understatement to suggest that the self-incrimination provision in *Miranda* protects a substantial privacy interest that is deeply rooted in common law. That is, people subject to government control have an intrinsic privilege against being compelled through torture, coercion, or deception to make confessions against themselves. The high Court in *Miranda v. Arizona* provided this account: "The cases before us raise questions which go to the roots of our concepts of American criminal jurisprudence: the restraints society must observe consistent with the Federal Constitution in prosecuting individuals for crime . . . . [and a] privilege under the Fifth Amendment to the Constitution not to be compelled to incriminate himself."[146]

Though *Miranda* provisions contain two constitutional tracks, self-incrimination and right to counsel, it specifically highlights a custodial suspect's Fifth Amendment guarantee that "[no] person . . . shall be compelled in any criminal case to be a witness against himself."[147] Two critical issues emerged from the original *Miranda* decision that bear restating. First, the *Miranda* warning must be given only pursuant to a custodial interrogation. Here, individuals must be in police custody or believe that they are under arrest and as such are not free to leave. Next, the arrestee is subjected to interrogation questions whose responses are incriminating.[148] Hence administrative information, such as name and address, are not protected because it lacks the ability to incriminate.[149] Arrestees have a constitutional right to remain silent and cannot be lawfully compelled to answer nonadministrative questions. Also generally speaking, once individuals in custody have invoked their right to have access to an attorney, the courts have consistently held that any subsequent testimonial evidence obtained through police interrogation is not admissible.[150]

A second important issue is any incriminating statement provided by the suspect in custody must be offered voluntarily to be admissible in court. This presumes that the arrestees knowingly waived their self-incrimination privilege. As applied in other situations, the courts may rely on the totality of circumstances measures to determine the validity of a *Miranda* waiver if disputed.[151] The privacy interest of the arrestee is greatly affected by coercive measures used by the police to obtain testimonial evidence. Thus, voluntariness in providing incriminating statements in the *Miranda*-type environs provides an important privacy protection for the person in custody. As further evidence of the emphasis placed on noncoerced confession, Justice Frankfurter in *Rogers v. Richmond* (1961) stated, "Our decisions under the [Fourteenth Amendment] have made clear that convictions following the admission into evidence of [involuntary confessions] cannot stand . . . not so much because confessions are unlikely to be true but because the methods used to extract them offend an underlying principle in the enforcement of our criminal law . . . "[152] The Supreme Court has consistently held that confessions obtained through physical abuse, psychological coercion or intimidation, trickery, or drugs must be excluded because they are constitutionally violative.[153]

Even after *Miranda* became institutionalized as a procedure in police interrogation, the courts were dissecting the decision to determine if circumstances could justify exceptions to the original rule. Within a few years the Court had established exceptions that would allow the police to use testimonial evidence obtained outside of the conventional *Miranda* context.

Exceptions to the *Miranda* Requirement

The courts have outlined several circumstances where the *Miranda* warning is not required. Since arrest is one of the requisites that activate *Miranda,* the Supreme Court in *Berkemer v. McCarty* (1984) ruled that it is not mandatory during ordinary traffic stops because the driver is not considered in custody—only temporarily detained.[154] Another circumstance where *Miranda* fails to be required is known as the public safety exception. In *New York v. Quarles* (1984), the Court ruled officers faced with an immediate danger to public safety, and contemporaneous to their arrest, can pose questions to a person in custody and use the responses as evidence.[155] In a third exception, the Court allowed incriminating statements made to an undercover police officer by his jail cell mate. In *Illinois v. Perkins* (1990), the Supreme Court held that since the inmate voluntarily divulged the information and was not subject to a police-dominated environment, such as during interrogation, the evidence was admissible in the absence of *Miranda.*[156]

The constitutional safeguards outlined in *Miranda* protect key privacy interests including the right to refrain from revealing incriminating information that could lead to a criminal conviction. However, the protection is not absolute as the Court has allowed the use of voluntary statements in some circumstances.

Surreptitious Audio Recording of Suspect

Together, *Miranda,* Fifth Amendment self-incrimination privilege, and reasonable expectation of privacy are intended to protect persons from having their statements used as criminal evidence if obtained through coercion, compulsion, or unlawful intrusion. However, these protections do not apply if the suspect voluntarily makes comments that are heard by a police officer, criminal informant, or recorded by a device in the operator's presence. Regardless of whether the officer is undercover or not, anything the suspect says directly to an officer or is overheard in a nonintrusive manner can be used as evidence. In essence, law enforcement officers or criminal informants can use surreptitious devices to record a conversation with suspects and their incriminating statements are admissible. In *United States v. White* (1971), the Court found there was no constitutional difference if an officer used a recording device "[i]f the ... revelations of an agent operating without electronic equipment do not invade the defendant's ... expectations of privacy, neither does a simultaneous recording of the same conversations ...."[157]

Several factors influence the internal workings and duration of criminal investigations. Moreover, given the widespread discretion at every level of the justice system, the fate of a criminal case is often unpredictable.

Police Criminal Case Disposition

There is no fixed time period that dictates the length of a criminal investigation. In fact, some homicide investigations last for years or remain open forever. These are commonly referred to as cold cases and become increasingly difficult to solve as time passes. An investigation begins with the initial police contact with citizen or crime scene and continues until the case is closed. In law enforcement nomenclature, a criminal investigation case is considered cleared, that is, administratively solved, when the alleged perpetrator has been arrested or identified. According to the FBI's *Uniform Crime Reports,* "law enforcement agencies can clear, or 'close,' offenses in one of two ways: by arrest or by exceptional means."[158] Exceptional means refers to closing a case when offenders have not been apprehended because they are at-large, deceased, or beyond reach.[159]

From the investigator's standpoint, physical and testimonial evidence collection begins with the crime incident and continues until the investigation is closed by identifying the offender and presenting a prepared case to the prosecutor. However, several other justice processes are under way at the same time and may continue throughout the life course of the investigation. Obviously, law enforcement officers make arrests to not only protect the community but to have the criminal suspect held accountable in court for the alleged offense. Once suspects are apprehended, they may enter a multifaceted justice apparatus that includes prosecutorial and judicial processes. Laws and procedures vary considerably across jurisdictions and offenses. Yet, at this point, arrestees move from investigatory and pretrial processes into the prosecution stream where they are screened for criminal charges.

PRIVACY AND THE PREINDICTMENT PROCESS

Even though a criminal investigation may be ongoing, police have two options in handling arrestees. They can release the person in custody if there is insufficient evidence to advance the case to the prosecutor. Or, in some misdemeanor offenses or minor cases, the arrestee may be released after receiving a court summons or posting bail at the station house. Otherwise, officials will pass arrestees onto the prosecutorial stage where they are booked into the justice system and bound over for screening with the aim of filing formal criminal charges.

Booking Processes

Booking, in criminal justice parlance, is the station house holding or admission processing of an arrestee into a jail facility prior to an appearance before a magistrate. Jail booking is more formalized and reduces privacy protections because the person is held in a secure correctional facility. In either case, authorities impact two areas of privacy interest when processing persons in custody. In this setting, arrestees have no expectation of privacy over their physical appearance, identity, or biometric identifiers. Therefore, officials can take photographs, fingerprints, and collect DNA samples.

Each of these identification measures is minimally intrusive and has been upheld by the courts, although DNA sampling continues to be challenged due to the absence of a specific Supreme Court ruling on the practice. The second privacy interest is possessory. Authorities conduct inventory searches of arrestees and their belongings when they enter the custodial institution. Of course, any criminal evidence discovered in the custodial inventory is just as admissible as that collected in the field as long as the search procedure is reasonable and within the permissible scope. As Justice O'Connor in *Hudson v. Palmer* (1984) commented, "[The] fact of arrest and incarceration abates all legitimate Fourth Amendment privacy and possessory interests in personal effects."[160]

Privacy rights in a secure correctional facility, such as a jail or prison, are viewed by the courts in an entirely different context than police field operations. If arrestees are housed in jail, as a pretrial detainee, their expectation of privacy is dramatically diminished and considered secondary to the institutional needs of security and effective operation. The high Court in *Bell v. Wolfish* explained, "[A prisoner's] reasonable expectation of privacy [is] of a diminished scope."[161] In this case, the Court upheld the strip search and visual body cavity inspection of a pretrial detainee after a contact visit with persons from outside of the institution.[162] John W. Palmer explains, "Although a pre-trial detainee may be subject to some of the same restrictions as convicted prisoners, the restrictions are not unconstitutional unless they amount to punishment."[163] As alluded to in *Wolfish,* jail officials must have individualized reasonable suspicion to conduct more intrusive strip or body cavity searches of pretrial detainees. In this setting, however, pretrial detainees must relinquish personal effects, submit to identification procedures, and comply with institutional rules because they have little expectation of privacy protection. However, if arrestees are simply being processed and not held in the facility, officials may not conduct a complete inventory of their belongings.[164] Holding an arrestee is not an end to itself but rather one stage in a justice process leading next to prosecutorial and judicial review. Among the American jurisdictions, there are various preindictment screening strategies.

Initial Judicial Contact

Though still considered in the investigatory stage, the prosecutor and court become actively involved after booking. The prosecutor may be engaged in reviewing the case at the same time the arrestee appears before a magistrate. In some circumstances or jurisdictions they may be independent screening processes; although judicial reviews are not constitutionally required as the Court commented in *Albright v. Oliver* (1994), "the accused is not entitled to oversight or review of the decision to prosecute."[165] This does not mean, however, that probable cause is absent since it is required to legally arrest, hold, or charge the suspect. Nor does it remove all screening options as Yale Kamisar et al. comment, "[A]ll American jurisdictions provide at least one procedural avenue for obtaining such a screening . . . jurisdictions [require] either . . . a grand jury indictment or a preliminary hearing bindover."[166]

As early as A.D. 1215, Clause 39 of the *Magna Carta* stated, "[N]o free man shall be . . . imprisoned or disseised [dispossessed] . . . except by the lawful judgment of his peers or by the law of the land."[167] American law assures a detainee the right to not be held without legal justification. Although, the Supreme Court has ruled there is no constitutional guarantee to a judicial preliminary hearing, in *Gerstein v. Pugh* (1975) it found that the Fourth Amendment "requires a judicial determination of probable cause as a prerequisite to extended restraint following arrest," but it can be determined in ways other than an initial hearing, such as the issuance of an arrest warrant.[168] Most persons detained by the police or jail are promptly brought before a magistrate after their arrest for a first appearance.

Often, the appearance occurs through teleconferencing using closed-circuit television rather than the detainee and magistrate having direct personal contact. This promotes security and efficiency since the arrestee does not leave the institution.

The purpose of the first appearance before a magistrate is multifold.[169] Initial hearings commonly have three principal objectives: first, to conduct a judicial review of the facts to ensure that sufficient probable cause exists to bind suspects over for charges; second, to confirm that arrestees have been properly advised of their *Miranda* warning and understand their right to counsel; third, to select an appropriate bail option for those suspects being forwarded for charges. Many of the arrestee's constitutional protections at this stage are procedural; however, the review conducted by a neutral magistrate safeguards communicative privacy interests pertaining to *Miranda,* as well as privacy and liberty interests affected by the bail determination.

Pretrial Release Process

There is no absolute right to bail guaranteed by the Constitution for arrested persons. Specifically, the Eighth Amendment states, "Excessive bail shall not be required, nor excessive fines imposed . . . ," which is designed to prevent bail from being used in a punitive fashion.[170] However, Fifth and Fourteenth Amendment protections do restrict jurisdictions from denying bail if it "deprives any person of life, liberty, or property without due process of law."[171] The purpose of bail is to assure that the released defendant appears in court when required. There are a significant number of bail options available in most jurisdictions. In some states, police officers issue citations, conduct station house releases, or accept predetermined bail amounts from arrestees in minor offense cases. Otherwise, many jurisdictions require the magistrate conducting the first appearance to make pretrial release or detention determinations. Pretrial release alternatives are separated into two categories. According to the Pretrial Services Resource Center,

Pretrial release alternatives are divided into financial and nonfinancial options. Among the forms of nonfinancial pretrial release are: summons, field citation, stationhouse release, release on recognizance (ROR), supervised release, third party custody, and house arrest. Under ROR and its derivatives, summons, citation, and stationhouse release defendants are released on their promise to appear in court as required and without further conditions except to refrain from criminal activity.[172]

Financial options available to the court are commercial surety bail, such as a bail bondsman, full cash bail, property bail, deposit bail, and unsecured bail. Even though financial bail options are offered to defendants, in many cases they are financially unable to obtain the amount needed. Under this circumstance they will not be released and become pretrial detainees until there is an official disposition of the case. Research shows that in state courts, in 75 of the largest counties between 1990 and 2004, 62 percent of defendants were granted pretrial release before case disposition.[173] However, not all defendants are offered financial bail or alternative pretrial release options by the court.

A majority of states include a right to bail in their constitutions or statutes but also incorporate exceptions that permit preventive detention in specific types of serious crimes or capital offenses.[174] Defendants may be denied the opportunity of bail or release using two justifications. If the court determines accused persons pose a threat to the community, it may refuse to release them.[175] Factors such as the seriousness of the offense, the behavior of the defendant, risk to the victim or witness, or likelihood of committing additional crimes are considered when refusing release based on potential threat. And if the court views defendants a high flight risk, meaning they may flee the jurisdiction if released, rejecting bail is justified. In both situations, courts may deny pretrial release without violating the defendant's constitutional rights if their determination is justifiable.[176] Experts have debated for years which pretrial release option has the greatest efficacy in terms of assuring that the defendant will return to court when scheduled.[177] According to research, property bail defendants are the most likely to appear in court when scheduled; yet, they are also the most likely, along with release on recognizance defendants, to be rearrested while released.[178] Defendant misconduct, while free on bail or release, is a matter of serious concern for the court.

Consider the case of Detroit, Michigan, mayor Kwame Kilpatrick. Mayor Kilpatrick was charged in March 2008 with several felony offenses including perjury. Earlier in the year the *Detroit Free Press* newspaper wrote a story accusing Kilpatrick of having an intimate relationship with his chief of staff, Christine Beatty. In the story the newspaper published excerpts of sexually suggestive text messages exchanged between Kilpatrick and Beatty. Both denied, under oath, they were involved in a relationship, which turned out to be false. Kilpatrick is also accused of perjuring himself in testimony regarding a law suit filed by two fired Detroit police officers. Kilpatrick was freed on bond and ordered not to leave the jurisdiction without court permission. On August 7, 2008, Kwame Kilpatrick's bond was revoked by District Court Judge Ronald Giles after he discovered the mayor had attended a meeting across the border in Canada without first obtaining the court's authorization. Judge Giles ordered Kilpatrick jailed the same day.[179] This incident illustrates the types of pretrial restrictions that can be imposed on persons released by the courts.

Pretrial Release Conditions

Certainly, liberty interests of the defendant are impacted by the pretrial release consideration. But conditional or supervised release also has tremendous bearing on the defendant's privacy. To receive pretrial release the defendant must agree to appear in court when directed and may be required to abide by additional court-imposed conditions or supervision. Defendants subject to pretrial release are presumed innocent and protected by constitutional rights similar to nonarrested persons. Also, some courts classify nonadjudicated pretrial defendants differently than released convicted offenders, such as probationers, when it comes to privacy and Fourth Amendment rights, except that the pretrial defendant's lawful arrest and court oversight during release status diminish their expectation of privacy.[180] In *Thornton v. United States* (2004), Justice Scalia commented, "The fact of prior lawful arrest distinguishes the arrestee from society at large."[181] Andrew J. Smith insists "the correct understanding of pretrial arrestee's status is that they are in the 'quasi-custody' of the state. 'Quasi-custody' most accurately reflects a pretrial arrestee's diminished expectation of privacy . . . ."[182] Many pretrial releasees are subject to conditions while those considered higher risk must agree to official supervision. Supervision can be carried out by direct contact with an official, technology surveillance, or third-party custody. Supervised release is designed to minimize the likelihood of failure to appear and rearrest.

Conditions fall into four categories—status quo, restrictive, contact, and problem oriented. The Pretrial Services Resource Center describes the types as follows:

> "Status quo" conditions require that defendants maintain their residence, school, or employment status . . . restrictive conditions limit defendants' associations and movement [such as house arrest, curfew, or avoiding contact with

the victim], ... contact conditions require the defendant to report by telephone or in person ... at designated intervals ... problem-oriented conditions
relate to specific defendant problems that could affect the likelihood of court
appearance [such as substance abuse].[183]

Depending on the type of release format or condition package, the defendant
could forfeit control over personal decision making, association, or movement. Some restrictive conditions, such as house arrest, curfew, and avoiding
restricted areas (that is, schools), severely limit activities and are often subject
to electronic monitoring to ensure compliance and to promote public safety
by tracking the defendant's location. The primary difference between conditional release and supervised release is that the latter involves active human or
electronic monitoring.

Both types of release may include problem-oriented conditions that
require the defendant to participate in counseling programs or submit to
drug or alcohol testing if it is directly related to reducing the risk of reoffend-
ing or failing to appear in court when scheduled. Starting in the 1970s,
the growing number of drug arrests brought scores of substance users into
the courts. At the same time, researchers were theorizing about a drug-
crime nexus that claimed a close relationship between drug use and criminality. They hypothesized that if drug-using criminals were identified upon their
entrance into the justice system, they could be treated more effectively.

Beginning in 1995 at the direction of President Bill Clinton, U.S. Attorney
General Janet Reno launched an initiative to require drug testing of all federal
arrestees before the court considered their pretrial release. Two years later
Congress used the Byrne Formula Grant to make federal funds available to
states to implement a similar model. Originally, early testing was viewed as a
complement to other drug treatment efforts. But by the 1970s it was also used
as a monitoring tool for those under probation or parole supervision and by
the 1980s was utilized to reduce pretrial misconduct. Jurisdictions drug tested
arrestees at various stages of the pretrial process. Some used the screening to
identify drug users at the point of arrest, before initial appearance, before pretrial release consideration, or for monitoring during pretrial release. Methods
used are urine, perspiration patch, and hair analysis to detect the presence of
illicit substances such as opiate, cocaine, amphetamine, phencyclidine, and
marijuana in the defendant's body.[184]

Research on the use of drug testing as a predictive tool to assess pretrial
release failure or misconduct produced mixed results. So many jurisdictions
use drug analysis during pretrial release to primarily monitor defendants
for compliance with conditions. A Department of Justice study showed that
approximately 68 percent of pretrial programs use drug testing to monitor

persons on release.[185] Secondarily, it is used to detect active drug use during conditional release so the defendant can be directed into proper treatment. As a result of the example provided by the federal Bail Reform Act of 1984, federal and state courts began to require defendants, in drug-related cases or who are drug users, to consent to random drug testing and searches to ensure compliance with pretrial release conditions.[186] As the monitoring programs gained wider use, defendants challenged the constitutionality of the drug testing and warrantless search consent agreement required for pretrial release. The federal courts consistently rejected these claims until a 2006 ruling of the Ninth Circuit Court of Appeals.

Raymond Scott was arrested on methamphetamine possession charges in Nevada. After he consented to random drug testing and warrantless search of his home, he received conditional pretrial release on personal recognizance. Pretrial officials received an informant tip that Scott had several firearms in his possession. Officer Douglas Swalm, along with other officers, went to Scott's home and directed him to provide a urine sample for drug testing, as required by his release conditions. The analysis result was positive, showing the presence of methamphetamine. A subsequent warrantless search of the home by the officers uncovered a prohibited sawed-off shotgun, so Scott was arrested. He was charged with federal firearm violations, but the trial court ruled that the home search was unreasonable under the Fourth Amendment, because the officers lacked probable cause, and suppressed the evidence. The government appealed arguing that using a totality of circumstances analysis the pretrial conditions were valid under a special needs rationale. The Ninth Circuit Court of Appeals in *United States v. Scott* (2006) disagreed. Judge Alex Kozinski reasoned,

> Warrantless searches, including random drug testing, imposed as condition of pretrial release in state prosecution, required showing of probable cause, even though defendant had signed [a] pre-release consent form; protecting community from further crime committed by defendant did not amount to [a] "special need," since crime prevention was [a] quintessential general law enforcement purpose, there was no showing that [the] problem of releasee's failing to appear in court as result of drug use justified intruding on privacy rights of every releasee . . . .[187]

Several aspects of this decision potentially affect the privacy and Fourth Amendment rights of pretrial releasees. Since the Supreme Court has not resolved the narrow constitutional questions that surfaced in *Scott*, lower courts and legal experts continue to debate the Ninth Circuit court's findings. As Andrew J. Smith asserts, however, "several lower court decisions . . . reveal a clear trend of courts upholding the constitutionality of pretrial release conditions."[188] And yet, the court's holding in *Scott* deviates from substantial precedent, thereby raising three important constitutional issues: first, whether persons can bargain away their Fourth Amendment and privacy rights in exchange for pretrial release; second, whether the defendant's consent in *Scott* was voluntary given the potentially coercive choice presented by the judicial officer, namely, either agree to the conditions or remain incarcerated; third, whether privacy rights of persons on conditional pretrial release differ from those of convicted probationers.

Some commentators insist that given the potentially coercive surroundings of practices such as plea bargaining in criminal cases, which is widely accepted, the Supreme Court would likely uphold the pretrial consent to drug test and warrantless search provided by Raymond Scott in exchange for his release. Melanie D. Wilson suggests,

> When a person is arrested and faces the real likelihood of pretrial detention in jail, the person risks not only a reduction in his privacy rights, but also a loss of his liberty. In such circumstances, the arrested person should be able to bargain away some of his Fourth Amendment rights in exchange for the additional freedoms associated with release to home.[189]

Courts recognize the validity of an arrestee's voluntary waiver of constitutional rights in both police custodial and pretrial circumstances. Just as the prerogative is available in a *Miranda* context to arrestees wanting to offer voluntary statements, pretrial release candidates may waive constitutional and privacy rights by consenting to have supervision or conditions imposed upon them in exchange for release. Thus far, no definitive constitutional prohibition prevents most jurisdictions from using drug testing, warrantless search, and other monitoring conditions to ensure compliance with court provisions to promote public safety, assure scheduled court appearance, and reduce pretrial misconduct. The impact of the *Scott* decision is difficult to assess, but thus far, the findings have neither been directly resolved by the high Court nor widely imposed on other jurisdictions.

Electronic Supervision

Another pretrial release monitoring method that affects privacy interests is defendant electronic monitoring. Electronic supervision technologies are widely used by officials and justified by two primary objectives—public safety and condition compliance. Electronic supervision is used in various community-based settings including pretrial release, probation, and parole. The principal role of electronic supervision technology is to generate information for correctional decision makers. According to Ann H. Crowe, offender monitoring programs consist of computerized automated reporting, identity verification, and programmed contact or automated calling. Offender tracking devices include portable field monitoring, group monitoring, and location tracking systems. Specific DUI systems involve remote alcohol detection and ignition interlock. And victim alert/notification systems are designed to prevent offender contact with the victim.[190]

The closest supervision of total movement occurs with location tracking systems using global positioning technology, while other monitoring methods are combined with restrictive conditions such as house arrest or curfew. Together, these electronic supervision technologies are designed to enable officials to protect the public, ensure condition compliance, and reduce misconduct among persons on pretrial release.

Because of the surveillance capability of these technologies, the risk of privacy invasion by monitoring officials is significant. Therefore, statutes in several states allow usage of visual images only of the defendant's face. Some laws also prohibit the use of auditory sounds or voices other than the defendant's, as well as eavesdropping. As South Carolina state law noted, "An approved electronic monitoring device may be used to record a conversation between the participant and the monitoring device, or the participant and the person supervising the participant, solely for the purpose of identification and not for the purpose of eavesdropping or conducting any other illegally intrusive monitoring."[191] Similarly, the state requires that the person subject to electronic supervision provide written consent to be monitored, and officials are responsible for "insuring that the approved electronic devices are minimally intrusive upon the privacy of the participant and other persons residing in the home."[192]

Although electronically supervised defendants have challenged the constitutionality of monitoring, courts have generally held that electronic monitoring does not unreasonably intrude on an expectation of privacy.[193] Claims based on privacy or Fourth Amendment violations are weakened because the pretrial releasee subject to condition, supervision, or electronic monitoring consented to the provisions imposed by the judicial officer and ordinarily waives such rights before being granted release. Electronic supervision de vices are intended merely to gather information, including defendant verification or location, to ensure condition compliance. The technology simply enhances or permits mechanical checks and surveillance of pretrial releasees akin to that performed by official contact.[194] As such, they are no more intrusive than an officer's visit to the defendant's home if used legally and properly. Legal limitations, however, prohibit the devices or monitoring officials from unlawfully eavesdropping or conducting law enforcement forays for criminal evidence from those under surveillance. The pretrial defendant retains constitutional protection against surreptitious collection of testimonial evidence, in violation of Fifth Amendment privilege, or nonconsensual search by authorities that reach beyond the scope of the court-imposed conditions.

Privacy interests of persons subject to pretrial detention or release are viewed in a postarrest context and, thus, have a diminished expectation. For those released, some classifications of defendants require problem-oriented conditions to ensure compliance and protect the community. Unlike a detainee, their privacy and constitutional rights are interpreted based on the conditional agreement that led to their release. Conditional release often includes periodic substance testing, search, or monitoring to assure compliance and minimize pretrial misconduct.

While defendants are in the pretrial stage of the justice process, their cases are still subject to further investigation. At this point, the police have referred the matter to the prosecutor who reviews it to determine if sufficient evidence exists to formally charge the person. Prosecutorial decision making is steeped in discretion that allows the official to consider all relevant facts regarding the filing of a criminal charge. For minor offenses, prosecutors can present charges based strictly on the factual information provided by the arresting police officer, without the benefit of grand jury or judicial review. Serious crime cases, however, are subject to the investigatory review of a grand jury to determine if sufficient evidence exists to indict the arrestee.

PRIVACY RIGHTS AND GRAND JURY INVESTIGATION

Given the inherent checks and balances in the American justice system, it would be expected that the Framers instilled a constitutional provision for reviewing the sufficiency of evidence before charging a person with a serious crime. The Fifth Amendment states, "No person shall be held to answer for a capital, or otherwise infamous crime, unless on a presentment or indictment of a Grand Jury . . . ."[195] Grand juries are independent investigatory bodies comprised of ordinary citizens. Their responsibility is to review evidence and render a decision on the validity of the prosecutor's allegation against the defendant. Grand jury reviews are neither adversarial nor adjudicatory; therefore, their role is simply to investigate the possible guilt of the arrestee based on evidence within their purview.

Reviewable evidence ordinarily comes from two sources: either information derived from the police or prosecutor investigation or original evidence independently obtained by the grand jury. In the latter case, grand juries are authorized to issue subpoenas for witnesses, documents, or exemplars. Although the legal rationale is somewhat different in the grand jury setting, the defendant is not constitutionally shielded from appearing or producing evidence upon request.

A federal grand jury in Illinois was investigating interstate gambling allegations against a group of persons. Among the submitted evidence were voice recordings obtained by police using a court order. To gather voice exemplars for comparison, the grand jury subpoenaed 20 persons implicated in the case, ordering them to report to the U.S. Attorney's office to record a reading of a prepared conversation script. Antonio Dionisio received a subpoena but refused to provide the voice exemplar insisting that the order violated his Fourth Amendment rights. The district court directed Dionisio to comply; when he again refused, he was jailed for contempt of court. He appealed claiming the grand jury compulsory order, both to appear and submit a voice exemplar, was a Fourth Amendment seizure and therefore required a showing of reasonableness. The Supreme Court in *United States v. Dionisio* rejected his argument reasoning

> [s]ince neither the summons to appear before the grand jury, nor its directive to make a voice recording infringed upon any interest protected by the Fourth Amendment, there was no justification for requiring the grand jury to satisfy even the minimal requirement of 'reasonableness' . . . A grand jury has broad investigative powers to determine whether a crime has been committed and who committed it.[196]

Similarly, the Court ruled in another case that the *Dionisio* reasoning also applies to grand jury–compelled handwriting exemplars, such that the subpoena recipient cannot refuse to provide the sample on constitutional grounds.[197]

The legal justification needed for a grand jury subpoena to request the compulsory production of biometric evidence, such as hair, saliva, or blood, slides on a continuum based on its relevance, need, and level of intrusion. Depending on the evidence requested, different courts have mandated standards ranging from search warrant to individualized reasonable suspicion. Yale Kamisar et al. assert, "Courts have agreed that a special showing is needed as to the taking of blood, which has long been held to constitute a search when performed at the direction of the police, but have divided as to whether the presence of a grand jury subpoena alters the character of the required showing."[198] The greater the privacy intrusion the higher legal standard courts may require in subpoenaing biometric exemplars from witnesses. As one court explained, "[A] subpoena requiring witness to furnish saliva falls toward the middle of the continuum extending from the procedures in *Dionisio* and *Mara* and the taking of a blood sample."[199] Hence, minimal intrusion exemplars such as voice, handwriting, scalp hair, and fingerprints typically do not require the grand jury to satisfy a search standard such as probable cause or individualized suspicion. Conversely, grand jury subpoenas for more intrusive biometric or DNA samples such as saliva, blood, or tissue may be subject to court requirements of a warrant, probable cause, or individualized reasonable suspicion depending on the jurisdiction.

Grand jury proceedings are not subject to the procedural rules required in criminal trials. As the Supreme Court explained, "[A grand jury] may compel the production of evidence or the testimony of witnesses as it considers appropriate, and its operation generally is unrestrained by the technical procedural and evidentiary rules governing the conduct of criminal trials."[200] The authority of a grand jury to investigate, subpoena, and gather evidence is not without some limitation, nor does it strip witnesses of all constitutional protections. Persons are not required to comply with the demands of unreasonable or oppressive subpoenas.[201]

Moreover, all witnesses are protected by the Fifth Amendment privilege against self-incrimination and have the right of refusal involving testimonial evidence that may incriminate them. However, the Fifth Amendment self-incrimination privilege is not available for information that has no risk of implicating the witness in a crime. Yet, it is in full force during grand jury testimony because witnesses may be subject to criminal prosecution, and if subpoenaed, their comments are subject to compulsion. The high Court in *Hoffman v. United States* (1951) held "[t]he [self-incrimination] privilege afforded not only extends to answers that would in themselves support a conviction ... but likewise embraces those which furnish a link in the chain of evidence needed to prosecute the [witness]."[202]

As in other interrogation processes, witnesses retain self-incrimination protection but anyone is subject to grand jury subpoena and may be questioned. Yet, arrestees cannot be compelled to divulge what they may know if it risks implicating themselves in a crime. A Fifth Amendment self-incrimination privilege closely intersects with individual privacy rights by protecting information within the arrestee's knowledge that is prohibited from being seized by the government through involuntary disclosure.

In *Murphy v. Waterfront Comm'n* (1964), the Supreme Court described the constitutional relationship between the Fifth Amendment self-incrimination privilege and individual privacy interests. Justice Arthur Goldberg explained seven fundamental values that underlie the privilege and their importance in protecting, among other things, the rights of the accused. These mirror historical and legal views of personal rights as a "reflection of our common conscience." Among the listed values is "... our respect for the inviolability of the human personality and of the right of each individual 'to a private enclave where he may lead a private life' ...."[203]

In *Murphy,* the Court treats self-incrimination as a privacy right joining those delineated in the Fourth and First Amendments as protections against government intrusion. Other courts have noted that the privacy aspect of the privilege is protecting what a person knows from government invasion. The Court in *Couch v. United States* (1973) commented that the self-incrimination privilege protected the "privacy of the mind" because it "respects a private inner sanctum of individual feeling and thought,"[204] thus insulating the arrested from self-condemnation brought about by pressure from authorities.

Arrestees or witnesses have a diminished expectation of privacy pursuant to grand jury investigations. They must comply with subpoenas to testify, produce document, and provide exemplar as long as the grand jury request is relevant to the investigation and reasonable. Subpoenas that demand intrusive biometric samples may be required by the courts to first obtain a warrant, support the request with a showing of probable cause, or have individualized reasonable suspicion. Those subpoenaed are subject to questioning but are protected by a constitutional self-incrimination privilege that defends them throughout the criminal justice process.

TRANSITION TO POSTINDICTMENT PROCEEDINGS

Arrestees continue to be the target of a grand jury investigation until they are indicted or their complaints are dismissed by the prosecutor. Theoretically, criminal investigation or inquiry into criminal activity continues until the case is disposed through conviction or acquittal. Just because a person is formally charged, the investigation may simply shift to the courtroom but it is "entirely proper to continue an investigation of the ... criminal activities of the defendant and his alleged confederates."[205] If the grand jury investigation fails to find sufficient cause to support a criminal charge, arrestees may be unconditionally released as charges against them will be dropped. Conversely, if ample evidence supports a grand jury indictment, arrestees will be bound over for adjudication. As indicted defendants, their legal status changes and they are subject to greater official control, and by extension, a further reduction in privacy rights. Yet, a full complement of constitutional safeguards is available during the adjudication process that follows grand jury indictment. Proceedings move to an adversarial setting once the defendant is indicted. Adjudication triggers a host of defendant constitutional and procedural rights during trial; therefore, defendants' liberty and privacy interests are viewed in that context by the courts.

Chapter 4

FINAL VERDICT ON
DEFENDANT RIGHTS

Federal agents in New York received an informant tip that crew members on the SS *Santa Maria,* sailing from South America to New York, were smuggling illegal drugs aboard ship. When the ship arrived, the officers conducted a search of the vessel and seized over three pounds of cocaine. Their investigation revealed that two merchant seamen on the ship, Winston Massiah and Jesse Colson, were connected to the illicit narcotics. Both were arrested, arraigned, and released on bail. Massiah retained an attorney prior to arraignment and pleaded not guilty at the hearing. A subsequent indictment charged the seamen with possession of illegal drugs while Colson and others were also charged with conspiracy. Unbeknown to Massiah, Colson agreed to cooperate with federal authorities. Agent Murphy installed a radio transmitter under the seat of Colson's car. Colson and the agent arranged to lure Massiah into the car to discuss the narcotics smuggling scheme. By eavesdropping on the conversation, the agent hoped to learn the names of the other traffickers. Massiah was unaware that agent Murphy was listening to the electronically transmitted conversation from a nearby car. Massiah made several incriminating statements during the private discussion with Colson. At his trial, Massiah's incriminating statements, obtained through warrantless eavesdropping, were introduced into evidence during agent Murphy's testimony. Defense objections were overruled by the trial judge, and Massiah was convicted of federal drug trafficking, due in part, to the recorded evidence.[1]

This case raises a number of constitutional and privacy issues. Since it was decided by the Supreme Court in 1964, it predates the *Katz* privacy and *Miranda* custodial interrogation doctrines; yet, it clearly implicates Fourth, Fifth, and Sixth Amendment protections because the police secret evidence collection occurred after Massiah was indicted and hired legal counsel. *Massiah* (1964) is a landmark case that guarantees defendants constitutional rights once they have retained an attorney and begun postindictment adversarial proceedings. Justice Potter Stewart commented,

Here we deal . . . with . . . a federal case where the specific guarantee of the Sixth Amendment directly applies. We hold that the petitioner [Massiah] was denied the basic protections of that guarantee when there was used against him at his trial evidence of his own incriminating words, which federal agents had deliberately elicited from him after he had been indicted and in the absence of his counsel.[2]

The Court failed to address in its ruling the issue of the agent's warrantless eavesdropping and seizure of Massiah's incriminating statements. It opted, instead, to focus on the right to counsel protection under the Sixth Amendment. The *Massiah* doctrine prohibits investigators from conducting interrogations in the absence of the defendant's attorney once adversarial proceedings have begun.[3]

DEFENDANT PRIVACY RIGHTS DURING ADJUDICATION

A guarantee of legal counsel is just one of the constitutional rights activated after formal criminal charges have been brought against a defendant. The Sixth Amendment is the principal guarantor of the rights during criminal trial proceedings; it states the following:

In all criminal prosecutions, the accused shall enjoy the right to a speedy and public trial, by an impartial jury of the State and district wherein the crime shall have been committed, which district shall have been previously ascertained by law, and to be informed of the nature and cause of the accusation; to be confronted with the witnesses against him; to have compulsory process for obtaining witnesses in his favor, and to have the Assistance of Counsel for his defence.[4]

As assured in *Gideon v. Wainwright* (1963), and later echoed in *Massiah,* the defendant has a right to be represented by legal counsel at every critical stage of the criminal process.[5] Furthermore, the defendant retains a full complement of constitutional and privacy safeguards including Fourth Amendment search and seizure, Fifth Amendment self-incrimination privilege, and Sixth Amendment evidence confrontation rights during the adjudication proceedings.

Some of the constitutional protections available during this stage of the criminal proceedings are procedural and not directly relevant to individual privacy rights. However, criminal defendants are able to protect their privacy interests using prescribed constitutional and procedural methods in the pretrial and adjudication phases. Defendants can challenge not only the adverse criminal evidence but also the method officials used to collect it when it is introduced against them in trial. Additionally, accused persons are protected from disadvantage if the government tries to undermine their presumption of innocence or privilege against compulsory self-incrimination during trial.[6]

Right to Privileged Communication

Defendants have a long-standing legal privilege protecting the confidentiality of communications with designated persons. Their discussions are privacy protected, and neither the defendant nor the other discussant can be compelled by officials to divulge the content of conversations covered by the constitutional or statutory privilege. Privilege relationships vary across jurisdictions. Some are derived from common law such as the attorney-client privilege, while others stem from statutes. For instance, some jurisdictions include husband-wife, physician-patient, or clergy-penitent privileges among those available to the defendant. If a privilege exists in a given jurisdiction, the privacy protection afforded the communication is absolute and cannot be lawfully obtained by criminal justice officials.[7]

Defending Privacy Interests through Confrontation of Evidence

Persons accused of a crime have a constitutional right to confront their accusers and the probative evidence presented against them. The confrontation clause gives the defendant a two-prong right—to face adverse witnesses and cross-examine them.[8] Defendants also have a constitutional right to present a defense to rebut the government's evidence, including introducing favorable exhibits and obtaining witnesses on their behalf.[9] In order to take advantage of this guarantee, the defendant has a right to be present at every critical stage of the justice process, including the trial proceeding. In spite of the constitutional assurance, accused persons may waive their confrontation privilege by choosing to be absent from trial or intentionally becoming disruptive, which results in their removal. The Supreme Court has authorized three methods for dealing with unruly defendants during trial. In *Illinois v. Allen* (1970), it explained, ". . . We think there are at least three constitutionally permissible ways for a trial judge to handle an obstreperous defendant . . . (1) bind and gag him, thereby keeping him present; (2) cite him for contempt; (3) take him out of the courtroom until he promises to conduct himself properly."[10]

The scope of the confrontation clause has been addressed by the high Court in a line of cases. For instance, consider the case of *Coy v. Iowa* (1988), where

> . . . [John Coy] was arrested and charged with sexually assaulting two 13-year-old girls . . . [yet] neither was able to describe his face . . . at the beginning of [Coy's] trial, the State made a motion pursuant to a recently enacted [Iowa]

statute . . . to allow the complaining witnesses to testify either via closed-circuit television or behind a screen. The trial court approved the use of a large screen to be placed between appellant [Coy] and the witness stand during the girls' testimony.[11]

The Supreme Court reversed the trial court's conviction finding

Appellant's right to face-to-face confrontation was violated since the screen at issue enabled the complaining witnesses to avoid viewing appellant as they gave their testimony. There is no merit to the State's assertion that its statute creates a presumption of trauma to victims of sexual abuse that outweighs appellant's right to confrontation.[12]

Though the defendant's conviction was based on the evidence, the Court in *Coy* defended the Sixth Amendment confrontation clause because it gives the accused a fundamental right to face the witnesses.

Yet, the right to face-to-face confrontation is not absolute as the Court later established an exception in the *Maryland v. Craig* (1990) child sexual abuse case. In *Craig,* the Supreme Court allowed child witnesses to testify from an adjoining room by one-way closed circuit television to prevent the "child [from] suffering serious emotional distress, such that he or she could not reasonably communicate."[13] The Court held that the "confrontation clause did not categorically prohibit child witness in child abuse case from testifying against defendant at trial, outside defendant's physical presence, by one-way closed circuit television" and the "finding of necessity for use of one-way closed circuit television procedure had to be made on case specific basis."[14]

Since the Court permits trial courts to apply the procedure on a case basis, the exception has been rejected by some jurisdictions on state law grounds; in other cases, courts found that the government failed to produce reasonable arguments why the defendant was not allowed to confront the witness. Thus, except with individualized justification, the general rule is that the accused has the right to know the identity of adverse witnesses and confront those offering testimony.[15]

Discovery Rules

A defendant's right of confrontation extends beyond witnesses to include discovery of evidence. The procedure enables the defense to request prosecution disclosure of witness and evidence to be used in the trial. Discovery rules vary by jurisdiction since the Supreme Court has not designated it a constitutional right. Most jurisdictions have enacted statutes or rules of court using the practice. For example, the Federal Rules of Criminal Procedure state the following:

> ... Upon request of the defendant the government shall permit the defendant to inspect and copy or photograph books, papers, documents, photographs, tangible objects, buildings or places, copies of portions thereof, which are in possession, custody, or control of the government, and which are material to the preparation of his defense or are intended for use by the government as evidence in chief at the trial, or were obtained from or belong to the defendant.[16]

In sum, the defendant can challenge any adverse witness or article of evidence introduced in trial.

Impeaching Evidence

The defense endeavors to impeach prosecution evidence by challenging the trustworthiness of witnesses and exhibits. Also, defendants may elect to take the witness stand to testify on their own behalf so as to refute or clarify adverse witness testimony.[17] However, this can be a risky trial maneuver because then the defendant must be available for prosecution cross-examination. Regardless, accused persons retain their constitutional privilege against compulsory self-incrimination. And the prosecution is barred from making comments that tend to coerce the defendant to testify.[18]

Motion to Suppress Evidence

Defendants protect their privacy interests in trial by opposing the introduction of prosecution evidence. Prior to the beginning of the criminal trial, the accused can file pretrial motions to suppress evidence before it is introduced. This is used to persuade the court to invoke the exclusionary rule to prevent a piece of evidence from being admitted. It is at this stage that the defense argues that police unlawfully invaded privacy, conducted unreasonable searches and seizures, or violated other constitutional safeguards. The accused can ask the court to exclude statement, pretrial identification, witness testimony, or physical evidence at any stage in the proceedings from pretrial to posttrial, except the Court has rejected the invocation of the exclusionary rule during grand jury investigation.[19] Requests to suppress evidence are a formidable weapon for the defendant, particularly if the court agrees to exclude evidence found to be improperly obtained or introduced in trial.

The manner in which evidence is searched and seized contributes to its susceptibility to suppression. If criminal evidence is obtained with a warrant, the search is more likely to have prima facie validity since probable cause was assured beforehand by the judicial officer. Conversely, warrantless searches rely on probable cause formulated by the police in the field. Since this class of searches does not enjoy the benefit of initial judicial review, it is more vulnerable to challenge. Once the defendant disputes the validity of an official intrusion, search, or seizure, the burden then shifts to the government to assuage the court that the police action was reasonable and lawful. If the government is unable to refute the defendant's claim, the evidence may be ruled inadmissible. In this situation, the prosecutor may have to dismiss the charges against the defendant if the loss of the evidence prevents the prosecution from proving the elements of the offense. Often, court imposition of the exclusionary rule decimates the government's case, particularly if it relied heavily on the omitted evidence.

Defendant's Access to Exculpatory Evidence

Defendants have a constitutional right to confront and try to discredit adverse evidence. In order to fully benefit from that entitlement, they must have access to all evidence used against them. The Supreme Court established the *Brady* rule in the 1960s, which imposes a duty on prosecutors to disclose material and exculpatory evidence that suggests the innocence of the accused.

In the *Brady* case, defendants John Brady and Donald Boblit were convicted of first-degree murder in a Maryland court and sentenced to death. In a separate trial, Brady admitted to being involved in the robbery but claimed that Boblit killed the victim. Before the trial began, Brady's attorney asked to examine Boblit's police statements that were being held by the prosecution. Several of the statements were shown to Brady's lawyer, but the prosecutor withheld one crucial statement where Boblit admitted to the murder. After conviction and sentencing, Brady learned of Boblit's admission statement and asked for a new trial in light of the undisclosed evidence. His request was denied and on appeal the Supreme Court ruled that Brady's due process rights had been violated by concealment of the co-defendant's confession. In *Brady v. Maryland* (1963), the high Court stated, "We hold that the suppression by the prosecution of evidence favorable to an accused upon request violates due process where the evidence is material either to guilt or to punishment, irrespective of the good faith of the prosecution."[20]

Later in *United States v. Agurs* (1976), the Supreme Court made the materiality of the exculpatory evidence central to a prosecutorial breach of duty.[21] The *Agurs* Court outlined intentional use of perjured testimony and failure to disclose material evidence as circumstances in which prosecutors are assigned a *Brady*-type duty to produce all material and trustworthy evidence in their possession. In two subsequent cases, the Court directed the prosecution to supply exculpatory evidence if there is a reasonable probability that the information will yield a different result in the criminal proceeding.[22] Similarly, in *Banks v. Dretke* (2004), the Court reversed a capital murder conviction where the prosecution withheld that a government witness, who denied any affiliation in sworn testimony, was a paid informant. By allowing the false testimony to remain uncontested and hiding the informant's identity from the defense, the prosecutor violated the *Brady* rule.[23]

Although the prosecutor has a duty to refrain from concealing exculpatory evidence, the Supreme Court has failed to rule that government officials must preserve evidence based on the possibility that it might exonerate the accused.[24] Similarly, the Court held that police do not have to abandon standard evidence handling procedures because the defendant files a motion of discovery. In *Illinois v. Fisher* (2004), the high Court upheld the police normal practice of destroying narcotics evidence after 10 years. It found that even though the defense had requested discovery before the defendant absconded, the police were not required to give up standard evidence handling procedures years later.[25]

The Supreme Court has not specifically applied the *Brady* rule to law enforcement investigators. In line with *Brady* thinking, the Court requires disclosure of evidentiary information that is material to a case regardless of its type.[26] Hence, the Court has ruled withholding impeachment information about the credibility of a witness is just as violative as not disclosing other exculpatory evidence. In *Giglio v. United States* (1972), the Court concluded, "When the 'reliability of a given witness may well be determinative of guilt or innocence,' nondisclosure of evidence affecting credibility falls within the general [Brady] rule."[27]

Assigning *Brady* co-responsibility to police officers investigating criminal cases follows two strands of reasoning. To begin with, officers are ordinarily the first officials to be involved in the search, seizure, and follow-up investigation. They are privy to the history of the evidence and had advance contact with the crime scene, physical evidence, exemplar, arrestee, interrogatee, victim, and witness. Second, investigators are essential prosecution witnesses because they compiled the criminal case components. Due to their familiarity with most aspects of the criminal case, the officers' credibility is a vital element in the government's case. Lisa A. Regini insists that prosecutors have a "... duty to learn ... any favorable evidence known to others acting on the government's behalf, including the police . . . ."[28] Some courts have extended this duty to disclosure of officer misconduct if it has a bearing on the veracity of law enforcement officer witnesses.[29]

In the Los Angeles Police Rampart Division scandal, officer credibility significantly influenced the integrity of criminal investigations, not to mention, had a determinative effect on the outcome of criminal proceedings.[30] To combat officer deception or misconduct, which may taint an investigation or subsequent prosecution, some police agencies have established a "no lies" policy. In doing so, police managers extend *Brady* duties to officers to reduce the risk of derailing the prosecution's case due to nondisclosure of exculpatory evidence. Jeff Noble asserts, "In a case where an officer will be testifying as a witness to an event, the officer's credibility is a material issue and his lack of credibility is clearly potentially exculpatory evidence and therefore sustained findings of untruthfulness must be revealed."[31]

The combined effect of court decisions, statutes, and agency policies places a *Brady* duty on police officers, prosecutors, and presumably other government agency participants, who contribute to criminal investigations and prosecutions. In addition to benefiting from the *Brady* rule, the defendant can utilize reciprocal discovery to develop potentially favorable evidence.

Under statutes in some jurisdictions, the defendant has the right of reciprocal discovery. Consistent with the Supreme Court's rationale in *Wardius v. Oregon* (1973), some courts have found that due process and fundamental fairness dictate "that the accused be given a reciprocal right to discover and utilize contrary evidence."[32] In those circumstances the defense can request to conduct independent scientific tests, lineups, or other procedures that could produce favorable results for the accused so as counter the findings of the government. Through the *Brady* rule and other due process doctrines, the courts have worked to ensure fundamental fairness in criminal proceedings and to protect defendants from the nondisclosure of evidence that is supportive of a claim of innocence. Unfortunately, police or prosecutorial misconduct involving the handling, credibility, or reporting of evidence can result in a miscarriage of justice.

As an illustration, consider the case of former Durham, North Carolina District Attorney Mike Nifong. On March 14, 2006, exotic dancer Crystal Mangum accused several Duke University lacrosse players of sexual assault. She was hired to perform at a team party held at an off-campus house. Durham, North Carolina District Attorney Mike Nifong called the team members "a bunch of hooligans"[33] amid extensive media coverage of the incident. Forty-seven members of the team complied with a court order to provide DNA samples for comparison. Later Mangum identified three players in a photographic spread as her attackers. Students Reade Seligmann, Dave Evans, and Collin Finnerty were indicted on sexual offense and kidnapping charges. All three maintained their innocence, while the accuser offered conflicting accounts of her story and player DNA samples failed to match evidence collected from the victim.

By the year's end, Nifong was being investigated by a state bar ethics committee for making misleading and inflammatory statements about the accused to the media, at the same time he was campaigning for reelection. And the director of the forensic lab testified that he agreed to Nifong's request to purposefully omit, from his laboratory report findings, information that DNA evidence found in the body and on the underclothes of Ms. Mangum did not match any of the accused players. Nifong then asked North Carolina Attorney General Roy Cooper to take over the criminal case and withdrew as the prosecutor. Nifong was charged with violation of several bar rules and professional misconduct. Attorney General Cooper criticized District Attorney Nifong, saying the "rogue prosecutor had pushed ahead unchecked."[34] Cooper further stated that "there were many points in this case where caution would have served justice better than bravado. This case shows the enormous consequences of overreaching by a prosecutor."[35] As the case unraveled, on April 11, 2007, Cooper announced,

> The result of our review and investigation shows clearly that there is insufficient evidence to proceed on any of the charges. Today we are filing notices of dismissal for all charges. We believe these cases were a result of a tragic rush to accuse and failure to verify allegations . . . we believe these three individuals are innocent . . . .[36]

On June 16, 2007, a North Carolina bar disciplinary committee revoked Nifong's attorney license for numerous counts of misconduct including lying to a judge, tampering with the DNA report results, improper statements to the media, and withholding exculpatory evidence in the Duke Lacrosse case. By January 2008, the disgraced former D.A. filed bankruptcy as he faced a barrage of lawsuits from the former Duke defendants.[37]

This disastrous case shows that in spite of duties and constitutional safeguards to protect defendant rights, official abuses can occur if authorities fail to handle evidence with integrity and disclose exculpatory information as required.[38]

PRIVACY RIGHTS IN CRIMINAL PROCEEDINGS

Fourth Amendment Rights

At this stage of the criminal proceedings all adversary participants, that is, the prosecutor, defendant, and defense counsel, interact directly with the court on matters pertaining to the case. Hence, if the prosecution wants to conduct an additional investigatory search or seizure, such as asking for fresh defendant exemplars, best practice suggests the prosecutor will request an order or warrant from the judicial officer. The defendant can file court motions anytime during the criminal proceedings to oppose government search requests or raise claims of privacy or Fourth Amendment violation that result from police or prosecutor investigations. Unless the government's request is unreasonable or immaterial to the case, challenges by the defense are unlikely to succeed. This is not a common occurrence since most Fourth Amendment searches and seizures occur during investigatory and preadjudication stages of the justice process.

If new information, fresh evidence, or fruits of searches and seizures during the adjudicatory proceeding surface, the prosecutor has a duty to inform the defense if it is material under the *Brady* rule. However, the prosecutor is not required to share every piece of information contained in a criminal investigation or reveal the contents of the government's case unless it satisfies the *Brady* criteria. For instance, in *Strickler v. Greene* (1999), the Supreme Court refused to compel the prosecution to disclose a police detective's interviewing notes because there was no showing that the information would have shed light on the defendant's innocence, thereby affecting the trial's outcome.[39] Infringement of defendant privacy interests can also occur as a result of their presence or testimony in court. Here, the Fifth Amendment self-incrimination privilege is implicated as defendants are participants in the proceedings pursuant to their rights under the confrontation clause.

Fifth Amendment Self-Incrimination and Due Process Rights

The Fifth Amendment self-incrimination privilege protects only testimonial evidence. The confrontation clause establishes defendants' constitutional right to be participants in criminal proceedings where they can examine and challenge the evidence presented to prove their guilt.

Similar to pretrial identification, witnesses are asked to identify the defendant in the courtroom. Defendants, however, have the benefit of legal counsel and the option of challenging court identification, which protects their constitutional rights. Individualized identification by witnesses, during trial, is a vital part of connecting the defendant to the crime. It is necessary for the judge or juror to confirm accurate identification of the defendant as the alleged perpetrator for the court record. Yet, this type of in-court identification is very suggestive. As the Supreme Court in *Moore v. Illinois* (1977) commented, it "is difficult to imagine a more suggestive manner in which to present a suspect to a witness for their critical confrontation."[40] However, the defendant's physical appearance alone is neither protected by the Fourth Amendment because there is no expectation of privacy nor assured by the Fifth Amendment self-incrimination privilege since it is not communicative.

Therefore, no constitutional safeguard precludes the defendant from being identified through direct confrontation in criminal proceedings.

There are circumstances, however, where the government takes extraordinary measures to present a defendant in court in a manner that stands to violate the person's privacy expectation. For example, the Court failed to find a compelling state security need in *Riggins v. Nevada* (1992) where Justice Sandra Day O'Connor stated, "[I]t was an error to order the defendant be administered antipsychotic drugs during the course of trial over his objection without findings that there were no less intrusive alternatives, that the medication was medically appropriate, and that it was essential for the sake of defendant's safety and the safety of others."[41]

As a general rule, the courts have held that defendants have a right not to appear at trial in jailhouse clothes, physical restraints, such as handcuffs or shackles, or in a chemically subdued state by using psychotropic drugs; any of which may unduly prejudice the jury. Compelling defendants to be seen in court under these conditions violates their constitutional and privacy interests since it forces them to indirectly incriminate themselves by appearing dangerous or guilty before jurors.[42] However, the Supreme Court has allowed exceptions where the government can show a compelling security need to prevent escape or ensure public safety.

Inferences can be drawn from a convicted person's appearance during sentencing in a way that could unconstitutionally prejudice a jury. Following his conviction on murder charges, David Dawson was sentenced to death by a Delaware court. During the sentencing hearing, the prosecution used descriptions of Dawson's hand tattoo depicting his affiliation with the white supremacist prison gang Aryan Brotherhood as associational evidence suggesting his dangerousness. Dawson appealed, claiming that the introduction of such evidence violated his First Amendment right of expression. The Supreme Court in *Dawson v. Delaware* (1992) concurred, holding that "even if the Delaware group to which Dawson allegedly belongs is racist, those beliefs, so far as we can determine, had no relevance to the sentencing proceeding . . . ."[43] The Court reaffirmed that defendants cannot be disadvantaged by their appearance in criminal proceedings and that such reference by the prosecution must be material and relevant to the case.

Just as constitutional and privacy rights are viewed differently when persons move from investigation to adjudication, a conviction disposition moves them to a significantly different legal status. Once defendants are convicted in court, their background, character, and behavior are subject to greater scrutiny as they enter the sentencing phase of the criminal proceeding. Likewise, their privacy rights are now viewed in the context of convicted offenders.

PRIVACY RIGHTS OF THE CRIMINALLY CONVICTED

Cliff Roberson asserts, "In no other area of the justice system is there greater variance between states than in the sentencing phase of justice proceedings."[44] In many American jurisdictions, adjudication and sentencing are a bifurcated process, that is, distinctly separate, while in others they may be seamless. Commonly, the judge has the duty to pronounce punishment on the convicted. But, considerable diversity exists across locales regarding who is authorized to make sentencing determinations. Some statutes allow juries to sentence, and others restrict the decision to the court. Like other stages of the criminal justice process, broad discretion rests with sentencing decision makers. Often the sentencing authority has a mélange of options to choose from ranging from community to institutional alternatives.[45]

Presentence Investigation

Placed in between the trial disposition and the pronouncement of the criminal sentence are a number of processes designed to assist the court in rendering an informed punishment decision that is constitutionally proportional, adheres to statute, and is best suited for the convicted. Probably the most common mechanism for informing judges prior to sentence pronouncement is the presentence investigation (PSI), also known as the presentence report, which is conducted following conviction and before imposition of sentence. The report is ordinarily prepared by a probation officer at the judge's direction or if required by law in the jurisdiction. Essential parts of the investigation include the offender background information and the officer's evaluation and sentencing recommendation. In many jurisdictions, the PSI is statutorily required, and its contents include offense detail, criminal history, and educational, social, psychological, financial, and family background information to assist the judge in formulating the most appropriate sentence that contributes to offender rehabilitation and serves justice.[46] The PSI is a common tool used to inform sentencing judges, and they tend to abide by the report's punishment recommendation a majority of the time. Harry E. Allen et al. comment, "[I]t is estimated that more than 85 percent of states do prepare some kind of presentence report in felony cases . . . judges tend to accept the presentence recommendation at a rate of about 83 percent for probation and 87 percent for imprisonment."[47] For instance, the PSI is required by the Federal Rules of Criminal Procedure to be completed by U.S. Probation and Parole Officers who in 2003 conducted 67,513 reports for the federal courts.[48]

Convicted offenders have limited privacy protection over the court's access or use of background information that factors into the sentencing decision. Jurisdictions are mixed regarding the convicted offender's statutory right to review the contents of the PSI or other information obtained by the court. Todd R. Clear et al. state that "16 states require full disclosure of the PSI. In the other states, the practice is generally to 'cleanse' the report [of confidential or clinical content] and then disclose it [to the defense]."[49] The Supreme Court has addressed this issue in the long-standing case *Williams v. New York* (1949).

A New York jury found Samuel Williams guilty of first-degree murder and recommended life imprisonment, which the trial judge rejected and instead sentenced him to death. Under New York statute, the sentencing judge was entitled to review the defendant's prior criminal record and consider other information. The Court commented, "To aid a judge in exercising this [judge's] discretion intelligently the New York procedural policy encourages him to consider information about the convicted person's past life, health, habits, conduct, and mental and moral propensities."[50] Prior to pronouncing sentence, the judge considered the defendant's history along with out-of-court witness statements. Williams appealed, claiming that the sentence violated his due process rights since he had no opportunity to confront or cross-examine the witnesses. The Supreme Court in *Williams v. New York* denied that Williams's due process rights were violated holding "[t]he considerations we have set out admonish us against treating the due process clause as a uniform command that courts throughout the Nation abandon their age-old practice of seeking information from out-of-court sources to guide their judgment toward a more enlightened and just sentence."[51]

Likewise, the Court in *United States v. Tucker* (1972) reasoned, "[Before] making [the sentencing] determination, a judge may appropriately conduct an inquiry broad in scope, largely unlimited either as to the kind of information he may consider, or the source from which it came."[52] In *Tucker*, the high Court upheld the trial court's authority to consider information from numerous sources, including that obtained from outside of the adjudication proceedings. However, one of the controversial issues that emerged from the decision was whether the convicted could review and rebut the contents of PSI reports or uncorroborated facts considered by the court in arriving at its sentence decision.

For the courts, the demarcation divides along capital versus noncapital punishment lines. In *Gardner v. Florida* (1977), the Supreme Court found that the trial court must disclose specific information that contributed to a determination of a death sentence.[53] In noncapital cases the courts have failed to provide clear guidance; therefore, jurisdictions that require court disclosure do so through statute. Similarly, the defendant's right to present favorable evidence on his or her own behalf during sentencing is ordinarily reserved for capital cases. Yale Kamisar et al. explain, "The right of the defendant himself to speak on his own behalf at sentencing, however, a privilege known as allocution, is protected in most jurisdictions by statute. Courts disagree whether this right is guaranteed by the Due Process Clause."[54] As a general rule, the convicted person is unable to sustain an invasion of privacy challenge regarding information used by the court to make sentencing determinations, and the Supreme Court has rejected Fifth and Fourteenth Amendment due process claims in most situations. Hence, the boundaries of the sentence imposed by the court are dictated by the constitutional principle in the Eight Amendment prohibiting cruel and unusual punishment and statutory guidelines.

Privacy Rights in Community-Based Corrections

Depending on the offense and the jurisdiction, the court imposing sentence tailors a punishment drawing options from two principal correctional categories—community based and institutional. Subsumed under each are variations of punishment sanctions. American courts sentence a significant number of defendants to punishments that require correctional supervision or incarceration. In 2006, 7.2 million persons were on probation, parole, or incarcerated; comprising 1 in every 31 adults in America. Persons locked up in America's jails and prisons by mid-year 2007 numbered approximately 1.67 million.[55] All told, the United States has the highest prison population rate in the world at 762 persons per 100,000 population.[56]

Community release consists of different forms that plot along a continuum, yet, the legal status of releasees is generally dichotomous: on the one hand, pretrial releasees, who have not been adjudicated, and on the other, convicted offenders. Probationers are convicted offenders who are subject to court-imposed conditions, while parolees are postprison releasees whose conditions and supervision are stipulated by parole authorities. The bifurcated legal distinction, between pretrial and posttrial, turns on criminal conviction. Hence, convicted offenders have a diminished expectation of privacy and often more restrictive conditions. At the far end of the spectrum are parolees who have been released after serving a custodial sentence in prison.

Courts use a variety of analytical perspectives depending on the person's legal status. Privacy protections lessen as the person moves down the continuum, from before trial to prison release. In addition to the legal differences, probation and parole have disparate objectives while both promote law-abiding behavior and community reintegration. Probation tends to focus on rehabilitation, and parole more so on reintegration. Moreover, parolees are more likely to have committed serious felonies than probationers and present additional challenges due to prison institutionalization effects, as well as they are presumed to have a greater predilection for new crime. Otherwise, the conditions and supervision circumstances are very similar. Regarding constitutional liberty and privacy interests, the courts approach cases from the standpoint of the legal status of the releasee.

Altogether, community-based correctional strategies include a wide range of options. Motivated by systemic institutional overcrowding, cost, and over-burdened justice agencies, court and correction systems have utilized an assortment of schemes to rehabilitate convicted offenders while placing them in the community. These alternatives span from deferred adjudication to prison.[57] In the former, the defendant's official conviction is discharged following successful completion of his or her conditional release term. Obviously, the latter is the most restrictive. Positioned in between are gradations of punishment alternatives such as restitution, community service, probation, house arrest, and split sentences. Similar diversity is seen in probation where there are four principal types—standard, felony, intensive, and shock.[58] Nationwide, in 2006, probation populations were divided evenly with 50 percent felony and 49 percent misdemeanor offenders. Of those, 73 percent were given probation for nonviolent crimes.[59] What differentiates the probation types is the level of supervision or restriction based on the offender category and rehabilitation needs. The most restrictive is shock probation that utilizes a split sentence approach combining short-term incarceration with conditional release. In recent years, courts have released greater numbers of serious felony offenders on probation who require close supervision and more restrictive conditions.

Probation Objectives and Conditions

More convicted offenders are released on probation than any other single sentencing option in the United States. In 2006, there were 4.24 million convicted persons placed on probation by the courts.[60] Probation is a form of punishment that involves community release with mandatory conditions and often under official supervision. Statistics show that 84 percent of probationers released in 2006 were subject to supervision.[61] Essentially, probation is a suspended sentence where the court imposes a criminal sentence and grants probation as an alternative to incarceration. Judicial decisions to grant probation are influenced by a myriad of factors that reach beyond PSI recommendations. These may include plea bargaining, prison overcrowding, correctional cost, or rehabilitation needs.

To receive probation, the offender must agree to conditions imposed by the sentencing court. General conditions include abiding by laws, mandatory officer visitation, remaining in the jurisdiction, and avoiding disreputable persons and places. A wide range of special or problem-oriented conditions is available to the court. The conditions selected are intended to target the specific rehabilitation needs of the offender. To be valid, court-imposed conditions must abide by certain legal stipulations, which include that they are reasonable, constitutional, clear, and related to the goals of rehabilitation.[62] Otherwise, court-imposed conditions are limited only by their reasonableness and relevance to the offender's rehabilitation goals. Judges are at liberty to impose specific conditions to respond to criminogenic causes or offender behavioral needs. Programs such as substance abuse treatment, mandatory education, vocational training, victim restitution, and others can be required. Courts have struck down conditions that are unrelated to the rehabilitation needs of the probationer or to protecting the community or severely infringe on fundamental constitutional protections. For example, conditions that are unreasonably capricious, discriminatory, violative of inalienable rights, or bear no relationship to the probationer's behavior or treatment have been found by courts to be impermissible.

Historically, the courts have been particularly vigilant about protecting the probationer from conditions that infringe on privacy rights relating to familial relations and procreation. With the exception of extraordinary circumstances involving child abuse and intrafamilial sexual offenses, higher courts as a rule have rejected conditions that seek to narrowly regulate family relations and procreative activities. Sentencing courts typically are unsuccessful in stipulating conditions that regulate marital sexual conduct, childbearing, or similar behaviors. In one exceptional case, the Oregon Court of Appeals upheld a trial court condition prohibiting a convicted child abuser from fathering additional children, during the course of the probation period, until he successfully completed substance abuse and anger management training.[63] To impose conditions that intrude into constitutionally protected privacy areas, the sentencing court must demonstrate a substantial compelling need to protect society. Ordinarily, rehabilitation goals will not permit the court to enforce conditions that restrict fundamentally private activities, such as procreation.

If convicted offenders reject the court's probation offer, they may be subject to mandatory incarceration in lieu of the suspended sentence. Courts regularly propose probation as an alternative to incarceration because it alleviates institutional overcrowding and is more cost-effective than institutionalization. Implicit within the probation agreement is the offender's acceptance of monitoring, supervision, and condition compliance. Probationers enter into a contractual arrangement with the court to participate through voluntary consent, pay stipulated probation or monitoring fees unless waived, submit to monitoring, and comply with imposed conditions. In spite of the restrictions placed on probationers, they do not relinquish complete constitutional protection but retain fundamental rights. Yet by its very nature, the probation arrangement reduces some privacy expectations and constitutional defenses.

Probation and Parole Search

Two factors substantially diminish the probationer's Fourth Amendment and privacy expectation safeguards. First, unlike pretrial release supervision and condition, probation is a postconviction punishment. Hence, the innocence presumption found prior to adjudication no longer applies, and convicted offenders are subject to greater government restriction. Second, probationers waive many constitutional protections through voluntary consent, thereby obviating many unreasonable search and seizure or privacy invasion challenges. As part of standard conditions, they agree to warrantless and suspicionless home and personal search to ensure condition compliance. Probationers also accede to other forms of monitoring such as random drug testing and electronic supervision.

Using different legal rationales, the Supreme Court has consistently held that probationers are subject to warrantless searches by officers pursuant to monitoring their compliance with conditions. In *Griffin v. Wisconsin* (1987), the Court relied on the special needs beyond law enforcement rationale to allow the warrantless search of probationer Joseph Griffin's home by officers. It reasoned, "[A] state's operation of a probation system . . . likewise presents 'special needs' beyond normal law enforcement that may justify departures from the usual warrant and probable cause requirement."[64] In finding government deterrence and supervision interests in the probation context compelling, the Court ruled that requiring probation officers to formulate probable cause to conduct compliance searches is "both unrealistic and destructive [regarding] the continuing probation relationship."[65]

Several years later, the Court revisited probation-compliance searches in *United States v. Knights* (2001). Mark Knights was convicted on illicit drug charges and received probation. As part of his probation condition, under California law, he was required to "[submit] person, property, place of residence, vehicle, personal effects, to search at any time, with or without a search warrant, warrant of arrest, or reasonable cause by any probation officer or law enforcement officer."[66] Unbeknown to probation authorities, a sheriff's detective conducted a warrantless search of Knights's apartment based upon reasonable suspicion that he was involved in a suspected arson. Using evidence discovered in the search, Knights was charged with conspiracy to commit arson, possession of a destructive device, and possession of ammunition by a felon. The trial and appeals court upheld the probationer's motion to suppress criminal evidence finding that the police search was investigatory rather than probationary.

But in a unanimous decision, the Supreme Court rejected this argument holding "when an officer has reasonable suspicion that a probationer subject to a search condition is engaged in criminal activity, there is enough likelihood that criminal conduct is occurring that an intrusion on the probationer's significantly diminished privacy interests is reasonable."[67] In using a balancing of competing interests test, as opposed to the special needs analysis of *Griffin,* the Court ruled the Fourth Amendment is not violated by a warrantless police search. In another recent case, the high Court eroded the constitutional protection against police warrantless search even further involving a known parolee.

Although *Samson v. California* (2001) involved a parolee, the legal jurisprudence is analogous. Donald Samson was released on parole from a California prison after serving time on a weapon conviction. State law stipulated that parolees "shall agree in writing to be subject to search or seizure by a parole officer or other peace officer at any time of the day or night, with or without a search warrant and with or without cause"[68] as a condition of release. Officer Alex Rohleder approached Samson on the street and asked him if he was wanted on a parole violation. Samson answered no, and the officer searched him because of his status as a parolee pursuant to authorization under state law. In the search, methamphetamine was discovered and he was arrested. At trial, Samson moved to suppress the evidence as a fruit of an illegal search; the court rejected his claim, sentencing him to prison. The California Appeals Court upheld the warrantless and suspicionless search finding it reasonable under state law and the Fourth Amendment. The U.S. Supreme Court agreed to hear the case to determine "whether a condition of release can so diminish or eliminate a released prisoner's reasonable expectation of privacy that a suspicionless search by a law enforcement officer would not offend the Fourth Amendment."[69]

In *Samson v. California* the Court held "that the Fourth Amendment does not prohibit a police officer from conducting a suspicionless search of a parolee."[70] In citing *Knights,* the Court reasoned "parolees are on the continuum of state-imposed punishments. On this continuum, parolees have fewer expectations of privacy than probationers, because parole is more akin to imprisonment than probation is to imprisonment."[71] Personal and property searches of probationers and parolees by government officials are the least intrusive types permitted by the courts. Drug testing has become commonplace across the spectrum of official searches conducted on persons under conditional release.

Probation and Parole Drug Testing

Drug testing is used with pretrial, probation, and parole releasees to ensure condition compliance, promote sobriety, and encourage a drug-free lifestyle. Aside from the practical considerations regarding the detrimental effects of drugs on society, American intolerance for drug and alcohol misuse has long been based on fear and anger.[72] This has contributed to the United States having some of the most draconian drug prohibition policies in the world.[73] Current research data support the long-standing concern over the role drug and alcohol use play in crime. For example, according to federal Arrestee Drug Abuse Monitoring Program data, in 2003, 73.9 percent of persons arrested tested positive for at least one of nine illicit controlled substances, such as cocaine, opiates, or methamphetamine or alcohol at the time of arrest.[74] This strong correlation between drug or alcohol use and criminality is evident across the justice system. Statistics show that in 2008 over 52.5 percent of all inmates in the U.S. Federal Bureau of Prisons were convicted of drug-related offenses.[75] And a 1995 government report found that "about two-thirds of probationers may be characterized as alcohol- or drug-involved offenders . . . 70 percent report using drugs in the past . . . [and] 40 percent report being under the influence of drugs or alcohol at the time they committed the offense."[76]

In spite of such compelling evidence supporting a drug-crime nexus, the fact is the causal relationship is based on conjecture. Researchers have long theorized about the cause and effect correlation between drug or alcohol use and criminality, yet empirical evidence fails to explain the relationship.[77] Regardless, the link between the two has become an accepted truth among law enforcement officers, offender rehabilitation specialists, and courts for decades. As a result, if persons under conditional release are suspected of being drug involved, they typically have drug testing as a condition of their release.[78] According to a 1997 government report, 32 percent of adult probationers were subject to drug testing.[79] Although being compelled to urinate for testing is intrusive, the courts allow drug testing using the same rationale as with other postconviction searches in the probation and parole context. Persons on conditional release have no expectation of privacy protection if the testing is a court or parole authority–imposed condition of release and officers use accepted practices to obtain offender samples for testing.

Probation and Parole DNA Collection

Another form of probationer or parolee compulsory testing that has generated debate and litigation is DNA typing. DNA testing and cataloging by law enforcement and correctional agencies have become so prevalent that few of the postconviction privacy challenges succeed. Each of the states and the federal government have statutes creating offender DNA databanks.[80] One report found "[a]s of January 2005, each of the 50 states has a DNA database of some kind, and each collects and enters information regarding all persons convicted of sex crimes and 38 states also collect genetic profiles of all felons."[81] Furthermore, American courts have settled the admissibility of DNA evidence question, finding the scientific testing reliable and valid. They have also resolved the matter of offender DNA databanks generally ruling them permissible. Although courts are mixed on the collection of warrantless DNA samples for investigations, except with voluntary consent of arrestees, postconviction collection is more widely accepted.[82] As with other searches, probationers, and more so parolees, have a substantially diminished expectation of privacy. Simon A. Cole and William C. Thompson explain, "In general, the taking of DNA samples from convicted felons can be justified with little legal difficulty, either on the basis of a 'special need' because of high recidivism or because convicted felons have 'diminished expectations' of privacy."[83] Given the minimal intrusiveness of DNA saliva or cheek swabs, as an example, many courts allow collection, storage, and agency dissemination of the offender's genetic fingerprint.

Although the specific issue of banking probationers' DNA samples has not been definitively resolved by the Supreme Court, three factors suggest that the practice will become more widely supported by the courts: first, the evolution of federal and state statutes allowing DNA sample collection from many types of convicted offenders; second, supportive parallel reasoning found in the jurisprudence involving arrestees and convicted offenders; and, third, a growing body of lower court decisions that permit the collection and storage of offender genetic materials. For example, the federal court in *United States v. Kincade* (2004) concluded that the compulsory collection of DNA samples from federal probationers, subject to conditional supervised release, did not violate the Fourth Amendment because it "serves the special needs of a supervised release system [quoting *Griffin v. Wisconsin*]."[84] Furthermore, in using a totality of circumstances analysis, the court concluded "the overwhelming societal interests so clearly furnished by the collection of DNA information from convicted offenders . . . [would overcome a] conditional releasee' . . . substantially diminished expectation of privacy."[85] Using a variety of rationales, a growing chorus of courts is authorizing postconviction offender DNA material collection and generally reasoning that, when balanced with government needs, it fails to violate Fourth Amendment or privacy prohibitions.[86]

Electronic Monitoring and Supervision

Another privacy concern for released offenders is electronic supervision. Even though pretrial releasees have minimal privacy expectations when it comes to electronic monitoring, they are even more reduced for postconviction offenders. Electronic supervision for probationers or parolees is multipurpose, whereas in pretrial settings its goal is primarily to ensure that the defendant reports to court. As Ann H. Crowe commented, "After adjudication, electronic supervision may be used for offender punishment, rehabilitation, and public safety."[87] Particularly with higher-risk offenders, such as intensive probation or sex-offender clients, electronic supervision technologies are used to not only ensure compliance, but perhaps more importantly, to provide community protection. Yet in spite of the widespread use of technology and supervision models, research is mixed regarding its overall efficacy in meeting those goals.[88] Though the rehabilitation objectives are broader in a probation or parole context, the applications and accompanying jurisprudence used in pretrial settings apply here as well.[89]

Although disparate treatment is contrary to constitutional equal protection, one class of offender receives special attention when released in the community. Given their behavioral characteristics, recidivism risk, and threat to the community, sex offenders are considered a distinctive criminal type.[90]

Sex Offenders: A Special Case

Because of their predatory nature, potential for violence, and skill at deception and manipulation, sex offenders are regarded as some of the most dangerous criminals in society.[91] Due to the difficulty in apprehending and rehabilitating them, legislators have created a host of statutes that impose extraordinary sanctions on convicted sex offenders. Generally, the courts have followed suit authorizing very restrictive punishments and community release provisions. For example, there is the case of Leroy Hendricks who in 1984 was convicted of indecent liberties with two children, and a Kansas court sentenced him to prison. Just prior to the completion of his sentence, the Kansas legislature enacted the Sexually Violent Predator Act. The Act provided for a civil commitment procedure for the long-term care and treatment of sexually violent predators. Hendricks was confined under the new Act and appealed the commitment on several constitutional grounds including due process, double jeopardy, and ex post facto.

The Kansas Supreme Court upheld the convict's challenge, but the U.S. Supreme Court disagreed. In *Kansas v. Hendricks* (1997), the Court held that "the Act does not establish criminal proceedings and . . . involuntary confinement pursuant to the Act is not punitive."[92] As such, the Act's provision for indefinite confinement for dangerous sex offenders did not violate the Constitution. The Court reasoned "[that his] admitted lack of volitional control, coupled with a prediction of future dangerousness, adequately distinguishes Hendricks from other dangerous persons who are perhaps more properly dealt with exclusively through criminal proceedings ... in that it narrows the class of persons eligible for [civil] confinement to those who are unable to control their dangerousness."[93] The *Hendricks* case is illustrative of the disparate treatment convicted sex offenders, who are classified as dangerous, can receive in the justice and legal system.[94]

In a later case, the Court in *Seling, Superintendent, Special Commitment Center v. Young* (2001) found that

> Washington State's Community Protection Act of 1990 (Act) [that] authorizes the civil commitment of "sexually violent predators" [and] persons who suffer from a mental abnormality or personality disorder that makes them likely to engage in predatory acts of sexual violence ... [is] An Act, found to be civil, [therefore] cannot be deemed punitive "as applied" to a single individual in violation of the Double Jeopardy and *Ex Post Facto* Clauses and provide cause for release.[95]

Together in the *Hendricks* and *Seling* decisions, the Supreme Court clearly signaled its support for the civil commitment of dangerous sex offenders in addition to any criminal punishment they receive.

Another public safety measure gaining traction is the use of mandatory sex-offender registration laws. By 1996, all 50 states and the federal government had enacted sex-offender registration laws, as required by the 1994 Violent Crime Control and Law Enforcement Act. Most recently Congress passed the Adam Walsh Child Protection and Safety Act of 2006, which expanded existing federal sex-offender monitoring laws and created the Office of Sex Offender Sentencing, Monitoring, Apprehending, Registering, and Tracking program to coordinate convicted sex-offender oversight programs for the U.S. Department of Justice.[96] Included in Title I of the Adam Walsh Child Protection and Safety Act is the Sex Offender Registration and Notification Act designed to establish basic guidelines for sex-offender registration and act as a federal resource to assist states in complying with registry requirements across all jurisdictions.[97] These types of statutes are commonly referred to as Megan's Law. They were named for seven-year-old Megan Kanka, the New Jersey girl who was raped and murdered by a twice-convicted paroled sex offender in 1994. The United States Department of Justice estimates that 614,000 sex offenders were registered in the United States in 2007.[98]

In recent years, more convicted sex offenders have received probation due to improved monitoring technology, rigid statutory supervision, and the practical problems posed by institutional overcrowding.[99] These offenders have special rehabilitation needs, but also pose a significant threat to public safety. This type of probationer has generated its own genre of problem-oriented conditions and strict monitoring protocols.[100] Often referred to as a containment approach, released convicted sex offenders are subject to extremely restrictive conditions that are intended to target and control their predatory tendencies and deviant characteristics.[101] Conditions focus on two principal objectives. First, requirements closely monitor offenders' movements through electronic supervision, global tracking, curfew, and other applications to trace their location at all times. Second, since deception, manipulation, and secrecy are common behavioral traits of sex offenders, conditions center on detecting their dishonesty. Extraordinary requirements such as periodic polygraph testing and clinical counseling are used to discover misconduct and noncompliance. While offenders retain their constitutional protection against self-incrimination, courts in a number of states have supported the use of the polygraph condition as a means of effectively supervising these unique types of offenders.[102]

As an extension of the sex-offender registration process, many jurisdictions use the "scarlet letter" shaming condition that includes public notification of registered sex offenders residing in a community.[103] Although criminal convictions are a matter of public record, the compulsory posting of offender name, residential address, and offense evoke privacy challenges due to the invasive nature of the disclosure. The Supreme Court has not directly addressed the invasion of privacy issue but has decided cases on other constitutional grounds.

In *Connecticut Department of Public Safety et al. v. Doe, individually and on behalf of all others similarly situated,* the Court held that it was not a violation of constitutional due process rights to disseminate public notifications about convicted sex-offender registrants to the community. John Doe was released as a convicted sex offender and under state law was required to register with the state's Department of Public Safety (DPS). The agency's responsibility was to post the offender's name, address, photograph, and description on its sex-offender registry Internet Web site, which is available to the public. Doe filed a class-action civil rights lawsuit in federal court to enjoin the DPS from distributing the information on the grounds that it violated his due process rights. Justice William Rehnquist explained,

> ... due process does not entitle him to a hearing to establish a fact—that he is not currently dangerous—that is not material under the statute. As the DPS Website explains, the law's requirements turn on an offender's conviction

alone—a fact that a convicted offender has already had a procedurally safe-guarded opportunity to contest.[104]

Even though convicted sex offenders want a constitutional expectation of privacy that would shield their personal information from public view, the courts have ruled two factors block that expectation. To begin with, they are convicted criminals, and more importantly, when balanced with government's compelling need to protect the public from dangerous persons, the sex offender's privacy expectation is outweighed. On the whole, convicted sex offenders fall into a unique criminal classification. Their inherent characteristics and potential dangerousness relegate them to being the most restricted category of offender, who is subject to an array of constraints designed to protect society. As such, their liberty and privacy interests are severely eroded by their offense type, thus leaving them with virtually no protected expectation of privacy. Monitoring is not the only constitutional right affected by postconviction community release.

Self-Incrimination Privilege

It is well established that persons in the criminal process have an inexorable Fifth Amendment self-incrimination privilege unless voluntarily waived by the arrestee, accused, or convicted. That principle applies equally in probation or parole situations. Persons subject to conditional release retain their self-incrimination protection and cannot be compelled to reply to questions that would implicate them in a crime. Although condition compliance obligates them to supply answers to officer questions, if those contain incriminating content the courts consider the response equivalent to a Fifth Amendment waiver because it was offered voluntarily.

Consider the Supreme Court's decision in *Minnesota v. Murphy* (1984). Marshall Murphy pleaded guilty to sex-related charges, and the trial court gave him probation after suspending his sentence. Among his standard conditions was a provision that Murphy attend sex-offender treatment. During a counseling session, he admitted to a rape and murder six years before. His counselor notified the probation officer who had Murphy report to her office. Upon further questioning by the officer, Murphy again confessed to the rape and murder. After indictment on murder charges, he moved to suppress the confession on the grounds that it was obtained in violation of his Fifth and Fourteenth Amendment rights. The trial court denied his motion and he appealed. The Supreme Court rejected his argument. In a six to three decision, the Court held "[t]he Fifth and Fourteenth Amendments did not prohibit the introduction into evidence ... admissions to the probation officer ... [and used in the] subsequent murder prosecution."[105]

In *Murphy* the Court clarified several issues pertaining to self-incrimination and admissions in probation settings. First, it found that probationer Murphy was not in custody; therefore, the probation officer was not required to provide a *Miranda* warning prior to questioning. Second, the Fifth Amendment self-incrimination privilege is not self-executing; thus, the probationer must assert the safeguard. Third, by voluntarily answering the officer's questions, to include an incriminating admission, Murphy effectively waived his constitutional privilege. Last, Murphy was under no compulsion to answer questions since he could have refused to respond or left the meeting in spite of a belief that those actions would result in revocation. Even though the probationer's conditions required him "to report to his probation officer periodically, and to be truthful with the officer in all matters,"[106] the worst repercussion from failing to answer was revocation. The *Murphy* Court found that such a prospect was not sufficiently coercive to compel the probationer to waive his self-incrimination privilege.

Although probationer and parolee agree to the terms of imposed conditions, such does not dispense with their constitutional self-incrimination privilege. Yet, they are subject to revocation by the probation-issuing court or parole authority if they violate any of the stipulated conditions.

Probation or Parole Revocation

Violations fall into two categories—technical and new criminal offense.[107] A term used in the justice system to describe the repetition of criminal behavior is recidivism.[108] It connotes new crime committed by persons previously convicted. In correctional settings, it is a common benchmark used to measure rehabilitation efficacy.

Technical violations involve a failure to comply with the conditions of release, such as not reporting to the parole officer as required or leaving the jurisdiction without permission. If probationers or parolees commit either a technical or criminal violation, they risk having their conditional release revoked by the court or parole authority.

The Supreme Court in *Morrissey v. Brewer* (1972)[109] and *Gagnon v. Scarpelli* (1973)[110] ruled parole or probation cannot be revoked without an administrative hearing that affords the violator due process rights. At a minimum the hearing must include notice of violation, presentation of adverse evidence, right of confrontation of evidence, and opportunity to rebut the evidence. Although the hearing does not require the full panoply of rights as in criminal proceedings, probationers or parolees nonetheless have a right to challenge the allegation against them to protect their privacy and liberty interests. Revocation officials generally have two options in responding to probationers or parolees who violate conditions. First, the court or parole authority may impose more restrictive conditions, referred to as "tourniquet sentencing," on the violator.[111] Second, the court can rescind the suspended sentence and pronounce the original punishment, or in the case of parolees, reincarcerate the offender in prison. Statistics show that approximately one in five probationers and one in six parolees are incarcerated.[112]

Since probation focuses more on community rehabilitation, in theory, probationers have more constitutional safeguards. Yet, they still relinquish liberty and privacy protections by accepting conditional release. Parolees forfeit many of the same interests; however, they are less protected in terms of constitutional rights due to prior incarceration and perceived propensity for new crime. Probationers and parolees have diminished privacy rights; however, convicted offenders in institutional confinement have the least expectation of privacy protection in the justice system.

PRIVACY RIGHTS OF INCARCERATED OFFENDERS

Convicted criminal offenders are held in two types of American custodial institutions—jails and prisons. Originally, jail and penitentiary inmate populations were quite different, and each institution had its own objectives. Jails operate in local jurisdictions and detain a diverse group of short-duration arrestees including minor offenders, civil commitments, pretrial detainees, and felony prison transfers. Conversely, prisons are maintained by state or federal governments and hold more serious offenders for longer terms. Whereas jails are a detention facility for local police and courts, penitentiaries incarcerate felony offenders for the purpose of punishment. In recent years, due mostly to prison overcrowding, jails have become increasingly congested. Approximately 48 percent of the persons incarcerated in 2006–2007 were held in jails with the remainder kept in prisons.[113] Large jail populations are attributable, in part, to felony prison transfers stranded in local facilities. The unintended effect is that jail inhabitants resemble the prison inmate population much more closely.

Among other things, these similarities have caused both types of custodial institutions to adopt comparable operational methods in terms of security, safety, discipline, and contraband control. As a result, the preponderance of privacy right jurisprudence is applied the same in both jail and prison settings.

General Philosophy of Inmate Rights

From a civil rights standpoint, American correctional institutions have passed through several transitional periods since the founding of the nation's first detention facility, the Walnut Street Jail in Philadelphia in 1790. Scholars have identified three eras in prisoner rights litigation: (1) the Hands-Off Period (before 1964), (2) the Rights Period (1964–1978), and (3) the Deference Period (1979–present).[114] A major shift in judicial thinking occurred during the Rights Period.

In 1871, the Supreme Court made known its position on inmate rights in *Ruffin v. Commonwealth* commenting, "The prisoner has, as a consequence of his crime, not only forfeited his liberty, but all his personal rights except those which the law in its humanity accord to him. He is, for the time being, a 'slave of the state.'"[115] Interestingly, by the time the Court decided *Ruffin*, Congress had passed both the Fourteenth Amendment to the Constitution in 1868, which required states to guarantee Bill of Rights protections to its residents, and the trilogy of civil rights laws, 1866–1871. These statutes provide criminal and civil remedies for civil rights violations committed by government officials acting under color of law. Later these laws became instrumental in the prisoner's rights movement that emerged in the 1960s.

Prior to that time, courts adopted a hands-off policy believing that jail or prison inmate constitutional challenges were best handled by the correctional system.[116] Federal judges considered these matters a function of the executive branch and generally opposed judicial meddling in prison affairs.[117] Beginning in the late 1950s, the Supreme Court shifted its priority toward a pro-libertarian point of view. Under the leadership of Chief Justice Earl Warren (1953–1969), the Supreme Court became much more proactive in hearing underdog litigant cases including ethnic minorities, juveniles, criminal defendants, and prison inmates.[118] Much of the Court's transition occurred parallel to the civil rights movement unfolding in 1960s America.

Two Supreme Court decisions in the early 1960s transformed judicial interpretation of inmate constitutional rights. In 1961, the Court ruled in *Monroe v. Pape* that state officials acting under color of law were subject to federal civil rights laws for constitutional violations.[119] Next, the Court's decision in *Cooper v. Pate* in 1964 marked an end to the hands-off perspective when it ruled that state inmates could seek redress for prison constitutional violations using the federal civil rights tort remedy found in 42 USC § 1983.[120] The decision turned out to be monumental as it opened a floodgate of inmate litigation that challenged every aspect of prison life, rules, and operations.

Inmate Privacy Rights

The courts in prisoner cases rely heavily on a balancing of competing interests weighing inmate rights against government compelling needs.

Jack E. Call found that the Supreme Court "... [when] comparing the needs of prisons to maintain discipline and security with the interests of prisoners in privacy [found] consistently that the prisoners' interests are outweighed by the prison interests."[121]

Contrary to the *Ruffin* Court perspective, by the 1960s an inmate was no longer viewed as a slave devoid of constitutional rights. The modern philosophy focused less on servitude and more on order, discipline, security, and rehabilitation.[122] There is wide variation among correctional institutions in terms of prison type, custody level, and operational philosophy. Regardless of the management approach, correctional institutions use a variety of coercive measures and regulations to manage inmates. These rules can impinge on inmate constitutional and privacy rights and are frequently challenged in court.

Constitutional Prison Regulations

Since *Cooper v. Pate* in 1964, the Supreme Court has been inundated with prisoner appeals and lawsuits contesting virtually every facet of prison management, operation, and inmate life. Institutional regulations are commonly targeted since they affect a myriad of constitutional rights. Inmate litigants have long preferred to file claims in federal courts to benefit from national civil rights laws, as well as, they perceive them to be more receptive to constitutional challenges.

Many prisoner lawsuits stem from institutional regulations that manage or restrict prisoner activities. In *Turner v. Safely* (1987), the high Court established standards to measure the constitutionality of prison regulations that impact individual rights. A class-action suit was brought by inmates challenging mail and marriage regulations in the Missouri Division of Corrections. Prison authorities instituted a policy that prohibited inmate-to-inmate mail correspondence, unless it involved family members or legal matters, because of security concerns. In citing similar security worries, another regulation forbids inmate marriage without official authorization based on a compelling need such as pregnancy or birth of an illegitimate child. Justice O'Connor wrote,

> ... (1) inmate-to-inmate correspondence rule was reasonably related to legitimate security concerns of prison officials, so as not to be facially invalid, but (2) inmate marriage regulation, which prohibited inmates from marrying other inmates or civilians unless prison superintendent determined that there were compelling reasons for marriage, was not reasonably related to any legitimate penological objective.[123]

In adopting a rational basis test, the Court outlined specific guidelines for determining the constitutionality of prison rules stating "when a prison regulation impinges on inmates' constitutional rights, the regulation is valid if it is reasonably related to a legitimate penological interest."[124] The multipart reasonableness standard created in *Turner* is the prevailing test used by the courts to assess the constitutional validity of prison regulations. By using a rational basis test, the Court gave prison authorities the flexibility to institute legitimate inmate regulations. Furthermore, it shifted the burden to the prisoner to demonstrate in court that there is no rational explanation for the rule in the operation of the institution.

Institutional Search and Seizure

Given the validity of security concerns in correctional institutions, prisoners are regularly subject to warrantless and suspicionless search of their persons and cells. In an effort to prevent the circulation of contraband, prison officials conduct frequent pat down outer body, visual body cavity, and cell searches. If inmates temporarily leave the secure facility, such as for medical care or court appearance or have contact with outside persons during visitation with family or attorney, they are subject to even greater search scrutiny. These circumstances give rise to increased risk that justifies more intrusive strip searches. Invasive body cavity searches can be conducted only in instances where a reasonable suspicion exists that the prisoner may have hidden contraband. Inmates have no protected expectation of privacy regarding reasonable searches, and the Supreme Court has authorized such measures as legitimate.

Two principal cases reflect Supreme Court rules for person and cell searches. In *Bell v. Wolfish,* the Court considered several challenges of confinement conditions and practices brought by a pretrial detainee. The prisoner held in the federal Metropolitan Correctional Center in New York City filed complaints involving cell double-bunking, prohibition of nonpublisher delivered reading materials, postvisitor contact body cavity searches, and mandatory removal during cell inspections. The Court rejected the detainee's challenges finding the procedures were reasonable except for a "condition or restriction [that] is arbitrary or purposeless . . . [and amounts to] punishment."[125] Justice Rehnquist wrote, "None of the security restrictions and practices described . . . constitutes 'punishment' in violation of the rights of pretrial detainees under the Due Process Clause . . . These restrictions and practices were reasonable responses by MCC [Metropolitan Correctional Center] officials to legitimate security concerns . . . ."[126]

Regarding the body cavity search, Rehnquist commented,

> Assuming that a pretrial detainee retains a diminished expectation of privacy after commitment to a custodial facility, the room-search rule does not

violate the Fourth Amendment . . . Similarly, the body-cavity searches do not violate [the Fourth] Amendment. Balancing the significant and legitimate security interests of the institution against the inmates' privacy interests, such searches can be conducted on less than probable cause and are not unreasonable.[127]

Five years later in 1984 the Supreme Court rendered a decision in a prison search case. Inmate Russell Palmer was serving sentences for forgery, grand larceny, and bank robbery in a Virginia penitentiary. Correctional officers conducted a random shakedown search of Palmer's prison locker and cell checking for contraband. During the search, officers found a torn pillowcase among the inmate's trash. Palmer was charged with disciplinary infractions for destroying state property. The prisoner filed a civil rights lawsuit in federal court arguing among other things that officials had conducted an unreasonable shakedown search and falsely charged him with a prison disciplinary violation. In *Hudson v. Palmer,* the Court held

> [a] prisoner has no reasonable expectation of privacy in his prison cell entitling him to the protection of the Fourth Amendment against unreasonable searches . . . imprisonment carries with it the circumscription or loss of many rights as being necessary to accommodate the institutional needs and objectives of prison facilities, particularly internal security and safety. It would be impossible to accomplish the prison objectives of preventing the introduction of weapons, drugs, and other contraband into the premises if inmates retained a right of privacy in their cells.[128]

The Court rejected the prisoner's claim that destruction of property during the cell search was also an unreasonable Fourth Amendment violation. Furthermore, it commented that "[the] loss of freedom of choice and privacy are inherent incidents of confinement . . . ."[129]

Together, these two Supreme Court decisions found, on balance, that prison authorities have a compelling need to ensure security and safety that outweighs inmate privacy expectation. In secure correctional settings, such as jails and prisons, detainees or inmates have no reasonable expectation of privacy that protects them or their cell quarters from valid searches to discover contraband. More invasive manual body cavity searches are also permissible if based upon a reasonable suspicion that the inmate is in possession of secreted contraband. Correctional officials are not required to obtain search warrants or judicial authorization to conduct searches and seizures involving prisoners in their custody or within the facility. However, authorities are restricted from seizing legal correspondence or personal belongings that are not identified as prohibited contraband.[130]

Protecting Private Activities

Some lower courts, however, have upheld inmate claims of privacy right violation where officials failed to take reasonable measures to protect inmates from being seen by strangers or opposite sex persons during institutional strip searches.[131] In the same vein, another court agreed with female jail inmates who challenged the condition of cell toilet facilities that were not shielded from general view in a manner that invaded their privacy.[132] Inmates have also objected to being monitored by opposite gender correctional staff when unclothed. The federal Seventh Circuit Court of Appeals in *Johnson v. Phelan* (1995) refused to impose correctional officer gender standards regarding inmate monitoring, noting that staffing should be determined by the operational and security needs of the institution rather than guided by inmate privacy concerns.[133] There is not an inmate privacy right that protects them from being viewed by other inmates or staff while unclothed. Though some lower courts have extended protection during strip searches, they are divided and the Supreme Court has not ruled specifically on this issue.

Inmate Control Measures

Broad privacy interests also include the right to protect one's body from invasion or harm by government officials. A related issue to prison search and seizure is the official use of force. Prisoners have filed suits challenging force used against them by correctional officers, claiming it amounted to cruel and unusual punishment. As a general rule, use of force by police is justified in instances of defense of self or third person and lawful arrest. Similarly, correctional officers are permitted to use force or deadly force for defense purposes. The Supreme Court has outlined standards for reasonable use of force in custodial institutions.

During a disturbance at the Oregon State Penitentiary, inmates took a correctional officer hostage and barricaded themselves in their cellblock. Gerald Albers, a prison inmate, was shot in the leg by an officer during a rescue operation to free the hostage. Albers filed a civil rights suit claiming the use of deadly force was a constitutional violation of his protection against cruel and unusual punishment. The Supreme Court disagreed and in *Whitley v. Albers* (1986) concluded that

[t]he shooting of respondent did not violate his Eighth Amendment [right] . . .
where a prison security measure is undertaken to resolve a disturbance, such as
occurred in this case, that poses significant risks to the safety of inmates and
prison staff, the question whether the measure taken inflicted unnecessary and
wanton pain and suffering ultimately turns on whether force was applied in a

good-faith effort to maintain or restore discipline or maliciously and sadistically for the purpose of causing harm . . . the shooting was part and parcel of a good-faith effort to restore prison security.[134]

In another use of force case, Keith Hudson, a Louisiana prison inmate, was beaten by correctional officers while shackled. He suffered facial bruises and loosened teeth. He brought a federal civil right action against the officers; the Court in *Hudson v. McMillian* (1992) held "[t]he use of excessive physical force against a prisoner may constitute cruel and unusual punishment even though the inmate does not suffer serious injury."[135] It reasoned,

> Whenever prison officials stand accused of using excessive physical force constituting "the unnecessary and wanton infliction of pain," violative of the Cruel and Unusual Punishment Clause, the core judicial inquiry is . . . whether force was applied in a good faith effort to maintain or restore discipline, or maliciously and sadistically to cause harm.[136]

As seen in these cases, the Supreme Court permits correctional authorities to use reasonable force in good faith to maintain discipline and order in the institution. Inmates have a valid constitutional claim if officials use force or cause injury for the purpose of inflicting unnecessary wanton pain and suffering.

Corrections officials on occasion encounter inmates who require mental health treatment. Since prisoners have limited privacy protections, they may be subject to control using antipsychotic drugs if they are deemed dangerous. In *Washington v. Harper* (1990), the Court considered an inmate's liberty interest to be free from the involuntary administration of antipsychotic drugs. Walter Harper was serving a sentence for robbery in the Washington state penitentiary system. While there he was under psychiatric care after being diagnosed with manic-depressive disorder. Because of episodes of violence he was considered a danger to himself and others. A prison psychiatrist prescribed antipsychotic drugs for Harper. Before using the drugs the Washington system required an independent medical review of the treatment to determine if the regimen was necessary and in the best medical interest of the inmate. During the medical review hearing the prisoner may appear, present evidence, and appeal the findings. The review board determined the drug treatment to be appropriate and prison medical staff administered antipsychotic drugs over Harper's objection. He filed a federal civil rights suit contending that the involuntary drug treatment violated his due process rights. A unanimous Court found that

> [t]he Due Process Clause permits the State to treat a prison inmate who has a serious mental illness with antipsychotic drugs against his will, if he is

dangerous to himself or others and the treatment is in his medical interest . . .
the [review] Policy comports with substantive due process requirements, since
it is reasonably related to the State's legitimate interest in combating the danger posed by a violent, mentally ill inmate.[137]

Institutions are also permitted to discipline inmates, in a manner that may
impinge a liberty or constitutional interest, for violating regulations. Further,
they may segregate prisoners for disciplinary purposes, protection, or to
maintain order. However, the Court has ruled that inmates subject to discipline must be afforded due process rights.[138]

Collectively, these cases show methods the Supreme Court allows correctional institutions to use to ensure safety, security, and order. Inmates in jails
and prisons have a significantly diminished expectation of privacy, and corrections officials are authorized to conduct reasonable suspicionless searches,
seize contraband, use force, enforce discipline, and administer restraining
drugs to protect inmate and staff.

Inmate Medical Condition and Record

From a penological perspective, security and safety have many dimensions. In addition to controlling violence and maintaining order, correctional
administrators contend with the problems caused by inmates with conta-
gious disease. Some airborne infections, such as tuberculosis, are particularly
difficult to control in facilities where persons are confined in close quarters.
And other virulent blood-borne diseases such as human immunodeficiency
virus (HIV), and its active condition, acquired immunodeficiency syndrome
(AIDS), present a lethal hazard to inmate populations, through sexual and
blood contact and to staff through blood contact. In the community, the
highest risk factors for contracting HIV are intravenous drug use and sexual
contact.[139] A significant portion of the criminal population is exposed to
these dangers prior to being incarcerated. As a result, many arrive at the jail
or prison already infected with HIV.

By year-end 2006, 20,450 inmates in state and federal prisons were HIV-
positive or had AIDS. That constitutes 1.6 percent of male and 2.4 percent
of female inmates nationwide. The same year, an estimated 155 state and
12 federal inmates died from AIDS-related causes. Due to the disease transmission risk, a number of states and the federal correctional system test inmates for
HIV. In 2006, 21 states tested inmates upon admission or at some point during their incarceration. Forty-seven states and the federal prison system HIV
test inmates who show symptoms of the disease or who request testing. Forty
states and the federal prisons test prisoners involved in incidents where they
are at risk of contracting HIV, such as sexual encounters or violent assaults

where blood is present. And 16 states and the federal system test inmates identified as being members of a high-risk group.[140]

Once authorities become aware that prisoners are HIV-positive, or have
AIDS, they take measures to separate them from general population inmates
to assure safety and security. Some institutions medically quarantine HIV-
positive prisoners, while others restrict them to segregated housing. Although
these responses promote institutional safety, they produce several disadvan-
tages for the segregated inmate including stigmatization, disclosure of
inmate's HIV medical condition, and increased risk of retaliation from other
prisoners.[141] The policies have been challenged in the courts by inmates
arguing they violated an expectation of privacy over their medical status, as
well as on other constitutional grounds. One court described "[t]he privacy
interest in one's exposure to the AIDS virus is even greater than one's privacy
interest in ordinary medical records because of the stigma that attaches with
the disease. The potential for harm in the event of a nonconsensual disclosure is substantial . . . ."[142]

As with other prison regulations, the courts employ a balancing of competing interests test and use the *Turner* standard to judge the constitutionality of
HIV inmate policies.[143] Since the Supreme Court has not specifically
addressed this issue, the lower courts have divided on the right of inmates to
protect the privacy of their medical condition or record in jails and prisons.
However, as a general rule courts have found that prison HIV inmate policies
outweigh the privacy rights of prisoners because they satisfy the legitimate
penological interests of the institution in protecting all inmates and staff from
the risk of HIV contagion.[144] For instance, the Ninth Circuit Court of Appeals
in *Camarillo v. McCarthy* (1993) upheld the prison's practice, arguing that
courts have not established "that a prison policy segregating HIV-positive
inmates from the general prison population is unconstitutional."[145]

Similarly, Robert D. Hanser et al. found that no constitutional privacy
right existed for jail inmates in protecting the confidentiality of their medical
information. In citing the federal court in *Sherman v. Jones* (2003), they commented, "The federal trial court held that there was no fundamental constitutional right to privacy for personal medical information in custodial
environments and that any judgment about whether such information
should be protected must be left to legislative action."[146] In sum, prisoners
have neither a constitutional privacy right to protect their medical status
from disclosure nor to oppose prison policies that seek to protect the institutional community from disease contagion. Here again, the courts have
deferred to prison authorities to implement inmate regulations and policies
as necessary as long as they reasonably relate to legitimate penological interests as outlined in *Turner v. Safely.*

Although prisoners experience a significant reduction in privacy rights, they retain other constitutional protections while in custody. Many of these pertain to access to the courts, due process, medical care, self-incrimination privilege, or conditions of confinement that have been mandated by the Supreme Court beginning with the inmate rights revolution of the 1960s. Yet, the Court has consistently given deference to correctional administrators promulgating policies to regulate and discipline inmates as long as the practices are sound and clearly relate to safety, security, and order maintenance.[147]

Persons who are arrested, adjudicated, or sentenced progressively forfeit individual privacy rights. In spite of a range of personal privacy, liberty, and possessory interests, the courts have interpreted these rights in relative degrees where convicted offenders have the least privacy safeguards. Using balancing of competing interests tests, the courts assess government interest in public safety and operational efficacy with individual privacy interests. A clear distinction is made between the general public and those subject to control of the criminal justice system. Although defendants or inmates retain some inviolate constitutional protections, overall expectations of privacy are dramatically reduced, on a diminishing scale, as they progress from police investigation to imprisonment.

Chapter 5

BEING WATCHED ON THE JOB

Monroe County Deputy Robert Baron's marked patrol car was seen parked in Linda Vaccaro's driveway overnight by Organized Crime Task Force investigators. The residence was under surveillance as part of an investigation into the criminal activities of reputed mobster Angelo Vaccaro. They informed Deputy Baron's supervisor, and he was ordered to terminate the affair with Linda Vaccaro, since she was married to a notorious gangster. After being warned, Baron was seen with Linda Vaccaro on three separate occasions. A year later, Angelo was convicted of federal racketeering charges and sent to prison. Meanwhile, Sheriff William Lombard brought administrative charges against Baron for insubordination, conduct unbecoming an officer, and bringing disrepute on the agency stemming from the deputy's refusal to disassociate himself from Linda Vaccaro. Baron was terminated from the Monroe County Sheriff's Department. He brought a federal civil rights suit against the department, claiming his constitutional right to privacy and association were violated by the employer's interference in his off-duty activities.

The federal court rejected Baron's claim and held "that sheriff's order that deputy sheriff cease associating with wife of reputed mobster did not violate deputy's constitutional right of privacy and order was not violative of the 'liberty' clause of the Fourteenth Amendment and, although harsh, termination for repeated violation was not unconstitutional."[1]

This case illustrates the complex challenges faced by criminal justice employers as they endeavor to effectively operate their agency, while at the same time, respect the constitutional privacy rights of their employees. The court in *Baron v. Meloni* (1983) provided a befitting summation of the officer privacy right issue when it commented,

> An individual joining a police agency must recognize that acceptance of such an important and sensitive position requires the individual to forgo certain privileges and even some rights that an ordinary citizen often exercises without restrictions or thoughts of sanctions, because a police force is a paramilitary organization with all the attendant requirements and circumstances.[2]

CRIMINAL JUSTICE EMPLOYMENT RELATIONSHIP

Privacy rights for criminal justice personnel differ from those of criminal suspects in many respects. For one thing, their privacy matters are framed in the context of public employment. This is important because they are subject to considerable regulation due to their position. There are several types of employment relationships in criminal justice public service. Some positions are filled by public election, such as judges and sheriffs, while others such as police and correctional officers obtain their jobs through appointments. Employees of elected justice officials are classified in most states as "at-will" where they hold their positions at the pleasure of the employers.

Employer authority to regulate employee privacy-related activities is affected by not only the employment arrangement but provisions of constitutional protection, statute, civil service law, or labor agreement. These vary depending on the employment classification and jurisdiction.

Employment Classification

Generally, criminal justice personnel are placed in three classifications—judicial officer, public safety sworn officer, and nonsworn staff. Employment position is important since it dictates policy-making capacity, enforcement authority, liability responsibility, and immunity protection. Judicial officers, such as judges, are in a capacity that gives them autonomy and decision-making immunity. Therefore, they are subject to minimal employment regulation.

A substantial amount of the privacy jurisprudence pertains to public safety personnel. These include prosecutors, law enforcement, probation, parole, and correctional officers who hold criminal justice authority or enforcement powers. What makes this group different is the legal capacity to act under color of law whereby they possess certain powers, privileges, or obligations due to their position of authority.[3] Not only does this designation assign legal powers, such as arrest, criminal prosecution, or supervision of offenders, but it imposes an array of criminal and civil liabilities upon them. Commonly, the same legal principles utilized in police officer privacy cases or policies are applied to other public safety workers.

As a general rule, the Supreme Court has held that safety position holders, such as police and correctional officers, possess a lesser expectation of privacy due to their public employment position.[4] Here, the courts rely on a balancing of competing interests test to determine the constitutionality of employer regulations that impinge on officer employee privacy rights. In this setting, much of the intrusion on officer privacy rights occurs through regulatory oversight by government employers.

Aside from the public employment common denominator, much of the employee privacy law is convoluted. Several factors contribute to the complexity, and often incongruence, of the jurisprudence. First, federal and state courts have gone in different directions in recent years regarding the workplace rights of officers and employer authority to regulate their activities. Will Aitchison commented,

> ... federal courts [are] more inhospitable to constitutional and statutory claims lodged by law enforcement officers, particularly in the areas of due process, freedom of speech, and the right to privacy ... [however] a concurrent development has been the increasing inclination of state courts to interpret state constitutions in a fashion more generous [to employees] than the federal courts.[5]

Second, the extraordinary diversity found among American law enforcement agencies and multidimensionality of a police officer's job creates many roles, tasks, and expectations.[6] For instance, in 2004 there were 17,941 federal, state, and local law enforcement agencies employing over 1 million persons, including 837,000 sworn police personnel. About half of local police departments employed less than 10 sworn officers.[7] Similarly, correctional officers make up a substantial portion of the total criminal justice workforce. In 2005, there were 1,821 American correctional facilities employing a staff of 445,055. Among those were 295,261 correctional officers responsible for guarding almost 1.6 million inmates.[8]

PRIVACY RIGHTS AND EMPLOYER REGULATION IN THE CRIMINAL JUSTICE WORKPLACE

Regulation of Employee Conduct

Since the Supreme Court concluded that public employees have a diminished expectation of privacy in the workplace, agency employers have substantial authority to regulate their activities. Government employers can stipulate proper behavior and enforce policies in both on- and off-duty settings. Agency regulations are not just intended to deter employee misconduct, but also to impose a professional standard upon those in public trust positions. Given their authoritative powers, officer-employees are held to high conduct expectations in their professional and private lives.

As a general rule, courts have supported regulatory policies that are legal, closely related to effective agency function, and include employee notification. Likewise, courts have upheld employer disciplinary actions for conduct unbecoming an officer, insubordination, on- or off-duty misconduct, or criminality using the same framework as valid policies. Discipline can range from verbal reprimand to discharge depending on the policy and violation. However, employers are barred from taking disciplinary actions that are discriminatory or violative of constitutional protections.

Employee expectation of privacy applies to behaviors and activities covering the person, workplace, forms of expression, and association rights. Courts are divided on some privacy-related issues, yet the Supreme Court has provided authoritative guidance in important workplace regulatory matters. One such area is warrantless search in the public workplace.

Workplace Search

Federal courts decided workplace search cases for several years with conflicting results. However, in 1987, the Supreme Court clarified the extent of employee expectation of privacy in the public workplace. In 1981, Dr. Magno Ortega was employed as a psychiatrist at Napa State Hospital. He was asked to take administrative leave while an investigation was conducted into his alleged misconduct. Ortega was suspected of improperly procuring state property and employee sexual harassment. While on leave, hospital officials searched his locked office, desk, and files without a warrant. They seized several items that were introduced as evidence at his disciplinary hearing, and after dismissal, Ortega filed a federal civil rights suit against the hospital.

In *O'Connor v. Ortega* (1987), the Court explained that employees in the public workplace have a diminished expectation of privacy; therefore, employers could conduct warrantless searches "for noninvestigatory, work-related purposes, as well as for investigations of work-related misconduct."[9] Justice Sandra Day O'Connor found that employer warrantless search of individual workplace contents should be determined on a case basis using reasonableness as the appropriate standard for the intrusion. Utilizing a balancing test, coupled with the special needs beyond law enforcement rationale, the Court concluded that the government had a compelling interest in the efficient and proper operation of the workplace such that noncriminal administrative searches were permissible. It found that a public employee's expectation of privacy in the workplace "may be reduced by virtue of actual office practices and procedures, or by legitimate regulation."[10] However, the courts made a clear distinction between work-related items and search of personal belongings, or for criminal investigation purposes. Personal material or investigatory searches constituted a greater intrusion on employee privacy whereby Fourth Amendment requirements of probable cause and warrant apply.

This case is significant because it paved the way for a broad application of government employer warrantless search policies and practices across public workplaces, including those in a criminal justice setting. Employers in the police and correctional workplace can conduct administrative warrantless searches, with few restrictions, if it involves government-issued property or pursuant to an employee misconduct investigation.[11] Perhaps more importantly, *O'Connor v. Ortega* established the principle that employees have a reduced expectation of privacy in the public workplace.

Search in the Criminal Justice Workplace

On several occasions the Supreme Court acknowledged the uniqueness of the law enforcement workplace.[12] After *O'Connor v. Ortega,* lower courts applied its doctrine to employer warrantless police workplace searches. As other courts began deciding police workplace cases, legal patterns and guidelines began to emerge. Employers are required to ensure that workplace search policies remain closely related to the operational function and efficiency of the agency. Further, employers must provide clear notification to employees that workspaces and all government-issued equipment, such as vehicle, desk, file cabinet, locker, or computer, is subject to warrantless search.

Courts have consistently ruled that accessible, shared, or highly regulated workspaces are subject to reasonable warrantless search as long as it is neither overly intrusive nor designed to uncover criminal evidence. The workplace provides limited employee privacy expectation, and employers may search offices and desks.[13] Other government-issued items, such as assigned vehicles, filing cabinets, and briefcases, are equally open to search as long as it complies with *Ortega* guidelines and applicable laws.[14]

Warrantless administrative searches, pursuant to employee misconduct investigations, may be conducted unless prohibited by state law or collective bargaining agreement. However, criminal investigation of employees must abide by Fourth Amendment requirements if it involves a search of employees or their workspace. While courts make a clear distinction between administrative searches and those designed to collect criminal evidence, criminal justice employees nonetheless have a reduced expectation of privacy over their workspaces and government-owned work materials. Only if employer searches involve person searches, more restricted individual access workspace, or personal belongings do police employees have a greater expectation of privacy. Even then, employers may be obligated only to provide justification for the search, which the *Ortega* Court instructed must be " . . . judged by a standard of reasonableness under all circumstances [including] both the inception and scope of intrusion."[15]

Work-Related Personal Search

Internal investigation of employee misconduct can involve personal searches of employees for evidence or to recover property. As a general rule, employers wanting to conduct searches of an employee's person or residence must comply with Fourth Amendment probable cause or warrant requirements. As one court explained, "If a police officer were required to open up his home whenever there was a reasonable suspicion that evidence may be found there, then officers truly would have watered-down constitutional rights."[16] However, in the case of administrative noncriminal workplace investigations, employers have been allowed by some courts to conduct warrantless limited intrusion person searches if it involves suspicion of employee misconduct. In these incidences the search, at a minimum, must be based on reasonable suspicion of misconduct.[17]

In situations involving more intrusive personal searches, courts have been divided and typically allow such warrantless invasions only where the employer has substantial legal justification.[18] As instructed by the Court in *Ortega,* public workplace search is intended to be a reasonable administrative tool to investigate employee misconduct on a case basis not to usurp the privacy protections outlined in the Fourth Amendment.[19]

Workplace Video Surveillance

Use of electronic surveillance in not only public spaces but also workplaces has become routine.[20] Criminal justice agencies make use of this technology to protect staff and property, deter employee misconduct, and reduce civil liability in police stations, courthouses, jails, and prisons. Persons in open, multiple access, common area, or public space do not have an expectation of privacy that blocks employers from using electronic video monitoring devices in the workplace. Hence, employers may also place accessible multiuse workspaces and locker rooms under electronic surveillance to deter employee misconduct.[21] Silent video surveillance is also allowed to be used in jail facilities.[22] Similarly, offices and other workspaces may be electronically monitored as long as that does not unduly invade personal privacy or restricted work areas. Due to privacy concerns, for example, employers would be prohibited from using video surveillance in private toilet facilities.

In *United States v. Taketa* (1991), the federal appeals court wrestled with several privacy issues stemming from an internal investigation of alleged officer misconduct. At the same time, investigators were conducting a criminal probe into an agent's suspected illegal activities. Drug Enforcement Administration (DEA) agent David Taketa shared an office at the Las Vegas,

Nevada, airport with Nevada state investigator Thomas O'Brien. Acting on an informant tip of illegal wire interception from a fellow DEA agent, internal investigators entered agent Taketa's office, searched the desk and other places, and installed a hidden video camera. As a result of information gathered during the warrantless workplace search, investigators obtained a search warrant. They returned to the office and seized criminal evidence, which, along with the videotape, was introduced at trial. Taketa and O'Brien were convicted in federal court of illegally intercepting wire communications. Upon appeal the appellate court reversed the convictions and held that the warrantless search of O'Brien's private office was permissible but rejected the use of videotape evidence because it violated the Fourth Amendment. The court found that the warrantless physical search of the agent's joint office was authorized under the *Ortega* doctrine because it involved an employee misconduct investigation. However, the court ruled that the warrantless video surveillance for law enforcement reasons violated the officer's expectation of privacy and the Fourth Amendment since the continuous videotaping was a search for evidence of criminal conduct.[23]

Employee Electronic Communication Monitoring

Employee expectation of privacy extends to areas other than just offices and desks. With the widespread use of advanced telecommunication devices, the matter of workplace interception of employee electronic communication commonly arises. When communications involve electronic wired transmissions, employer monitoring is governed by federal wiretapping laws. Specifically, the Electronic Communications Privacy Act of 1986 (Wiretap Act) regulates the lawful interception of electronic wire transmissions.[24] Under the Wiretap Act, federal law prohibits the interception, recording, or monitoring of employee telephone conversations or recorded voice mail information. However, the statute provides a law enforcement exemption if the monitoring is part of the agency's "ordinary course of business." Employers can use several methods to facilitate monitoring and reduce employee expectation of privacy.

Ordinarily, agency employers provide employees with written notice that they monitor electronic communications as a regular practice in the ordinary course of business. Notice acts to further diminish any expectation of privacy over transmission contents. Moreover, when employees give implied or actual consent, it lessens the chances for privacy challenges of telephone monitoring.

Although some courts have allowed agency employers to intercept and record telephone conversations, others are divided about whether the exemption is absolute. In police operational areas such as the radio dispatch center[25] and jail,[26] courts view these as ordinary course of business units where monitoring is practical and routine. In these situations, courts have ruled that employees have no reasonable expectation of privacy over telephone conversation content.

Agency employers can also monitor computer messaging. As a general rule, e-mail and other computer messages exchanged between government-owned computers in the workplace are not considered personal property, and employees have only a modest expectation of privacy over the information.[27] Employers are able to rely on the same Wiretap Act exceptions that allow telephone transmission interception and monitoring.

In spite of ongoing debate in the courts regarding the extent of Internet use monitoring, many have allowed agency employers to check employee cyber activity in the government workplace.[28] Again, agency workers have little expectation of privacy over accessed Internet addresses or sites, and employers can monitor the activity to assure compliance with business only use policies. A number of monitoring technologies can be used to conduct surveillance on employee Internet activity. Those include software that tracks unauthorized program installation or download, network spyware, and analyzes Internet use.[29] Some courts have supported both monitoring and warrantless search of employee computer files.[30] And the practice is even more likely to be authorized if it involves alleged employee misconduct. In one case a federal appeals court allowed the police employer to conduct a warrantless search of an employee's computer files, who was suspected of downloading Internet pornography on the job. The court in *United States v. Slanina* (2002) found that the search was valid basing its reasoning on *Ortega* rationale that the intrusion was pursuant to an internal investigation of employee misconduct.[31]

Courts have decided cases that involve employer interception or monitoring of government-issued pagers used by employees. Given the nature of the technology involved in pager transmission, federal wiretap laws are often implicated in the regulation of their use. In *Bohach v. City of Reno* (1996), the federal court ruled that the interception of employee Alphapage information violated neither federal wiretap laws nor employee privacy rights because the employer's recovery of the officer's messages was related to an internal investigation.[32]

Conversely, a federal court of appeals held that the warrantless interception of officer wireless alphanumeric text messages, to verify that the content was work related as required by department policy, violated the employee's expectation of privacy and Fourth Amendment rights. Since the pager data obtained from the service provider were not related to an employee misconduct investigation and the department's search policy did not include pager messages, the court in *Quon v. Arch Wireless* (2008) ruled that the interception was unauthorized.[33]

Employers are using workplace surveillance, monitoring, and recording technology to track and document employee movements, productivity, and equipment use.[34] In criminal justice agencies, wireless radios, cell phones, and patrol vehicles can be equipped with Global Positioning System navigational tracking devices that record the location of the equipment and officer when in use. Though employee privacy jurisprudence does not keep pace with advances in technology, current federal laws and post-*Ortega* principles suggest that employee privacy right challenges to tracking would be unlikely to succeed. Few privacy right protections are available under these circumstances, inasmuch as officers are using government-issued equipment in public space.

In sum, criminal justice employees have a reduced expectation of privacy in the workplace. Employee privacy rights are further weakened if employers provide notification of agency surveillance and search policies that are promulgated, reasonable, and lawful. Warrantless intrusions connected to administrative internal investigations of employee misconduct have been widely accepted by the courts. Criminal justice personnel are subject to other forms of workplace search such as employee drug testing.

Employee Drug Testing

Following the surge in illicit drug use in the 1960s, President Richard M. Nixon in 1971 launched a war-on-drugs campaign that spawned draconian crime control measures and widespread antidrug programs all designed to reduce drug abuse and ameliorate its harmful effects.[35]

Law enforcement drug interdiction at the borders, and on the streets, became preferred frontline responses to the problem. Yet, antidrug policy planners also considered schools and workplaces prime locations to detect and deter drug use among mainstream Americans. They also chose drug testing as the best method to discover illegal substance users. By the 1980s, cases were streaming into the Supreme Court challenging the constitutionality of urinalysis drug screening. The Court soon created warrantless drug testing doctrine for the public sector by analyzing Fourth Amendment and privacy claims brought by students, public transportation workers, and police officers. Meanwhile, drug testing had become routine in the private sector as more companies used pre-employment and disciplinary-related urinalysis to exclude or control illicit drug use in the workplace.

Federal courts applied administrative search and special needs rationales to authorize warrantless, and at times, suspicionless drug testing searches of students and some public employees. The Court's 1987 ruling in *O'Connor v. Ortega* signaled its acceptance of warrantless searches and reduced expectation of privacy for public employees.

In criminal justice settings, drug urinalysis had long been routinely used to detect and deter illicit substance use by criminal suspects, from conditional prerelease to parole. Among criminal justice personnel, the Supreme Court's groundbreaking decision in *National Treasury Employees Union v. Von Raab* (1989) established a precedent that allowed law enforcement agencies to require officers in some assignments to submit to compulsory drug urinalysis without suspicion or warrant.[36] Prior to *Von Raab,* lower courts viewed employee drug testing as a Fourth Amendment search and required agency employers to comply with its requirements or exceptions. At the same time, the courts were divided over the warrantless drug testing of police employees, particularly in the absence of individualized reasonable suspicion of substance abuse.[37]

In the *Von Raab* case, the U.S. Customs Service promulgated a policy requiring law enforcement agents to submit to drug urinalysis if they requested transfer or promotion into an assignment that required (1) interdiction of illegal drugs, (2) carrying of firearms, or (3) access to sensitive or classified materials. Under the program employees who tested positive for illicit drugs would be dismissed but not criminally prosecuted. The National Treasury Employees Union brought suit in federal court, and eventually the case was appealed to the Supreme Court. In a five to four decision, the Court upheld the interdiction and firearm provisions and rejected the sensitive material portion of the policy. Although the Court ruled that drug testing is a Fourth Amendment search, it held that it was permissible if it satisfied a reasonableness requirement. The Court relied on a balancing of competing interests test and special needs rationale in contending that the government has a compelling interest in ensuring that the Customs Service maintains a fit and sober police force that ". . . is our Nation's first line of defense against one of the greatest problems affecting the health and welfare of our population."[38] Furthermore, the Court found that drug testing programs for certain officer-covered positions were reasonable as an operational reality in law enforcement agencies. The *Von Raab* Court reiterated its position that "it is plain that certain forms of public employment may diminish privacy expectations."[39] This seminal case became the standard for criminal justice personnel drug testing programs.

Public Safety Drug Testing Programs

In spite of the influence of the *Von Raab* decision, not all lower courts supported suspicionless drug testing. But in the years that followed, criminal justice agencies not only refined their drug testing policies and procedures, but courts formulated guidelines for authorized practices. Agencies can use drug testing for pre-employment, deterrent, or individualized suspicion purposes involving covered position employees. Covered employees, such as police officers, in these circumstances have a decreased expectation of privacy due to the agency's interest in maintaining a drug-free workforce to ensure public safety.

Two drug testing methods have gained acceptance—compulsory and random. Compulsory or mandatory urinalysis screening is ordered by agency employers in several circumstances. First, pre-employment conditional drug testing of job applicants is valid if the procedure is systematically used and proper notice is given.[40] Second, if the employer has individualized reasonable suspicion that officers are drug involved or engaged in related misconduct, it can direct them to undergo drug testing.[41] Third, employees in designated covered positions, akin to the criteria noted in the *Von Raab* case, can be ordered to submit to testing as long as the position reasonably relates to the agency's need to assure a drug-free workplace.[42] This typically involves law enforcement or critical agency positions. Fourth, employers use compulsory drug testing to determine medical, postaccident, or postinjury fitness of officer employees. To assess fitness for duty, postincident or annual medical examinations can be required by employers, which include drug screening.[43]

The other drug testing method is random selection. Employee random drug testing is commonly used as a means of deterring drug use. Police and correctional agencies have established random drug testing regimens for sworn and civilian employees. Generally, the courts have supported these programs if they are standardized, systematic, and utilize a valid random selection scheme.[44]

Courts consistently find that government agencies have a compelling interest in maintaining a drug-free workplace, particularly when it involves police and correctional employees. If employers devise drug testing programs that are reasonably related to drug deterrence or individualized reasonable suspicion of drug-involved misconduct objectives, they have been found valid. Public safety applicants or employees may be subject to compulsory or random testing regimens depending on the circumstances. In these situations, they have a reduced expectation of privacy, and legal challenges seldom succeed if based on privacy grounds. However, some employees have brought suits stemming from privacy intrusions pertaining to specimen urination procedures.[45] And others have contested agency drug testing as a privacy violation on state constitutional grounds and experienced greater success than relying on federal courts in light of the *Von Raab* decision.[46] On the whole, courts have ruled that criminal justice employer drug testing does not violate the privacy rights of employees if the programs comply with constitutional and judicial principles. In spite of contentious debate among legal experts, the *Von Raab* ruling cleared the way for police employers to add suspicionless testing to other warrantless practices, which is a significant departure from previous court decisions.[47]

Criminal justice personnel have privacy interests over a number of behaviors and activities that agency employers want to regulate. In addition to surveillance and search, employers also use interview and polygraph questioning of employees to conduct internal investigations into alleged misconduct. Just as with other intrusions, agency employees have a privacy expectation regarding their comments when questioned during pre-employment or disciplinary investigations in the workplace.

Compulsory Questioning and Polygraph Examination

Private employers are prohibited by the federal Employee Polygraph Protection Act of 1988 from requiring an applicant or employee to take a polygraph test or use its results in adverse employment actions. However, the Act specifically exempts government agencies, intelligence and security services, and handlers of drug-controlled substances from its provisions.[48] As a general rule, courts allow criminal justice agencies to use compulsory polygraph testing for pre-employment or discipline-related questioning. This area of public employment privacy law remains unsettled, but the lower courts have provided some policy and procedure guidance. However, courts have developed specific guidelines for the constitutional questioning of employees in internal investigations for misconduct whether by interview, written statement, or polygraph. Two Supreme Court decisions, *Garrity v. New Jersey* (1967)[49] and *Gardner v. Broderick* (1968),[50] formulated valid procedures for use in employee questioning. The doctrine outlines two principal provisions. First, justice employees retain their privilege against compelled self-incrimination under the Fifth Amendment. Employers are prohibited from forcing applicants or workers to waive their privilege by making incriminating statements during interviews or polygraph examinations. Second, employers must grant employees immunity from criminal prosecution covering any evidence obtained through internal investigation questioning. Moreover, the employer is forbidden from using evidence derived from questioning for prosecutorial purposes. If employees are protected by immunity, they may be disciplined for refusing to answer questions unless the employer fails to formulate questions "specifically, directly, and narrowly to the performance of [the officer's] official duties."[51] To be valid, the questions must be closely related to the alleged misconduct; however, they may involve both on- and off-duty conduct.

Courts are far from unified on the point of employer-compelled answers or discipline for refusal to submit to questioning. Furthermore, a number of states have enacted statutory protection for employees that prohibits employers from taking adverse employment actions against government workers who decline to cooperate in the internal investigation. However, even states that provide legal shelter to employees on this point may allow agency employers to discipline officers for insubordination as part of a broad authority to regulate employee conduct.[52]

Some courts have ruled that police and related agency employers can command employees to submit to a polygraph examination or answer questions during an internal investigation.[53] Employee refusal can result in a range of disciplinary actions, including discharge, as long as the employer does not use the answers as criminal evidence or compel the involuntary waiver of Fifth Amendment self-incrimination privilege. If, however, employees voluntarily choose to waive their self-incrimination privilege and answer questions in the absence of immunity, their responses can be used as criminal evidence in a subsequent prosecution. Other than a guaranteed constitutional self-incrimination privilege, agency employees have minimal privacy expectation protection over their voluntary or compelled comments when subject to polygraph or internal investigation questioning. Unlike private employees, criminal justice public employees may be ordered to submit to questioning related to workplace conduct, and their refusal to cooperate is grounds for disciplinary action except where prohibited by state law. In spite of the divisions among courts on the validity of compulsory answers, some allow agencies to include directed questioning as part of a general employer authority to maintain an efficient and reputable criminal justice agency. Employee documentation about personnel matters, such as medical or financial condition, can also be the source of violation of employee expectation of privacy in the government workplace.

Compulsory Disclosure of Personal Matters

Consistent with the Supreme Court's reasoning in *Ortega,* government compelling interests in efficient agency operations, and a need to maintain public trust, criminal justice agencies are given the authority to intrude into the private activities of its employees. In line with the diminished privacy expectation of public employees and guidelines in internal investigation questioning, employers are permitted to compel the disclosure of employee confidential information if the data requested are directly related to job performance. Ordinarily, requests involve three categories of information—personal, financial, and medical. This area of employee privacy law is mostly settled in the courts, particularly when it pertains to public safety employees such as police officers. The *Garrity-Broderick* doctrine applies here as well in that employees retain their constitutional self-incrimination privilege but can be subjected to narrowly drawn questions about restricted matters if the information is not used as criminal evidence. Similarly, employers may compel employees to divulge confidential information beginning with applicants and extending to active duty personnel. In general, employees have a minimal privacy protection since the courts have given employers extensive authority to use this type of information to maintain efficient agency operation and employee fitness for duty.

Given the risk of official corruption, coupled with high public trust expectations of criminal justice personnel, employers commonly conduct background investigations on applicants and monitor confidential information that is related to employee official duties. Courts balance agency need to prevent official corruption, maintain efficient operation, and ensure public trust with the privacy interests of employees. In order for employers to obtain information about work fitness, conduct, or performance, they must demonstrate that their request is legitimate, closely related to job duties, and on a need-to-know basis.[54]

If employers demand compulsory disclosure of confidential information, it must satisfy these criteria for courts to allow its collection. Moreover, employers are expected to protect the confidentiality of employee private information and take measures to ensure that it is not mishandled or disseminated unless required by law.[55] For instance, many official actions involving officers or internal disciplinary matters are accessible to the public through public disclosure, open meeting, or freedom of information laws. However, courts have blocked agencies from disclosing some types of highly personal information such as identification numbers, home addresses, and telephone numbers of police officers working in sensitive or covert assignments because it violates their right to privacy.[56] Agency employers regularly collect work-related information from employees.

For example, law enforcement employers often use questionnaires to obtain information about employee personal matters or job conduct. Consider the case of *Broderick v. Police Commissioner of Boston* (1975). A large group of Boston Police Department officers attended the Law Day parade in Newport, Rhode Island. Several days after the celebration, the Boston Police Commissioner's office received complaints about raucous and inappropriate conduct by uniformed Boston officers during the parade and afterward in area hotels. As part of an internal investigation, the department distributed questionnaires to the involved officers, soliciting information about their conduct in Newport. The officers brought suit to enjoin the department from requiring completion of the questionnaire. After appeal, the Supreme Judicial Court of Massachusetts ruled in favor of the department finding that the specific questions sought information that bears a rational connection to the officer's "official acts [and] fitness and ability to serve in governmental service."[57] The court held that the questionnaire did not violate the officer's constitutional privilege against self-incrimination and was permissible because it inquired into specific conduct while they acted "under the cloak of officialdom" during the parade and thereafter.[58] This case illustrates the authority given to agency employers to gather information to assure employee fitness to serve and professional conduct. As one court commented, "society has the right to hold police officers to a higher standard of conduct than other citizens."[59]

Questionnaires requiring the reporting of employee financial information are also commonplace and used to deter official corruption and maintain public trust in agency personnel. Courts have consistently supported government employers in monitoring the confidential financial affairs of employees that are relevant to their official duty and integrity.[60] As the court in *O'Brien v. DiGrazia* (1976) explained, "[S]ociety's interest in an honest police force is strong."[61]

Confidential medical information is the third category typically gathered by criminal justice agencies. Federal law bars employers from using medical condition or disability to discriminate against employees.[62] Other federal statutes protect the privacy of personal medical records and restrict their disclosure except as permitted by law.[63] Yet, agency employers can use medical condition as a measure of fitness for duty, particularly for police and correctional officers. In several cases, courts allowed employers to gain access to employee medical records with consent or to compel the release of medical information following accident, injury, or illness to determine an officer's fitness for duty reinstatement.[64] Courts acknowledge the heightened employee privacy interest over confidential medical information, but, on balance, have found that the employer has a legitimate interest in ensuring the fitness of officers and promoting employee and public safety. Employers are able to inquire into and regulate private behaviors along with information.

Employee Freedom of Association

Because criminal justice agencies are responsible for ensuring public safety, and hold the public trust, they are given the authority to regulate many aspects of employee work and private lives. Courts seek a reasonable balance between government employer operational interests and individual employee privacy rights. In *Roberts v. United States Jaycees* (1984), the

Supreme Court explained, "... choices to enter into and maintain certain intimate human relationships must be secured against undue intrusion by the State because of the role of such relationships in safeguarding the individual freedom that is central to our constitutional scheme."[65] In spite of the Court's cautionary note, when it comes to agency operation, employers can dictate the limits of private relationships if they demonstrate an adverse effect on the organization or its personnel. Historically, courts afford greater privacy protection to marital, or other close family relationships, than to social associations.

Right of Intimate Association

Few other activities are more private, or evoke greater emotion, than intimate relations. This privacy expectation falls squarely in the right to be let alone in the view of criminal justice employees.[66] Understandably, this area of employer regulation has been heavily litigated as employees have challenged their right to privacy and First Amendment freedom of association in personal relationships and sexual activities. And yet, agency employers closely regulate these on- and off-duty conducts because of their effect on department operation, employee morale, public confidence, and community reputation. Courts are divided on exactly which types of intimate association can be regulated. Nonetheless, employers exert regulatory control on employee fraternization, adultery, fornication, cohabitation, dating, and homosexuality.

In cases where personnel engage in criminalized sexual behavior, such as sexual relations with a minor, employers find it less problematic to impose discipline. Yet, many other sexual behaviors are regulated by agency policy rather than by law. As in other areas, courts balance the agency's interest in employee becoming conduct, efficient operation, and public confidence with the individual privacy interests of personnel. Often, the balance pivots on the presence of an adverse impact on the agency. To lawfully regulate off-duty intimate behaviors, employers must demonstrate that there is a valid nexus between the conduct and effective agency operation. Otherwise, the courts tend to block employer efforts to govern employee private relationships.

Several factors contribute to the complex nature of employee privacy law regarding intimate relations. First, there are two tracks of sexual behavior that are subject to regulation—lawful and unlawful. Some states criminalize adultery, fornication, and sodomy based on notions of morality.[67] Moreover, every state and federal criminal code prohibits sexually related conduct involving children, such as child pornography and pedophilia. Obviously, employee illegal sexual conduct is banned. Second, employee sexual behaviors that are not prohibited by law are regulated by agency policy based on interpretation of community or professional standards of good conduct.[68] Third, these behaviors overlap two key constitutional interests—privacy rights and First Amendment freedom of association rights. This widens the constitutional field to challenge employer control of private sexual conduct. Fourth, variations in state law result in considerable differences in agency regulatory policies.

Extramarital Sexual Conduct

One of the most common types of regulated behavior is extramarital relations. Depending on the employer interpretation of unbecoming conduct, agencies may prohibit these relationships because of the adverse effect on the operation and reputation of the agency.[69] Some courts allow employers to discipline employees for adultery if they can demonstrate that it has a rational relationship to unsatisfactory officer job performance.[70] In some cases, courts ruled that since adulterous conduct is not a constitutionally protected First Amendment association right, employers can dismiss employees who engage in the prohibited behavior,[71] whereas other courts have blocked efforts to regulate off-duty extramarital affairs if no adverse impact on department operations can be shown.[72] As one case illustrated, a substantial risk to agency efficiency comes from fraternization among co-workers, particularly involving extramarital affairs.

Teresa Mercer was hired as a probationary police officer in Cedar Rapids, Iowa. Within a few months she began an extramarital affair with Captain Phillip Rivers, a veteran police commander and her former academy instructor. On several occasions Officer Mercer had confrontations with her estranged husband, a Cedar Rapids Reserve Officer, who was suspected of damaging her property in retaliation for the affair with Rivers. During an internal investigation, Officer Mercer admitted to the extramarital relationship with Captain Rivers. After the investigation, a panel of assistant chiefs recommended the termination of both Officer Teresa Mercer and her husband, Reserve Officer Shawn Mercer, for conduct unbecoming a police officer. Captain Rivers was laterally transferred to another assignment, which was essentially a demotion. Teresa Mercer filed suit, challenging her dismissal on privacy and discrimination grounds. On appeal, the federal Eighth Circuit Court of Appeals upheld the firing commenting, "We have no doubt that an extra-marital affair between two co-workers, one of whom is married to a third co-worker, can damage the morale, discipline, and reputation of a work force, particularly when the employer is a paramilitary organization such as a police department."[73] Similarly, agency policies regulate employee fraternization, cohabitation, and dating because these activities produce detrimental effects on operations and morale.

Fraternization and Cohabitation

Interestingly, a number of courts failed to allow agencies to discipline employees who fraternize or participate in cohabitation with co-workers, finding that it did not have an adverse effect on department operations.[74] Similar to the outcome in *Mercer*, however, other courts permitted employers to discipline employees who fraternized or cohabitated in intimate relationships with department peers because it had a deleterious effect on department efficacy.[75]

Employers can also regulate employee dating relationships that negatively influence agency operation or reputation. In *Jackson v. Howell* (1982), a police lieutenant had a dating relationship with a woman he met during an official criminal investigation. After dating and having sexual relations with the officer, the woman filed a complaint against him with the department. An ensuing internal investigation ruled that the officer's unbecoming conduct violated department policy and adversely affected operations. The court supported the officer's demotion and transfer as reasonable discipline.[76]

In other situations, courts allowed the regulation of off-duty relationships such as the termination of police officers for dating a known drug addict[77] or felony probationer.[78] Another often-cited case involved the termination of several vice officers who engaged in on-duty sex with known prostitutes, who were also paid police informants. The court in *Fugate v. Phoenix Civil Service Board* upheld the officers' terminations, finding their unbecoming conduct directly affected job performance that was "threatened by the obvious conflict of interests [thereby] threaten[ing] the department's legitimate interests."[79]

Regulating Social Relationships

Unlike in the private sector, criminal justice agencies are careful to control employee external social relationships to ensure internal security, effective operation, and public reputation. This can be a delicate task when dictating to employees whom they may befriend. Yet, in some situations courts have allowed employers to prohibit worker association with persons deemed to present a risk to agency security, compromise employee integrity, or bring disrepute on the organization. For example, the court in *Baron v. Meloni* upheld the termination of a deputy sheriff who refused to sever his relationship with the wife of a reputed mobster.[80] Commonly, in correctional settings the agency prohibits off-duty relationships between officers and convicted offenders, inmates, or their family members. The courts have upheld narrowly drawn rules that restrict employee off-duty association with these persons.[81] In an opposite ruling, the federal Ninth Circuit court supported a correctional officer's relationship with an ex-felon.[82] As a general rule, when these regulations are challenged by employees, the agency has the burden of showing that the policy is closely connected to officer work performance or department efficacy. Employers have greater success in controlling casual social associations than intimate familial relationships.

Homosexual Conduct

Regulating employee homosexual conduct in criminal justice agencies is a complicated task. Prior to the Supreme Court's ruling in *Lawrence v. Texas* (2003),[83] many departments relied on state criminal sodomy laws or the Court's previous position in *Bowers v. Hardwick* (1986),[84] where it held that homosexual behavior was not constitutionally protected. In some cases before *Lawrence,* courts permitted agencies to reject applicants or dismiss active employees for homosexual conduct.[85]

However, the Court's decision in *Lawrence v. Texas* changed the ability of agencies to depend on the criminalization of homosexuality in state statute to regulate the behavior among its employees. County police in Houston, Texas, responded to a reported gun disturbance at a private residence. Upon arrival they entered the apartment of John Lawrence. They observed Lawrence and Tyron Garner engaging in same-sex sodomy, and both were arrested for violating Texas' criminal deviate sexual intercourse statute. Lawrence and Garner were jailed, charged, and convicted in Justice of the Peace court. On appeal, the Supreme Court held that the Texas law criminalizing sodomy was unconstitutional. In a six to three decision, Justice Anthony Kennedy reasoned,

> Texas statute making it a crime for two persons of the same sex to engage in certain intimate sexual conduct was unconstitutional, as applied to adult males who had engaged in consensual act of sodomy in privacy of home, as impinging on their exercise of liberty interests protected by the Due Process Clause of the Fourteenth Amendment . . . [this case] involve[s] two adults who, with full and mutual consent from each other, engaged in sexual practices common to a homosexual lifestyle. The petitioners are entitled to respect for their private lives. The State cannot demean their existence or control their destiny by making their private sexual conduct a crime. Their right to liberty under the Due Process Clause gives them the full right to engage in their conduct without intervention of the government. "It is a promise of the Constitution that there is a realm of personal liberty which the government may not enter" . . . The Texas statute furthers no legitimate state interest which can justify its intrusion into the personal and private life of the individual.[86]

Since consensual homosexual conduct in private can no longer be criminalized by state statute, agencies wanting to prohibit employee homosexual behavior must rely on other grounds, such as department effectiveness. Will Aitchison predicts ". . . the logical extension of the Court's opinion

[in *Lawrence v. Texas*] is that state laws criminalizing homosexual behavior
are unconstitutional and law enforcement agencies will not be able to discipline or discharge employees solely because of their homosexuality."[87]
In light of the *Lawrence* Court's decision, and given the absence of post-
Lawrence case law, it is unlikely employer antihomosexual behavior policies
will be able to withstand challenges in court.[88]

Employees have certain rights of association in less intimate circumstances
than sexual or social relationships. Given the nature of criminal justice agencies, employees may choose to affiliate themselves with political or labor
organizations. These constitutional protections come from First Amendment
freedom of association rights that overlap a right to privacy in relationships.

Right of Political or Organization Association

Two factors have bearing on employee organizational affiliation in the
criminal justice workplace. First, some law enforcement or prosecution
employees work under at-will circumstances where they serve at the pleasure
of an elected or politically appointed official, such as a sheriff, constable, prosecuting attorney, or judge. By its very nature this employment arrangement is
politicized since the agency head is selected by popular vote or appointment.
In some states at-will employees have less protection from adverse employment
action. Hence, their political or organization affiliation can have ramifications
in the workplace if viewed as oppositional by the agency employer.

As an illustration, consider the controversy surrounding the termination
of nine U.S. Assistant Attorneys by Attorney General Alberto Gonzales in
2006. Allegations claimed that the dismissals were politically motivated.
In a related incident, the personal political views of U.S. immigration judge
candidates were allegedly screened by Department of Justice officials during
the selection vetting process, which is a violation of federal civil service
laws.[89] In a report issued in July 2008, Office of the Inspector General investigators concluded that numerous Department of Justice job candidates were
subjected to interviews illegally probing their views on abortion, same-sex
marriage, and a host of other political topics as part of an improper hiring
process prohibited by law.[90] These situations show the political climate in
which criminal justice or judicial personnel may be appointed to positions.

Second, many criminal justice employees belong to organized labor
groups. For instance, in law enforcement, "The Fraternal Order of Police is
the world's largest organization of sworn law enforcement officers, with more
than 325,000 members in more than 2,100 lodges."[91] Courts have consistently ruled that employer policies cannot restrict employee membership or
participation in organized labor groups.[92] Organized labor collective

bargaining agreements can have a direct impact on employer regulations. In some cases labor contracts stipulate the conditions of employer privacy intrusion. Of course, other policy limitations may be imposed on agencies by state constitutions, statutes, or civil service laws.

Although there is considerable disagreement in the courts regarding regulation of employee political activity or patronage, the Supreme Court has provided guidance in this area.[93] The Court in *Elrod v. Burns* (1976) established a distinction between the right of employee political affiliation involving nonpolicy makers and those who were in policy-making capacities. The *Elrod* Court prohibited employers from taking adverse employment action against public employees in lower-level non-policy-making positions because of their political patronage.[94] Subsequently in *Branti v. Finkel* (1980), the Court clarified the employee policy-making issue by holding that public employers must demonstrate a rational and direct connection between their adverse employment action and the effective operation of the agency.[95]

Beyond adhering to these basic guidelines, lower courts have issued diverse and conflicting decisions across the spectrum of political activities. For the most part, the cases involve three types of employee activities including political party affiliation, political activities or patronage, and support for political candidates. Several courts protected sheriff employees from discipline or termination due to their support or candidacy opposing the incumbent elected sheriff.[96] However, other courts have allowed adverse employment actions against employees who backed an opposing sheriff candidate.[97]

In one case, the court blocked the dismissal of two deputy sheriffs because of their political party affiliation,[98] and in others, they allowed employee termination depending on the type and extent of political activity involvement.[99] Finally, courts have upheld state police policies forbidding employees from displaying political yard signs[100] or running for a political office.[101] Aside from the high Court's *Elrod-Branti* doctrine separating policy-making employees, there are few clear principles or patterns evident in lower court decisions regarding political activities of public employees. In spite of the significant litigation involving at-will law enforcement employees, it is hard to locate the boundaries of employee First Amendment constitutional protection when engaging in political activities as a criminal justice agency employee.

Other First Amendment rights, such as speech, expression, and religion, have also been challenged by criminal justice personnel.

Freedom of Speech and Expression in the Workplace

First Amendment rights such as association, speech, and religion intersect with broader privacy interests in the criminal justice workplace. These rights have been interpreted in that context by the courts as they establish employer regulation guidelines. Agency regulations optimally control employee behaviors and activities that detract from the mission of the organization. Pursuant to that objective, employers restrict employee speech that is disruptive or damaging to the operation or reputation of the agency.

Employee Freedom of Speech

The Supreme Court has established a constitutional litmus test that determines whether an employee's speech is protected. In *Pickering v. Board of Education* (1967), the Court created a public employee speech standard that holds that expression of views that pertain to a matter of public importance or interest is protected by the First Amendment.[102] Courts make this determination based on a balancing test between the government's ability to effectively perform its function and the employee's constitutional right to make the remarks. The high Court clarified the *Pickering* measure in *Connick v. Myers* (1983), where it explained that to be protected, the public employee speech must "be fairly considered as relating to any matter of political, social, or other concern of the community [and] be determined by the content, form, and context of a given statement."[103]

Agency policies can regulate employee speech both on and off duty if it has a deleterious effect on the organization. However, employee comments regarding public concern matters are protected as long as they are truthful and not intentionally disruptive.[104] The leading case on criminal justice employee speech is *Rankin v. McPherson* (1987), where the Supreme Court ruled that a police constable could not restrict comments made by an employee to a co-worker because they pertained to matters of public concern.[105] Furthermore, courts have generally barred employers from promulgating policies that are designed to restrict free speech.[106] Other types of employee speech that may be protected involve content unrelated to the job, artistic or nonverbal expression, area of expertise, or whistleblowing.[107] Perhaps one of the most common employee speech claims stems from discipline that is triggered by criticism of the department leadership. Courts have upheld an employee's right to disparage the agency head as long as the comments are truthful and a matter of public concern or interest.[108] State and federal statutes also protect public employee whistle-blowers who report official corruption or misconduct to an appropriate government agency.[109]

Yet, not all employee speech is protected. Employee remarks about personal, internal, or nonpublic concern issues are not constitutionally safeguarded and are subject to discipline.[110] Other unprotected speech is that

which is intentionally disruptive, vulgar, or hate motivated. The court in
Pappas v. Giuliani (2002) upheld the termination of an officer who anonymously distributed antiblack and antisemitic materials at the police
station.[111]

In sum, criminal justice agency employers are permitted to restrict
employee speech, on and off duty, through policy or directive, if it is not a
matter of public interest or concern spoken truthfully. Otherwise, workers
have a First Amendment–protected right to make honest remarks, even if
critical or unwelcome, as long as they pertain to specific matters of public
interest. Speech is only one form of employee expression that occurs in the
criminal justice workplace. Nonverbal forms of expression such as clothing,
grooming, or other aspects of appearance can be regulated by employers.

Freedom of Expression through Appearance

Fashion choices are very individualized and can be a reflection of self-image. For many, it becomes a form of expression. However, in criminal
justice agencies, employers can closely regulate employee appearance and
grooming. Narrowly drawn policies that relate to the legitimate operation
and reputation of the agency have consistently been upheld by the courts.
Much of this area of law is settled and has been guided by the Supreme
Court's 1976 decision in *Kelley v. Johnson*. In *Kelley*, the Court held that
police agency policies regulating officer hair length and style did not violate
First Amendment constitutional rights. The Court reasoned, "The [appearance] choice may be based on a desire to make police officers readily recognizable to members of the public, or a desire for the esprit de corps which
such similarity is felt to inculcate within the force itself. Either one is a sufficiently rational justification for [grooming and appearance] regulations."[112]
Although the *Kelley* decision provided the original guidepost, much has
changed in popular fashion since 1976.

Agency employers must develop policies that address employee hairstyle,
accessory, and body art. As a general rule, courts have supported department
efforts to establish and enforce employee appearance standards.[113]

For instance, in *Weaver v. Henderson* (1993), the court upheld the Massachusetts State Police no-mustache policy finding that the rule was not arbitrary
and followed the Supreme Court's *Kelley* ruling.[114] In two subsequent cases,
courts issued opposite holdings based on religion rationale. Two Muslim
Newark, New Jersey, uniformed police officers sought an exemption from the
department's no-beard policy on religious grounds. Since the city provided
medical exemptions to the policy, the officers claimed religious discrimination
in their case. The court in *Fraternal Order of Police Newark Lodge No. 12 v.*

City of Newark (1999) agreed and enjoined the department from enforcing the no-beard ban on the officers.[115] Similarly, a Rastafarian correctional officer filed suit against the department because its grooming policy prohibited the wearing of dreadlocks, in violation of his religious beliefs. The court upheld the officer's claim and ordered the department to provide an exemption to the policy.[116] A similar challenge, however, brought by a Rastafarian police officer was rejected by the court in *Booth v. State of Maryland* (2003), which found that the department's grooming standard was legal.[117]

Another appearance issue that has generated employee challenges is the prohibition against wearing ear stud jewelry by on- and off-duty male police officers. The federal Seventh Circuit court in *Rathert v. Village of Peotone* (1990) ruled that the department was permitted to prohibit male employees from wearing the jewelry because professional appearance was a legitimate government interest in operating an effective agency; thus the policy did not violate employee First Amendment rights.[118]

Tattoo body art prohibition policies have also been contested by police employees. In 2002 a Hartford, Connecticut, police officer wrote a letter to the labor union and police chief expressing concern over the display of visible spider web tattoos by fellow officers. The complaint alleged that the tattoos depicted hate symbols commonly worn by racial extremists. The chief issued an internal memorandum directing employees with the tattoos to cover them so they were not visible while the officers were on duty. Five affected officers filed a federal civil rights suit claiming their due process and equal protection rights were violated since the policy did not require the covering of all tattoos. The federal district court in *Inturri v. City of Hartford* (2005) denied the employees' claim and upheld the department's policy finding that no constitutional violation had occurred.[119] Similarly, the court in *Riggs v. City of Fort Worth* (2002) allowed the department to require an officer deployed on bicycle patrol to wear long pants and a long-sleeve shirt to cover visible tattoos. The court found no employee constitutional rights had been violated because the agency's rationale that the tattoos detracted from the professional appearance of an officer was a legitimate government interest.[120]

In related cases, courts have supported correctional department regulations prohibiting female officers from wearing skirts while on duty. The agency policy required the women to wear trousers for uniform standardization and safety reasons.[121]

In essence, employers can develop grooming, appearance, and uniform policies setting specific standards if they are not arbitrarily applied and reasonably relate to the agency operation.[122] The last area of employee First Amendment association right is the free exercise of religion.

Employee Freedom of Religious Practice

Freedom of religion is one of the most fundamental rights enshrined in the First Amendment to the Constitution where it states "Congress shall make no law respecting an establishment of religion, or prohibiting the free exercise thereof...."[123] Protection of religious rights was further fortified by Title VII of the Civil Rights Act of 1964, making it illegal under federal law for employers to discriminate against a person on the basis of race, color, religion, gender, or national origin.[124] Although there are several legal avenues for employees wanting to contest agency policy or practice believed to infringe on religious freedom, Title VII discrimination, disparate treatment, or harassment are common modes of redress.

Ordinarily, employees object to duty assignment or days off because one or more conflict with religious practice or belief. In several cases, courts rejected employee discrimination claims where police officers refused duty assignments based on religious grounds. In *Rodriguez v. City of Chicago* (1998), the court found that the department's offer of a duty reassignment to an officer charged with protecting an abortion clinic, in violation of personal religious belief, constituted a reasonable accommodation.[125] The court in *Parrott v. District of Columbia* (1991) held that a police sergeant's refusal to perform assigned duties requiring the arrest of antiabortion protesters neglected his lawful responsibilities and the department was authorized to take disciplinary action.[126] Similarly, the federal Seventh Circuit court in *Ryan v. Department of Justice* (1991) disallowed an agent's religious discrimination claim involving a case assignment investigating crimes by antiwar groups. The court found that the agent's refusal to accept an offered duty transfer nullified his legal action because the agency had made a reasonable accommodation to address his grievance.[127] Along the same line the termination of a state trooper, who declined to accept an assignment investigating crimes at a gambling casino on the basis that it violated a religious belief against facilitating gaming, was upheld by the court that reasoned that broad accommodation of every religious tenet by the department was unreasonable.[128]

Allegation of employer religious discrimination is not the only circumstance that may impinge on employee rights. Agencies are prohibited from fostering a work environment that is illegally hostile to employee religious freedom. In one case, an officer was terminated for wearing a Christian cross pin on his uniform in violation of the department's policy prohibiting the display of unapproved accessories. After his request for religious exemption from the regulation was denied, his refusal to comply with the rule resulted in dismissal. The court upheld the officer's firing stating, "the no-pins policy does not target religion but only incidentally affects Daniels' individual religious practice, and thus is acceptable. A police department cannot be forced to let individual officers add religious symbols to their official uniforms."[129]

In *Venters v. City of Delphi* (1997), the court held that a police dispatcher was improperly terminated because the work environment promoted religious establishment due to the relentless proselytizing of the police chief. The court reasoned that the pressure to adopt a religious belief by the zealous chief created such coercive conditions that it violated the employee's freedom of religion.[130]

Some employees request religious accommodation in scheduling days off to avoid conflicting with their Sabbath observance. In *Balint v. Carson City, Nevada* (1999), the court ruled in favor of a correctional officer whose request for a work schedule change to enable Sabbath attendance was denied. The agency's failure to make reasonable accommodation for the officer's religious practice was held to be unlawful discrimination under Title VII.[131]

Criminal justice personnel have a constitutional freedom of religion right as outlined in the First Amendment. While employers are not required to oblige every employee request in assignment, work schedule, and appearance standard that poses a claimed obstruction to religious freedom, courts have indicated agencies are expected to make reasonable accommodations as long as they do not place an undue burden on department operations.

First Amendment rights in the criminal justice workplace entwine with overarching privacy interests of employees. Agency employers are permitted to promulgate and enforce policies that impinge on some individual preferences of expression or religious belief if the regulations are narrowly drawn, nondiscriminatory, and reflect a close connection to the effective operation of the organization. Although the courts have afforded employees some First Amendment protections in the areas of speech and religion, their balance has mostly tilted toward the needs of government to maintain operational efficacy in the workplace.[132]

The Supreme Court ruled in *O'Connor v. Ortega* that public employees have a diminished expectation of privacy. Due to the public safety and trust responsibilities of criminal justice agencies, the courts authorize employers to regulate various on- and off-duty personnel activities. Using the ubiquitous balancing of competing interests test, courts have generally found that the demands of criminal justice agency operation necessitate giving administrators leeway to develop policies that may adversely affect employee privacy interests. Although justice personnel do not relinquish all expectation of privacy in the government workplace, they forfeit some of the rights enjoyed by private citizens.

Chapter 6

PROTECTING CRIME VICTIMS

L os Angeles Lakers basketball superstar Kobe Bryant was accused of sexually assaulting a 19-year-old woman at a Colorado resort in July 2003.
The two met at the mountain lodge where Bryant was a guest and the
alleged victim worked. In a statement to police detectives, the accuser
reported that she and Kobe Bryant flirted when they first met and then mutu-
ally kissed. Their stories conflict beyond this point. Kobe Bryant admitted to
having sex with the hotel clerk, but insists it was consensual. The accuser
claims that Bryant refused to stop his sexual advances in spite of her objections, grabbed her around the neck with both hands, and raped her.

Kobe Bryant was indicted by an Eagle County, Colorado, grand jury and
charged with felony sexual assault. Bryant pled not guilty, and his attorney
filed pretrial motions challenging the accuser's credibility and asked for
access to her psychological and medical records. Furthermore, they requested
that the judge provide an exemption under Colorado's rape shield law to
allow them to introduce evidence of the alleged victim's extensive sexual history. In a closed hearing, Judge Terry Ruckriegel ordered that the accuser's
records remain confidential but agreed to allow a limited amount of victim
sexual history as evidence. In spite of the judge's ruling, the alleged victim's
identity was divulged when the court reporter mistakenly sent closed hearing
transcripts, bearing the accuser's name, by e-mail to local media. Immediately, the alleged victim asked the court to bring the case to trial, complaining
she was being subjected to threat, humiliation, relentless media scrutiny, and
probes by defense team investigators.

The case was scheduled for trial, but in early September the prosecution
informed the court it wanted to withdraw the criminal charges against Kobe
Bryant because the accuser, who was critical to its case, had become uncooperative and refused to testify. Charges were dismissed, and less than a week
later the alleged victim filed a federal lawsuit against Bryant. Kobe Bryant
issued a public statement apologizing "for my behavior that night and for
the consequences she [accuser] has suffered in the past year."[1]

This highly publicized case illustrates the significant risk posed to victim privacy when one is involved in criminal proceedings. The Bryant case lends support to the claim that crime victims can be victimized by both the offender and the criminal justice system. Unlike this case, however, not all criminal victimizations are so widely known. Most crime victimization is difficult to accurately measure, and researchers estimate a significant portion of actual crime is undetected. They refer to the unknown amount as the dark figure of crime. As a result, justice officials and researchers are left to speculate how much crime occurs.

OFFICIALS MEASURES OF CRIME

Official crime measurement in the United States comes from two primary sources—Uniform Crime Reports (UCR) and National Crime Victimization Survey (NCVS). Both are administered by the U.S. Department of Justice "to measure the magnitude, nature, and impact of crime in the Nation."[2] The primary crime reporting system is the UCR, which compiles police recorded crime data and is maintained by the FBI in Washington, D.C. Next is the official measure of crime victimization using the NCVS, which is managed by the Bureau of Justice Statistics, a research arm of the Department of Justice, in conjunction with the U.S. Census Bureau. Together, data derived from these sources constitute the official measure of crime in the United States for that year.[3]

National Crime Victimization Survey

The NCVS, begun in 1973, is the primary source of crime victimization data in America and is derived from a nationally representative sample of households. Researchers interview household members regarding their crime victimization over a given period. The NCVS consists of predetermined questions posed to respondents in telephone interviews. In 2006, the prearranged panel consisted of 76,000 households involving over 130,000 persons selected for the annual survey. With the exception of homicide, the NCVS measures the same offenses as the UCR and provides data on violent and property crimes. Information gathered from the NCVS shows a greater incident of crime than the UCR, which suggests that only about one-half of actual crime victims report their incidents to the police. Importantly, the NCVS gathers a wealth of information about the dynamics of the crime and victimization. In doing so, it provides valuable insight into the crime incident, offender, and victim.[4]

Crime Victimization in America

In 2006, the NCVS estimated that 25 million persons were crime victims in America.[5] That year, only 49 percent of violent crimes and 38 percent of property crimes were reported to the police. There are several explanations for crime victim failure to contact the police following a criminal incident. First, some crime victims want to avoid interaction with the police because of intimidation or fear of detection. Second, others may be acquainted with the offender and do not want to implicate the person in the crime. Third, victims may believe that the police will be unwilling or unable to provide them with assistance after the crime. Fourth, victims may have concerns about being humiliated or stigmatized by the crime perpetrated against them. For example, some fraud victims are reluctant to admit they were duped, while sexual assault victims want to avoid the social stigma associated with that crime.

Nowhere is the stigmatization perception more pronounced than with sex crime victims. Between 1992 and 2000, official estimates suggest that only about 36 percent of rape or sexual assault victims actually reported to the police.[6] This alarming statistic reveals the hidden nature of these crimes as their occurrence is not accurately reflected in official crime measures due to underreporting. Furthermore, low reporting hampers official efforts to protect the community and prosecute sex offenders. Excluding or abusing the victim in the justice process compounds the person's emotional victimization and reduces his or her willingness to participate, which begins with reporting the crime to the police.

CRIME VICTIM'S LEGAL RIGHTS

Given the number of criminal victimizations each year, advocates have called for greater government support and statutory protection for crime victims and their privacy rights. Beginning in the 1970s, they insisted that laws, policies, and procedures safeguard victim rights and allow them to become more active participants in the handling of their cases. Advocates argued that crime victims have been lost in the criminal justice maze, which results in their second victimization by a bureaucracy focused exclusively on the defendant. These movements led to the creation of government victim assistance agencies, and every state and federal jurisdiction has enacted a statutory crime victim's Bill of Rights to facilitate the victim's support and protection.

Although provisions of crime victim rights laws vary among jurisdictions, together they include the following:

- Right to notification of criminal justice proceedings and other legal remedies;
- Right to attend or participate in criminal justice proceedings;
- Right to speedy trial provision and to confer with the prosecutor;
- Right to protection from intimidation and harassment;
- Right to notice of release or escape of offender;
- Right to privacy and confidentiality of records;
- Right to prompt return of personal property stolen or used as evidence;
- Right to victim compensation and restitution.[7]

In support of these aims, Congress enacted the Crime Victims' Rights Act of 2004 (CVRA) that enabled crime victims to become full participants in federal criminal proceedings.

Federal Crime Victims' Rights Act

The CVRA gave crime victims a greater voice. Paul G. Cassell contends, "The CVRA transforms crime victims into participants in the criminal justice process by (among other things) guaranteeing them notice of court hearings, the right to attend those hearings, and the opportunity to testify at appropriate points in the process."[8] The federal statute's eight points embodied the same core principles as state victim rights laws focusing on the entitlement to notification, protection, and privacy. It emphasized "the right to be treated with fairness and with respect for the victim's dignity and privacy."[9]

Perhaps most importantly, the CVRA includes several enforcement mechanisms. Victims can assert their individual rights while their legal representative or the government attorney takes measures, such as motions or appeals, to ensure that officials comply with the law, thereby guaranteeing that the victim is afforded the protection prescribed by law.

A right to privacy is central to victims' rights and a crucial component in protecting them from intimidation, harassment, stalking, or harm. In this context privacy protection has a number of facets including identity, anonymity, and confidentiality.

CRIME VICTIM PRIVACY RIGHTS

Protecting the privacy of crime victims is a high-stakes obligation. Although divulging the identity of crime victims or their role in providing criminal evidence could result in unwanted media attention, embarrassment, humiliation, or stigmatization; it can also pose a realistic danger to the person. There are legitimate concerns for victim safety where violent crimes or intimate relationships are involved. One-fifth of the criminal victimizations against women in 2006 involved intimate acquaintances. Sexual assault crimes have provided much of the impetus for laws designed to protect the identity and private activities of victims. Often called rape shield laws, these statutes are designed to enhance the safety of sex crime victims, reduce further humiliation or stigmatization, protect victim privacy, and promote offense reporting.

Privacy and Rape Shield Laws

Victim Identity

A national survey reported that 66 percent of women questioned said they would be more inclined to report rapes if their identity was concealed.[10] These findings reflect an important aspect of privacy protection insofar as it encourages victim reporting and leads to more offender prosecutions. Maintaining sex crime victim anonymity has proven to be difficult. All jurisdictions have enacted some type of rape shield law, which was originally designed to provide evidentiary rules in rape cases. Several states have also passed legislation prohibiting the disclosure of rape victim identity by government agencies. Yet, these laws lack continuity and have demonstrated that they are ineffective in guarding victim identity.

Many rape victim identity protection statutes target the media as being the principal source of personal information disclosure. This legislation has not faired well since the Supreme Court has struck down laws that limit free press rights. The lead case is *The Florida Star v. B. J. F.* (1989), where the Court held that state laws that restrict the media's decision to publish the victim's identity violate fundamental First Amendment rights. Justice Thurgood Marshall wrote, "Although the interests in protecting the privacy and safety of sexual assault victims and in encouraging them to report offenses without fear of exposure are highly significant, imposing liability on the Star [newspaper] in this case is too precipitous a means of advancing those interests."[11] The Court found that the Florida rape shield statute could neither prohibit nor punish the media for distributing victim information that was lawfully obtained and truthful.[12]

In this case, B. J. F. filed a report with the Duvall County Sheriff's Department that she had been robbed and raped at knifepoint by an unknown assailant while walking to a bus stop. A police report, which included the victim's full name, was posted in its pressroom for media distribution. A staff

member of the *Florida Star* newspaper obtained the crime and victim information from the police report, and it was published in the local edition.
The victim's name was inadvertently included in the story, in violation of
the newspaper's internal policy, which requires the removal of sex crime
victim identity.

The inclusion of the victim's name also violated Florida's criminal statute
that makes it "unlawful to publish or broadcast information identifying sexual offense victim. No person shall print, publish, or broadcast, or cause or
allow to be printed, published, or broadcast, in any instrument of mass communication the name, address, or other identifying fact or information of the
victim of any sexual offense . . . ."[13] B. J. F. filed a suit against the department
and the *Florida Star.* The newspaper was found civilly liable for publishing
the victim's name and it appealed. The Supreme Court in *The Florida Star*
ruled that the Florida law was unconstitutional and reasoned that "where a
newspaper published truthful information which it has lawfully obtained,
punishment may be lawfully imposed, if at all, only when narrowly tailored
to a state interest of the highest order."[14] Although the Court's holding leaves
rape victim identity information obtained from government public records
open to media dissemination, it implied that states could restrict access if
they showed an interest of the highest order.[15]

Some state statutes sought to protect rape victim identity by barring the
media from criminal proceedings. The Supreme Court rejected this
approach. It disallowed a Massachusetts law ruling it was unconstitutional
to deny the public access to criminal trials. However, the Court reiterated
its position that restrictions may be imposed if the government shows a compelling interest on a case basis, such as involving juvenile victims.[16]

Given the Supreme Court's invalidation of laws that punish the media for
disclosing sex crime victim identity, many jurisdictions have instead focused
on protecting victim anonymity by restricting government disclosure. State
laws can prohibit the release of victim name only, complete description and
contact information, crime incident details, and pseudonyms. Sex crime victims are using pseudonyms more often in criminal proceedings, and some
courts have supported plaintiff anonymous pleadings in civil actions stemming from sexual assaults. The Ninth Court of Appeals in *Does I Thru XXIII
v. Advanced Textile Corp.* explained that plaintiff pseudonyms may be needed
to protect the victim from retaliation, preserve privacy, and ensure the privilege of self-incrimination.[17] In promoting greater anonymity, Meg Garvin
insists, "Too often victims are forced to a Hobson's choice: protect your
privacy or pursue justice."[18]

Some jurisdictions suppress victim information only at certain stages of
the criminal proceedings, while others conceal it throughout the criminal

process. As instructed by the Supreme Court, states can allow trial courts to rule on the use of victim details based on the government's compelling interest in withholding the information to protect the complainant. As Daniel M. Murdock asserts, ". . . the Court clearly suggests that concealing a rape victim's identity is a constitutionally sound method of protecting a rape victim's privacy."[19] Hence, many jurisdictions have extended privacy protections to sex crime victims by safeguarding at least their identities in government records and criminal proceedings.

Sexual History

The second prong of the rape shield laws deals with the protection of victim sexual history. Many jurisdictions have enacted evidentiary rules to control the use of victim sexual activity as evidence in sex crime cases. For example, Rule 412 of the Federal Rules of Evidence prohibits the use of evidence regarding other sexual activity of the victim in criminal or civil cases unless it fits within three narrow exceptions, mostly focused on the probative value of the information.[20]

States have also added provisions to their rape shield laws restricting the use of victim sexual history as evidence in the perpetrator's trial. The Supreme Court has allowed statutes to prohibit the use of victim sexual history on a case basis where the government can demonstrate there is a compelling need to limit victim privacy invasion, negative impact, or obstruction of prosecution. In the Kobe Bryant sexual assault case, Colorado rape shield laws permitted the trial court to consider defense requests to release the identity of the victim and introduce victim sexual activity as evidence. During the closed hearings, the judge ruled that the victim must remain anonymous but permitted the limited use of her sexual history as evidence. Typewritten transcripts of the judicial hearing, containing the name and sexual history information of the alleged victim, were accidentally disseminated to media outlets by the court reporter. When the court became aware of the unintentional distribution, it immediately notified recipients that ". . . [t]hese transcripts are not for public dissemination. Anyone who has received these transcripts is ordered to delete and destroy any copies and not reveal any contents thereof, or be subject to contempt of Court."[21] Several media organizations petitioned the Colorado Supreme Court to rule on the permissibility of the trial court's order.

In *People v. Bryant* (2004), the court upheld the trial court's action finding

Trial court's order forbidding media entities from publishing transcript of in camera [closed] proceedings they mistakenly received from court concerning evidence and arguments relating to alleged victim's sexual conduct before and after her sexual encounter with defendant constituted prior restraint, but, narrowly tailored, such prior restraint was constitutional; state had interest of highest order in providing confidential evidentiary proceeding under rape shield statute, because such hearings protected victims' privacy, encouraged victims to report sexual assault, and furthered prosecution and deterrence of sexual assault.[22]

The Colorado court ruled that the state had an interest of the highest order in protecting the private activities of the accuser. The court's reasoning here is a clear example of the government's rationale for wanting to protect the victim's privacy in sexual crime prosecutions. In *Bryant,* the court conducted a three-way balancing of media First Amendment interests, victim privacy interests, and state interests in protecting rape victims, in arriving at its conclusion that the victim and state interests should prevail. David E. Fialkow commented, "The distinguishing factor in *Bryant* was the impact of the privacy interest being weighed. The privacy interest violated was not only the release of the victim's name, but her complete sexual history."[23]

In spite of yeoman efforts by state and federal jurisdictions to protect sexual crime victim privacy using rape shield laws, they generally lack adequate enforcement mechanisms and contain loopholes that allow courts to admit sexual history information on a case basis.[24] Moreover, the proliferation of sophisticated telecommunications enables the instant dissemination of victim private information that outpaces many statutory restrictions. Nevertheless, sexual assault victims possess a statutory right to privacy in all jurisdictions that is designed to guard their identities and private sexual histories. In addition to concerns about harassment, retaliation, or anonymity in public record and court testimony, victims who participate in postcrime counseling worry about their confidentiality.

Privacy Rights and Counseling Communication Privilege

Various types of communication are protected from disclosure by privilege statutes. Every jurisdiction recognizes the attorney-client privilege that prevents either party from being compelled to divulge the contents of their communication. Recognition of other privileges, such as husband-wife, physician-patient, or clergy-penitent, varies according to state or federal laws. In 1996, the Supreme Court recognized that the psychotherapist-patient privilege was needed to protect the confidentiality of counseling communications. The Court in *Jaffe v. Redmond* (1996) noted that

confidential communications between a licensed psychotherapist and his or her patients in the course of diagnosis and treatment are protected from compelled disclosure under . . . the Federal Rules of Evidence [and] . . . the reasons for recognizing a privilege for treatment by psychiatrists and psychologists apply with equal force to treatment by a clinical social worker.[25]

Further in supporting an absolute psychotherapist-patient privilege, the Court commented "making the promise of confidentiality contingent upon a trial judge's later evaluation of the relative importance of the patient's interest in privacy and the evidentiary need for disclosure would eviscerate the effectiveness of the privilege."[26]

Even though all state and federal jurisdictions have enacted some form of psychotherapist-patient privilege, they do not provide blanket protection in every situation. For instance, victims who seek postcrime counseling from victim advocates or services within the criminal justice system may not be covered by the privilege in all locales. Under evidence discovery rules, government records generated by criminal justice personnel may be available to criminal defendants, thereby invading the privacy of victims in counseling. The *Jaffee* Court's ruling paved the way for states to extend a psychotherapist-patient privilege to all crime victims receiving counseling. Particularly in sex crime and domestic violence cases, such therapeutic methods are seen as valuable tools in contributing to the victims' recovery and promoting their full cooperation in the investigation and prosecution of the crime committed against them.[27]

Considerable attention has been devoted to the privacy rights of sex crime victims; however, personal data crimes increasingly threaten individual privacy as more people utilize electronic media to make transactions and disseminate information.

PRIVACY RIGHTS AND PERSONAL DATA

In 2004, the NCVS added questions to measure the incidence of criminal misuse of personal information. Based on the period July–December 2004, NCVS data reported 3.6 million households were victims of identity theft during the previous six months, losing an average of $1,290. Federal Trade Commission data showed 670,000 complaints of consumer fraud or identity theft were reported to law enforcement agencies in 2006.[28]

The centerpiece of identity theft victimization is the invasion of privacy to illegally obtain personal information for criminal profit. Obviously, victims engage in financial transactions that require personal banking or identification descriptors with a degree of expectation of privacy. Yet, victim willingness to divulge personal or financial information to fraudsters or expose such data to illicit acquisition by using unsecured electronic media significantly reduces individual expectation of privacy.

A victim right to privacy in protecting similar personal information in the possession of criminal justice agencies is subject to applicable state privacy laws. Regarding the statutory safekeeping of personal information maintained by federal departments, law enforcement organizations are exempt from the Privacy Act of 1974, which provides privacy protections and remedies for the handling of personal data.[29] In sum, personal information maintained by criminal justice agencies is generally considered public record and can be lawfully obtained. Except for statutory restrictions on personal information, pursuant to rape shield or similar laws, official data held by criminal justice organizations have no privacy protection that prevents acquisition by interested parties.

Chapter 7

SURVEILLANCE OF NONTRADITIONAL SUSPECTS

On the morning of November 5, 2003, 14 police officers took strategic positions around the main building of Stratford High School in suburban Charleston, South Carolina. Within 30 seconds, officers with guns drawn entered the main hallway and ordered 107 students to lie flat on the floor. Lt. Dave Aarons said, "12 to 14 students were placed in handcuffs due to their failure to respond to repeated police instructions to get on their knees."[1] A drug-sniffing dog alerted officers to 12 student book bags that were searched by school officials. No drugs were found and no arrests were made.

School officials requested the police intervention after a student tip led them to review surveillance video showing organized drug activity on campus. The police claimed the search tactics were appropriate even though school officials denied knowing that the surprise raid would involve drawn guns and handcuffing of innocent students. Scores of frightened students and angry parents accused officials of overreacting and using excessive force in a search that netted no arrests. Amid widespread recriminations, police and school officials agreed to review their drug-search procedures.[2]

As police extend their reach to combat problems such as illicit drug use in schools, they impact a group of nontraditional suspects who were once immune from crime controls. The Stratford High incident shows the effect of far-reaching anticrime campaigns that cast a large net of suspicion in unlikely places.

Since the 1970s, crime control policies have incorporated improbable persons, such as suspected drug-using students and airline passengers, in response to emerging crimes. As such, police investigations extended to persons not previously considered crime risks. However, this is not the first time that government has used extraordinary, and on occasion, extralegal measures to protect society from named threats.

Historically, new criminal menaces spawned urgent anticrime initiatives, which when applied to nontraditional suspects such as during alcohol

Prohibition, created a fresh class of unlikely offenders and invariably eroded liberty and privacy rights. Once threats become credible, they gain political traction and eventually produce statutes and court decisions that obligate the police to take enforcement action. When perceptions of pressing dangers entwine with powerful technology, the result can have Orwellian effects producing more government surveillance.

Official investigations are substantially more encompassing because police now collect data from widely used communication and transaction platforms such as cellular telephony and the Internet. In an unprecedented move, law enforcement after 9/11 placed significant emphasis on information as the best source of criminal intelligence and evidence. And electronic surveillance became the ideal investigative method for gathering troves of informational data used to combat crime and terrorism.

UNCHARTED CRIME THREATS AND NONTRADITIONAL SUSPECTS

Originally, common law crimes were viewed as trespasses against person or property that resulted in physical harm or dispossession. Yet when drug abuse spiked in the 1960s, illicit drugs became thought of as an imminent threat to public safety elevating the issue to the national agenda. Soon the drug scourge was seen as a priority with lawmakers and courts. Although various controlled substances had been illegal in America since the Harrison Narcotics Act of 1914, the new threat perspective added a nascent class of potential drug offenders. By the 1980s, a string of Supreme Court cases expanded warrantless administrative searches allowing them to reach into public school, workplace, and public transportation. A dubious group of potential drug suspects was caught in the sweep including extracurricular program students,[3] police and correctional officers,[4] and train engineers.[5]

In a series of landmark cases, the Court declared that persons in the public school and workplace had a diminished expectation of privacy and were subject to warrantless and suspicionless search. Official surveillance and search had expanded from a focus on the underworld to an all-inclusive strategy to detect drug use or wrongdoing in ordinary places.

Globalization Effects and Transnational Crime

Globalization effects such as advanced telecommunications, reduced border controls, extensive human migration, and multinational economic interdependence have facilitated the proliferation of transnational organized crime.[6] The current generation of organized criminal poses a global threat because of its ability to reach across borders to traffick goods or victimize citizens beyond their country of residence. After receiving an endorsement from 125 countries, the United Nations established the Convention against Transnational Organized Crime in 2000. Provisions of the agreement classified a crime as transnational if "an offense is . . . committed [or has substantial effects] in more than one state."[7] The multinational dimension presented a number of challenges for police. Unlike local crime, the transnational variety involved more sophisticated networks of drug traffickers, human traffickers, smugglers, and cybercriminals with international connections and technological capabilities spanning across many jurisdictions.[8] Their criminal connections involve corrupt officials, legitimate businesses, technical associates, and lawbreakers in many locations. Law enforcement simply lacked the expertise and intelligence-sharing tools to effectively prevent or investigate transnational crimes and criminals.

In response to the challenges posed by transnational crime, police sought greater surveillance authority and resources. Expanded powers were incorporated in statutes and supported by courts authorizing additional surveillance and data gathering to combat the formidable transnational crime threat. Much of the success of multinational criminal enterprises is linked to their use of complex smuggling structures, advanced telecommunications, and global money laundering networks. Predictably, police countermeasures targeted these strategic points using multijurisdiction task forces, improved intelligence networking, and more electronic surveillance. Given the sophistication and diversity of transnational criminal actors and schemes, police investigations naturally extend to a host of suspects at home and abroad.

Global Terrorism and 9/11

Although terrorism has been used as a tool of political violence since nineteenth-century European revolutions, it was not considered a serious threat in modern America. That changed with the catastrophic 9/11 attacks in New York and Washington, D.C., by radical Islamists. As the 9/11 Commission report states, "The 9/11 attacks were a shock, but they should not have come as a surprise. Islamist extremists had given plenty of warning that they meant to kill Americans indiscriminately and in large numbers."[9] Thereafter, Islamist terrorism was considered an imminent national security and public safety threat. The attacks revealed America's vulnerability to foreign terrorism because, among other things, it is an open liberal democracy that imposes strict constraints on its police and vigorously protects civil liberties. Restrictions on law enforcement surveillance were instantly cited as part of America's failure to prevent the 9/11 attacks. At the same time, the ease with which the terrorists entered the United States and carried out their attacks stunned officials and the public alike.[10]

Government officials called for more powerful investigative tools and the authority to use them. Within a few weeks, Congress enacted several statutory provisions expanding police and intelligence agency surveillance and data-gathering capabilities to combat the new threat. Some of these laws modified existing surveillance, search, and seizure authority leading to the collection of more data and deeper government intrusion. Two factors contributed to the widening of the net of suspicion. First, before the attacks, the 9/11 terrorists were not considered criminals in the traditional sense. Second, they entered the country using fraudulent travel documents and easily blended into America's diverse population as students or workers. These circumstances caused authorities to more carefully scrutinize foreign visitors, émigrés, travelers, financial networks, electronic communications, and criminal and terrorist connections.

To compound the challenge and further enlarge the pool of potential suspects, experts were convinced that transnational criminals, drug traffickers, and global terrorists shared best practices and illicit networks. As one U.S. military counterterrorism report explained, "Although terrorism and organized crime are different phenomena, the important fact is that terrorist and criminal networks overlap and cooperate in some enterprises . . . the phenomenon is growing . . . because [they] use similar approaches to promote their operations."[11] Likewise the narcoterrorism theory, which posits that terrorist groups derive operational funding from the global drug trade, gained momentum with decision makers.[12]

Illicit drugs, transnational crime, and global terrorism have joined more traditional street crimes not only expanding the public threat assessment but leading officials to adopt a more inclusive suspicion perspective. After 9/11, American police agencies placed greater emphasis on homeland security, which promotes preparedness and countermeasures that focus on external dangers.[13] Inherent to that approach is the notion that a panoramic survey of potential hazards is most effective in protecting society.

Under the aegis of preventive law enforcement, police have developed an appetite for intelligence data. In doing so, they are dedicated to collecting massive amounts of public and private information from surveillance and other sources.[14] The information itself is viewed as a valuable commodity that can be used to detect, investigate, or convict criminals and terrorists. The data range from raw information to criminal evidence used in prosecutions.

Clearly, the courts have also supported law enforcement use of surveillance and search in crime fighting. Moreover, imminent crime, drug, and terrorism threats have persuaded the courts to give greater surveillance and search authority to police, using primarily a special needs justification for expanded warrantless and suspicionless searches. Ordinarily, official electronic surveillance powers are outlined in federal and state laws. Likewise, statutes are a common source of citizen privacy protection against improper government electronic interception or misuse of personal information. Since the 1960s, Congress has enacted several laws that provide guidelines for police surveillance and outline individual privacy safeguards.

Federal Privacy Laws

A significant amount of information on citizens is collected and stored by government agencies. The data include a wealth of identification, transaction, and legal proceeding details. Officials gather information on personal identifiers, family relations, addresses, telephone numbers, as well as property, voting, and criminal records. Many of these public records are easily available due to Internet access. Both lawmakers and courts have worked to balance the two competing interests—transparency and privacy—in the handling of personal data by government agencies.[15] To address the disclosure of information of interest to the public, Congress enacted The Freedom of Information Act (FOIA) in 1966.[16] And to provide statutory protection for private information held by government agencies, Congress passed the Privacy Act of 1974.[17]

The Freedom of Information Act

The original provisions of the FOIA were amended in 1996 to allow electronic access to some documents. Essentially, the Act enables persons to obtain copies of documents stored by federal agencies. Requests must specify the needed record, and the agency is required to provide a response within a reasonable time period and may charge a fee for search and copy costs. If access or copy is denied, the federal agency must provide an explanation, and the requestor has a right of appeal unless the wanted document is protected by disclosure exemptions under the Act.

Among the nine categories of exemptions are records stored by law enforcement agencies. The law allows police to refuse document requests if disclosure would jeopardize enforcement proceedings, impede a defendant's right to a fair trial, constitute an unreasonable invasion of privacy, disclose the identity of a confidential source, disclose internal guidelines or operational practices, or endanger the safety of an individual. Additionally, law enforcement personnel records have restricted access under FOIA, and employers can decline requests for personnel or medical file contents.

Privacy Act of 1974

The counterweight to the FOIA is the Privacy Act of 1974 where Congress codified individual privacy safeguards for information stored by government agencies. In essence, the law provides restrictions on agency document dissemination and gives individuals consent and control over their personal information. Persons are given access, review, copy, and release privileges over their own records. Only in cases where private data are shared among government agencies for lawful and public policy purposes is dissemination allowed. The agency is civilly liable for safe handling and protecting the records against misuse or unlawful disclosure.

As with the FOIA, some law enforcement information is exempt under the Privacy Act. Records maintained by the Central Intelligence Agency or law enforcement agencies may be protected from provisions of the Privacy Act if the information pertains to criminal identification, history, investigation, confidential informant, or enforcement procedure. However, if persons are denied access to their own information, as prescribed by federal law, the agency must release the material, except that which discloses the identity of a government confidential informant. Congress has also passed laws that provide guidelines for official surveillance.

FEDERAL ELECTRONIC SURVEILLANCE LAWS

Although federal electronic surveillance law originated with the Federal Communications Act of 1934, changes in technology provided the impetus for Congress to enact several laws since then. Since the 1960s, federal statutes have given law enforcement greater authority to conduct electronic surveillance of criminal suspects. The powers include the use of wiretaps, as well as pen register and trap and trace devices that are designed to record telephone number or computer Internet protocol (IP) address traffic. Although these investigative tools require a court-issued warrant, they may be covertly installed to gather evidence on criminal suspects. The Supreme Court in *Dalia v. United States* (1979) held, "[t]he Fourth Amendment does not prohibit *per se* a covert entry [by police] performed for the purpose of installing otherwise legal electronic bugging equipment."[18]

Both federal and state electronic surveillance laws create specific eavesdropping procedures that do not necessarily parallel Fourth Amendment provisions. As Daniel J. Solove et al. contend, "[E]lectronic surveillance law operates independently of the Fourth Amendment. Even if a search is reasonable under the Fourth Amendment, electronic surveillance law may bar the evidence [and vice versa]."[19] Part of this can be explained by the rigid standards required by courts to obtain wiretapping warrants due to the degree of privacy invasion.

Omnibus Crime Control and Safe Streets Act of 1968, Title III

The same year that the Supreme Court decided the groundbreaking *Katz v. United States* (1967) case, establishing the expectation of privacy doctrine, it also outlined specific requirements for police electronic surveillance warrants in *Berger v. New York* (1967).[20] In that case, the *Berger* Court required that wiretap search warrants contain the specific conversation to be monitored, probable cause, time limitation, named suspect, and documentation returned to the court that the warrant was carried out.

In response to *Katz* and *Berger,* along with rapid changes in technology, Congress in 1968 enacted Title III of the Omnibus Crime Control and Safe Streets Act, as the Wire and Electronic Communications Interception and Interception of Oral Communications Act.[21] It is commonly referred to as the Wiretap Act, even though there are several subsequent federal wiretap laws that bear the same name. This law became the centerpiece of federal wiretap statutes and established guidelines for the interception of wire and oral communications. The law protects persons from the unauthorized wiretapping or interception of voice transmitted over telephone lines or through oral communication. It applies only to the nonconsensual interception of two types of aural, heard by ear, communications: voice over telephone line and oral voice, and not to electronic digital transmissions. The law concerns both private and law enforcement wiretapping or communication interception. However, it included provisions allowing police to obtain a surveillance or wiretap warrant issued by a court of competent jurisdiction.

Protection afforded by the Wiretap Act did not extend to the newer forms of electronic communication. But between 1970 and 1986, Congress amended the original law on several occasions because of advances in electronic and wireless communication technology.

First, the current version of the Act prohibits the interception and disclosure of wire, oral, or electronic communications. Second, the manufacture, distribution, possession, and advertising of interception devices are prohibited. Third, it establishes procedures for the authorized interception, disclosure, evidentiary use, and reporting of intercepted communications by law enforcement. Fourth, the law imposes criminal penalties and civil damages for the illegal or unauthorized use of intercepted communications.

Electronic Communications Privacy Act of 1986

In 1986, Congress substantially modified the original Wiretap Act with the Electronic Communications Privacy Act (ECPA).[22] ECPA amended the earlier wiretap law by creating three major sections: the wiretap provisions, Stored Communications Act, and Pen Register Act. Since ECPA was passed before Internet use became common, it was enacted primarily to extend Title III protections to the next generation of digital communication.

Specifically, the ECPA-revised Wiretap Act prohibits the interception of communications through aural eavesdropping or electronic devices of wire, oral, or electronic communications. Wire communications involve any aural transfer of voice over wire or cable between its origin and destination. Oral communication is defined as "uttered by a person exhibiting an expectation that such communication is not subject to interception . . . ."[23] Electronic communication refers to digital information and includes transfers of electronic mail or data.

Congress also expanded protection to include stored communications. Often, communication service providers store electronic communication data for backup purposes or as part of an electronic junction used in the delivery of information. The law prohibits the acquisition of electronic communications either through interception or retrieval of stored data.

LAW ENFORCEMENT ACCESS TO ELECTRONIC COMMUNICATIONS

Though the primary goal of the Wiretap Act is to protect individual privacy, as a practical matter circumstances arise that require access to transmitted or stored electronic communications. Obviously, communication providers are permitted to handle and store the data as long as they do not violate the privacy of the users or unlawfully disclose the information. Additionally, official investigations may require access to this information.

As outlined in the *Katz* and *Berger* decisions, officials must have a sufficient justification to lawfully intercept a person's private communication. The courts have developed procedures for police to request wiretaps for the interception of electronic or oral communications using surveillance devices. Officials are required to submit a sworn statement, to a court of competent jurisdiction, explaining the details of their probable cause and describing the person or communication they want to place under surveillance.

The proliferation of cellular telephones, digital communication devices, Voice Over Internet, and electronic messaging has changed communication modes used by criminal suspects. This has hampered police surveillance effectiveness, which is primarily designed to tap wire communications in fixed locations. Given the ephemeral nature of digital data and communications, law enforcement officials have struggled to maintain a viable surveillance capability.

At the same time, Internet and communication service providers constantly upgrade their equipment to remain competitive and provide cutting-edge features for their customers. By the 1990s, law enforcement surveillance equipment had become incompatible with much of the leading digital technology. Once again, Congress modified the surveillance laws to enable criminal investigations to keep pace with changing technology.

Communications Assistance for Law Enforcement Act of 1994

In 1994, Congress enacted legislation to facilitate the use of wiretap devices by investigators. The purpose of the Communications Assistance for Law Enforcement Act (CALEA) is to require service providers to give easy access to law enforcement for court-ordered surveillance, wiretapping, or data mining.[24] CALEA mandates that service companies, which use circuit-based telephone or packet-based data networks, calibrate their equipment so that it is more compatible with court-ordered wiretap devices. The statute enables the police to access information through technology such as DSL-telephone connected and Broadband Internet, cable, satellite, wireless, commercial push-to-talk, and Voice Over Internet Protocol technology. CALEA allows officials to locate cellular telephone users, identify callers, or determine telephone features used by patrons. Though many service providers opposed the CALEA legislation, in 2004 they were required by the Federal Communication Commission to comply with the law.

Technological change is not the only influence on the lawful interception of communications. After 9/11, Congress passed sweeping laws giving government officials new electronic surveillance powers.

FEDERAL ANTITERRORISM LAWS

The deadly 9/11 attacks were the catalyst for a paradigmatic shift in American policing.[25] They caused law enforcement agencies to amend their priorities and increasingly emphasize homeland security. Meanwhile, new statutes gave police enhanced investigative capacity to defend the homeland. Perhaps no other law depicts these changes more vividly than the voluminous USA Patriot Act. Passed by Congress six weeks after 9/11, the 342-page Bill revised existing federal laws with the aim of providing police more surveillance authority to battle the new terrorism threat.[26]

The USA Patriot Act of 2001

In 2001, the Uniting and Strengthening America by Providing Appropriate Tools Required to Intercept and Obstruct Terrorism Act, better known as the USA Patriot Act, was enacted.[27] This statute modified 15 federal laws, focusing primarily on counterterrorism and foreign intelligence investigation, while increasing police surveillance and search authority. It substantially altered provisions of the Foreign Intelligence Surveillance Act (FISA) and ECPA.

Patriot Act provisions relaxed restrictions on law enforcement wiretapping methods allowing agencies to request both blank and roving-multi-point electronic surveillance warrants. It enabled the police to monitor the communications of an unspecified suspect across all domestic U.S. jurisdictions. This was a major departure from traditional wiretap orders that required a named suspect and stationary location.

Another change affected police use of pen register and trap and trace surveillance devices. These instruments are designed to record called or received telephone numbers. Though both are time-honored wiretap methods, Patriot Act provisions now permit the equipment to be used to record Internet IP location addresses accessed by computer users.

Also new to the Patriot Act is the use of "sneak and peek" warrants that enable police to execute a search warrant or install a surveillance device without notifying the suspect if they believe disclosure will have an adverse effect on their investigation. This provision replaces the announcement and notification requirements for standard search warrants.

To ease constraints imposed by the Title III Wiretap Act, Patriot Act revisions expanded wiretap access letting police request a warrant for foreign intelligence, terrorist, or computer crime investigations by merely certifying that it is related to a law enforcement purpose. This provision reduced the stricter Fourth Amendment probable cause standard typically required to obtain an electronic surveillance warrant.

Additionally, Patriot Act National Security Letter (NSL) provisions let law enforcement authorities directly request records from a third party such as Internet Service Providers, telephone companies, or libraries by certifying that the information is relevant to an authorized investigation. Use of the letters replaced judicial orders, such as subpoenas.

The Act permits the court to impose a gag order on libraries, bookstores, colleges, or financial institutions that receive NSL requests for records or if police install a wiretap. Persons having knowledge that a police investigation is under way are prohibited from divulging any information.

Patriot Act terms modified banking and educational institution record-keeping practices. Changes to the federal bank reporting laws require financial institutions to provide federal authorities access to customer financial records upon receiving a written NSL request. Similarly, educational institutions must release student records with a NSL request pursuant to a foreign intelligence or terrorism investigation.

The Patriot Act has had a substantial effect on police surveillance and search powers.[28] Moreover, it has significantly impacted individual privacy rights by reducing statutory and judicial restrictions on law enforcement and intelligence agencies when collecting data through third party and electronic surveillance sources. The Patriot Act promoted greater information sharing among government agencies, thereby spreading the risk of official privacy invasion. In revising provisions of the FISA, the Patriot Act reduces the wall that blocked government access to a wealth of personal business, communication, education, and financial records maintained by private and public entities. Many stipulations shifted more authority to executive branch decision makers, sidelined traditional Fourth Amendment and judicial review safeguards, and gave law enforcement greater authorization to independently engage in surveillance and data collection in the absence of long-standing procedural safeguards intended to protect individual privacy rights. Finally, with the potential for pervasive use of gag orders, the Act increases the prospect of government secrecy and jeopardizes needed transparency.

Patricia Mell predicts,

> Removal of the checks and balances on governmental action by the Patriot Act could diminish the already waning protection afforded by the Fourth Amendment. By increasing the scope of information subject to government access and reducing the independent judicial review of the government's actions, the Patriot Act lowered the threshold for legitimate governmental intrusion into the individual's privacy under the Fourth Amendment.[29]

Congress followed the Patriot Act with other legislation designed to transform and improve counterterrorism laws, policies, and practices dedicated to homeland defense.[30] In 2002, the Homeland Security Act was enacted, which consolidated 22 federal agencies, in whole or part, into the new Department of Homeland Security. The aim was to eliminate agency turf battles and combine resources to establish a united front against transnational crime and terrorism threats, while focusing on homeland security.[31]

In response to recommendations of the 9/11 Commission, Congress also passed the Intelligence Reform and Terrorism Prevention Act to restructure the American intelligence community and promote a culture of information sharing.[32] The 9/11 Commission called for "unifying the many participants in the counterterrorism effort and their knowledge in a network-based information sharing system that transcends governmental boundaries."[33]

REAL ID Act of 2005

In another effort to standardize information after 9/11, Congress passed the REAL ID Act of 2005 requiring states to adopt a uniform "smart" driver's license that contains an embedded microchip that stores personal data about the license holder.[34] Microchip data are designed to be remotely read by radio-frequency identification devices (RFID) to enable authorities to easily access the card holder's information. When fully implemented, federal mandates stipulate that anyone entering federal facilities, commercial aircrafts, border points, or who obtain government services must possess the REAL ID or a valid U.S. passport. The law imposes rigid documentation, technology, and verification requirements on states that transform the driver's license ostensibly into a national identification card. Critics argue that the personal data stored in the ID card far surpass the information needed for an ordinary driver's license. Moreover, the REAL ID Act repealed a key provision of the Intelligence Reform and Terrorism Prevention Act of 2004 that prohibited the creation of a national identification card for Americans, thus thwarting Congress's original intent. In January 2008, the Department of Homeland Security announced it was extending the deadline for nationwide implementation and would not require encryption of the license's microchip data as a cost-saving measure.

The REAL ID program has undergone several revisions and implementation delays amid opposition from states estimating the program cost could exceed $11 billion over the first five years. At the same time, privacy advocates have raised concerns about the risks posed by REAL ID, citing the vulnerability of the card's unencrypted personal data to hacking, as well as the effort to establish a mandatory national identification card under the guise of an ordinary state-issued driver's license.[35]

Researchers at the University of Washington recently discovered that the wireless barcode microchips, imbedded in REAL ID driver's licenses and U.S. Passport Cards, could be easily scanned as far away as 50 meters. Known as skimming, the wireless retrieval of personal data from the microchip tag, by nefarious hackers, poses a serious threat to the card holder's privacy.[36]

Each of these federal statutes was a reaction to the advancing technology and shifting threats facing society. Though already under way, the events of 9/11 accelerated changes in laws, policies, and practices when it came to electronic surveillance and counterterrorism. Police had been gradually adopting the use of new technologies to investigate crime in spite of bemoaning their inability to keep pace with technologically sophisticated criminals. Yet, the gap has closed considerably since 9/11.

GOVERNMENT SURVEILLANCE AND SEARCH IN PUBLIC SPACE

Closed Circuit Television Surveillance

Electronic surveillance has become a favored method to gather official data on persons. It entails law enforcement monitoring of public arenas and cyberspace. One such method is the use of closed circuit television (CCTV), which has grown exponentially in both private and public applications. For example, it is estimated there are over 2,400 CCTV cameras in New York City's Manhattan alone. American cities large and small are installing CCTV to monitor public spaces.

It is undeniable that official surveillance in public space affects individual privacy and anonymity; however, American courts have consistently held that persons have limited or no expectation of privacy in these locations. Some lower courts have raised the prospect of legal challenges on state constitutional privacy grounds, but that is a minority view.[37] More commonly, court analysis relies on the main tenets of the *Katz v. United States* expectation of privacy doctrine. Courts have found that CCTV surveillance in public spaces, such as shopping centers, parking lots, subways, airports, schools, and government buildings, is not an illegal invasion of privacy. If persons voluntarily enter those premises, they expose themselves to electronic watching and relinquish a general claim of privacy expectation. Not to mention, one's public persona is not protected by an expectation of privacy. However, courts have ruled there are some areas that should be shielded from cameras, such as toilets and dressing areas, because they have a much higher privacy expectation. Courts interpret the validity of government intrusion in public spaces based on the degree of personal privacy expectation, level of intrusion, and extent of government interest.

Suspicionless Searches on Public Premises

Police are allowed to stop persons in public places and establish roadblocks as long as they have reasonable suspicion, probable cause, or specific procedures that focus on a narrow public safety threat such as preventing driving under the influence of drug or alcohol. Otherwise, the Supreme Court has rejected the use of police roving patrols or checkpoints intended to detect ordinary criminal wrongdoing where no individualized suspicion exists. As Justice Sandra Day O'Connor explained in *City of Indianapolis v. Edmond* (2000), unless there is an exigency or "appropriately tailored roadblock setup to thwart an imminent terrorist attack or to catch a dangerous criminal who is likely to flee by way of a particular route," general checkpoints violate the Fourth Amendment.[38] Unbeknown to Justice O'Connor, such an imminent terrorist threat would become a reality on 9/11 and forever change police countermeasures.

Public Transportation Search

In 2004, terrorists bombed a commuter train in Madrid, Spain, killing hundreds of people. The following year on July 7, explosives were detonated on London's subway, again killing or wounding scores. Within two weeks, the New York City Police Department launched a program to conduct random suspicionless searches of passenger bags on its public subway system. A component of the search strategy entailed using portable monitors to detect traces of explosives.[39] A group of commuters filed a federal civil rights suit claiming the warrantless, suspicionless searches violated their Fourth Amendment rights. On appeal, the Second Circuit Court of Appeals in *MacWade v. Kelly* (2006) upheld the searches finding them to be valid under the special needs beyond law enforcement exception to the Fourth Amendment. The court stated, "... we hold that the Program is reasonable, and therefore constitutional, because (1) preventing a terrorist attack on the subway is a special need; (2) that need is weighty; (3) the Program is a reasonably effective deterrent; and (4) even though the searches intrude on a full privacy interest, they do so to a minimal degree."[40] The court did not conclude that passengers have a reduced expectation of privacy; it did, however, rule that the government's compelling interest in deterring terrorism outweighed rider privacy interests. Schools are also a location where surveillance is routinely used to protect children and prevent contraband from coming on campus.

School Monitoring and Search

Following the Supreme Court's lead in *New Jersey v. T.L.O.* (1985), lower courts have consistently ruled that reasonable suspicionless administrative searches of students and their belongings in public schools are constitutional.[41] This case established the special needs exception in Fourth Amendment jurisprudence and reasoned that students have a diminished expectation of privacy while at school. The school's need to maintain a controlled and safe environment outweighs student privacy interests in the Court's view. To achieve that objective the high Court reasoned that school administrators must not be encumbered by Fourth Amendment constraints, such as probable cause or warrant, and should be allowed to keep weapons, drugs, and other contraband out of the school.

Schools have become the focus of preventive law enforcement measures not only in the general interest of protecting students but because they have tragically been the site of deadly violence. For example, 2004–2005 government data show 21 homicides occurred on public school campuses, involving youth ages 5–18, and 81 percent of schools report incidences of violence.[42] Even more alarming is the 2007 shooting rampage at Virginia Polytechnic Institute and State University (Virginia Tech) where student Seung-Hui Cho killed 33 persons. Beginning at 7:15 A.M., Cho gunned down fellow students in a dormitory and an academic building before taking his own life.[43] In recent years there have been a number of highly publicized shooting incidences involving public school students. For some time, police departments have assigned resource officers to schools for security and campus crime intervention purposes. Other measures have also been used to promote school safety, including reducing student drug use. The Supreme Court authorized warrantless and suspicionless drug testing to deter students involved in extracurricular activities from using drugs.[44]

Airline Passenger Surveillance and Search Programs

Investigators determined that the nineteen 9/11 terrorists entered the United States with fraudulent travel documents and then used airliners as guided missiles taking aim at the World Trade Center Twin Towers and the Pentagon. Understandably, this caused security officials worldwide to focus more on commercial air travel as a terrorism risk environment. In the United States, new surveillance and screening programs were implemented to avert unlawful entry and protect airline passengers. As one report commented, "Travelers and workers at transportation facilities such as airports have come to be regarded as objects of suspicion, potential terrorists, and targets of surveillance."[45]

Airport Passenger Search

Generally, courts have ruled that airport suspicionless searches are not an unreasonable intrusion on passenger privacy. The screening involves x-ray, magnetometer metal detector, or cursory pat-down search to check passengers and their bags. This is generally settled law as courts have consistently ruled that these types of warrantless, suspicionless searches are valid if advance notice is provided. Informing passengers beforehand gives them the opportunity to avoid the search by not passing through the security checkpoint. Airport suspicionless searches are permissible using two justifications. First, government has a compelling special needs interest in deterring crime and terrorism on aircraft. Passengers who choose to board the aircraft are receiving notice and are giving consent to search.[46] This is the same legal rationale used to permit warrantless, suspicionless border searches. Often cited as the leading case on airport check-point searches, the court in *U.S. v. Edwards* (1974) explained,

> When the risk is jeopardy to hundreds of human lives and millions of dollars of property inherent in the pirating or blowing up of a large airplane, the danger alone meets the test of reasonableness, so long as the search is conducted in good faith for the purpose of preventing hijacking or like damage and with reasonable scope and the passenger has been given advance notice of his liability to such a search so that he can avoid it by choosing not to travel by air.[47]

Officials use scanning technology to detect dangerous weapons before passengers enter an aircraft. Recently, a number of U.S. airports began using clothes-penetrating backscatter x-rays that scan the passenger's body for weapons that would be ordinarily missed by metal detectors. Called a virtual strip search, Thomas Frank explains,

> The scanners bounce harmless 'millimeter waves' off passengers who are selected to stand inside a portal with arms raised after clearing the metal detector. A . . . screener in a nearby room views the black-and-white image and looks for objects . . . that are shaded differently from the body. [Officials say they] protect privacy by blurring passenger' faces and delete images right after viewing. Yet the images are detailed, clearly showing a person's gender.[48]

Passenger Name Records

Human surveillance methods such as passenger behavioral profiling and screening through known threat watch lists were instituted after 9/11. Authorities relied on commercial air carriers and global computerized reservation systems for passenger data while federal homeland security officials developed personal traveler dossiers known as Passenger Name Record. The profiles contain a substantial amount of personal information regarding the traveler, itinerary, method of payment, and air travel details such as requested medical assistance or special diet. Additionally, federal authorities required Advance Passenger Information from airlines to facilitate watch list comparison on all international flights to the United States.

Secure Flight Program

At the same time, homeland security officials launched passenger pre-screening programs to identify potential threats. Thus far, each plan has been abandoned due to widespread problems. Yet, the one program scheduled to be reintroduced is the Secure Flight regime that checks passenger data against threat, no-fly, and selectee watch lists maintained by the FBI's Terrorist Screening Center. Estimates are that in 2006 the program screened approximately 270 million travelers each month against a combined watch list containing around 700,000 names. Following a Government Accounting Office report citing flaws in watch list and screening accuracy and inadequate privacy controls, Secure Flight was suspended in 2006. Officials announced plans to later reintroduce the program with improved guidelines for implementation.[49]

US-VISIT Program

A second program was introduced in 2004 to monitor foreign visitors entering the United States at air, sea, and land border points. Named the United States Visitor and Immigrant Status Indicator Technology (US-VISIT), the system checks foreign VISA applicants, including nationals from VISA waiver countries, against criminal and terrorist lists before granting entry. The program requires the foreign visitor to provide biometric and biographical information such as digital photograph and fingerprint scan of all 10 fingers prior to arrival. US-VISIT is designed to monitor entry and reentry of foreign nationals visiting the United States. By verifying identity and prescreening visitors, it is intended to secure national borders and reduce the likelihood of criminals and terrorists gaining admission.

Clearly, these surveillance and search measures impinge on passenger privacy, yet they have been upheld by the courts based mostly on a special needs rationale. Beyond public venues, government electronic surveillance applications have increased significantly in recent years.

GOVERNMENT ELECTRONIC SURVEILLANCE METHODS

Many of the modern surveillance and investigative technologies, including CCTV, had been in existence for years before being adopted by criminal justice officials to fight crime and terrorism. Although police had their own set of investigation devices, nascent technologies originally developed for intelligence or military applications have been added to the law enforcement repertoire.[50]

Biometric Measure Technology

Humans have relied on individual physical characteristics to differentiate one another for thousands of years. Historical records show that Babylonian and Chinese merchants used fingerprints to bind transactions as early as 500 B.C.E.

By the 1870s, French criminalist Alphonse Bertillon had introduced his anthropometry identification method that used body measurements to identify criminal offenders. It was replaced by fingerprint classification in the early twentieth century when adopted by police and prison officials. In the 1960s, automated identification systems were developed leading to a scientific explosion by the end of the century.[51]

Labeled as nature's barcode, biometric measures consist of methods to identify and verify persons based on their unique physiological or behavioral traits. The science is based on the assumption that each person has distinctive characteristics that will reveal his or her identity. Biometric measures are divided into two branches—physiological and behavioral. Physiological modalities consist of analysis of fingerprint, DNA, facial, eye, walk, sweat pore, body geometry, odor detection, and thermography. Behavioral modalities include speaker, handwriting, and keystroke analysis.

Physiological Modalities

For over a century, fingerprint identification has been a mainstay in criminal investigation. In 1999, the FBI launched the Integrated Automated Fingerprint Identification System that classifies, compares, and disseminates digital fingerprint images across a network of criminal justice agencies. Though the physical characteristics of the print remain unchanged, computerized images can be quickly and accurately processed through criminal databases and stored indefinitely.

DNA profiling was developed by the British scientist Alec Jeffreys in 1985. Since each body cell contains genetic materials, the typing method isolates and reads DNA markers from trace biological samples such as body fluids or tissue cells. Profiling techniques have evolved since first developed and are able to match DNA samples with an accuracy that surpasses other human identification measures. In 1998, the FBI introduced the Combined DNA Index System that enables networked crime laboratories to match DNA sample profiles from crime scenes with those of known criminals in the nationwide database.[52]

Facial analysis methods include geometric mapping of the face or ear. Facial applications use a computer algorithm to geometrically map the digital image of an individual's face to confirm identity or alert to a recognized person of interest based on a match in its database. Once the system has isolated the facial image, it measures nodal points, such as the distance or ratios between designated chin, eye, or cheekbone sites, and compares those dimensions to facial geometric profiles in the government database.[53] By 2000, automated systems using face recognition technology, Eigenface, and hidden Markov model computer algorithms were in use.[54] Similarly, ear mapping is an identification technique that relies on discrete biometric measurements.

Eye analysis consists of two types—iris and retina scanning. Both techniques use algorithms to map the unique features of the iris or retina and are utilized for verification of identity. Iris recognition analyzes the random pattern of the iris muscle, which has distinctive characteristics. The system relies on infrared lighting and captures a digital image of the iris. Computer formulas then measure and calculate the features into an Iriscode, which is used to verify identity by matching a code in its database. Retinal recognition methods scan and map blood vessel patterns in the eye. Once a digital image is captured, the retinal verification process is similar to iris matching.[55] In 2005, testing began on the iris-on-the-move technology, which uses a camera to obtain a digital image of a person's iris from a distance, then analyzes its pattern for identification or verification. Increasingly, airports and other facilities are using iris scans to verify identity before giving personnel access to secure areas.

Other physiological methods include body geometry that uses mapping techniques to measure hand dimensions or plot vascular patterns in the face or eye. Sweat pore pattern mapping is also being developed as a biometric method to identify persons. Thermographic modes measure physiological heat signatures. One experimental application involves using body temperature fluctuation, along with other psychophysiological indicia, to detect deception in the same manner as polygraph.[56] Two additional methods to determine or verify identity are individual odor detection and walk or gait traits. The latter profiles a person's distinctive walking patterns and matches digital images with a database profile.

Behavioral Modalities

There are three principal behavioral modalities that measure individual characteristics—speaker, handwriting, and keystroke. Voice recognition techniques were developed in the 1970s but are substantially more sophisticated today because of advanced computer processing. Speaker recognition is a biometric measure based on combined physiological-behavioral influences, whereas speech analysis examines spoken word patterns. Speaker recognition applications rely on the physical vocal tract and individual behavioral traits together. Each speaker produces unique acoustic sounds that are resonances stemming from an interface between an individual's vocal tract, airway, nasal, jaw, and tongue dimension and motion. Though susceptible to distortion when intercepted through dynamic audio collection, this method is inexpensive and can be effective if compared to a quality exemplar in the database. To use this method, the suspect's voice sample must be collected in compliance with electronic communication interception laws. Hence, if the control sample is collected voluntarily, the person simply records predetermined spoken phrases to be used for matching with samples obtained in the field.[57]

Handwriting and keystroke are two other behavioral methods that measure finger or hand use patterns during handwriting or keyboarding. These functions are believed to be affected by behavioral influences. Handwriting analysis is a long-standing forensic investigation method used to detect counterfeit documents. Biometric comparisons look for distinctive writing or keyboard typing motions to identify or verify persons.

Official use of automated biometric measures is increasing. In spite of challenges to their accuracy, more agencies are adopting surveillance regimens that include biometrics. Their acceptance is due in part to the premise that all persons possess physical and behavioral characteristics that are unique. Together, these traits form one's identity; therefore, official use of biometric measures affects privacy interests. With the exception perhaps of DNA sample collection, most of the biometric methods rely on informed consent or are captured in public places through electronic video surveillance. Only DNA specimen collection and eye analysis methods are intrusive, whereas the other measures generally are not. Hence, in spite of the potential loss of anonymity and the chilling effect of being electronically monitored, few privacy safeguards are available to persons unless biometric samples are obtained by government officials through coercion, deception, unlawful interception, or illegal search and seizure. These measures are designed to be used in settings that are considered probable transit or target locations for criminals and terrorists.

Other surveillance methods are being utilized by law enforcement officials to scan motor vehicles and persons in public places with the aim of identifying known or potential criminal or terrorist threats.

Recognition Technology

Two primary forms of recognition technology are used by police to monitor possible threats or compare information against watch lists of known criminals, terrorists, or stolen motor vehicles. Using CCTV video image data, computer algorithms compare the information to stored watchlist records. One application is the Automated License Plate Recognition (ALPR) system originally developed in the 1970s. Units are either fixed location, remote, or mobile. It works in conjunction with CCTV or road-rule enforcement video images to optically recognize license plate characters and then process them through police computer databases. Camera systems can be equipped with infrared technology to ensure images are readable regardless of lighting conditions and can also be configured to photograph the driver. Other ALPR applications include recording toll road usage, parking usage, and traffic violations.[58]

These systems are being employed by a growing number of American police agencies. The New York City Police Department introduced Operation Sentinel in 2008, which uses ALPR technology, coupled with radiation sensors, to monitor all vehicles entering Manhattan from a 50-mile radius around New York City.[59] This program joins the Lower Manhattan Security Initiative launched in 2007 that is installing scores of police-monitored CCTV surveillance cameras in Manhattan patterned after London's ring of steel that electronically blankets the center city.

A second recognition category is the biometric applications, which pair digital images with physiological measures to determine identity. In spite of the interest expressed by officials in using the technology, research has shown it is susceptible to error based on the quality of captured image depending on lighting or pose. A pilot study in Boston's Logan Airport showed approximately a 61 percent accuracy rate using digital photographic images.[60]

Both of these surveillance and identification methods can be interfaced with any source of digital imaging. Depending on the computer algorithm-based threat assessment or database, police officials can capture digital camera images of persons, license plates, or other objects in public places to identify suspects. Homeland security officials plan to integrate face recognition technology in the US-VISIT and REAL ID programs to compare digital photographs with watchlist databases. Officials have also devoted substantial resources to monitoring and gathering comprehensive data sets from a number of electronic sources.

GOVERNMENT SURVEILLANCE AND DATA MINING

Computer Surveillance and Search

Everyday use of electronic communications has grown exponentially in recent years. Internet usage and e-messaging have replaced earlier forms of information exchange. The expansion of cyberspace and virtual platforms is stunning as more Americans rely on computing for personal and business communications. Not only has the World Wide Web become a global marketplace and primary information source for legitimate transactions, but it is also a favorite of criminals and terrorists. They use it for communication, information, propaganda, and as a criminal instrument. For that reason, police are monitoring cyber activity using several approaches. First, with a search warrant investigators are able to seize criminal evidence stored on a computer. Computer drives can contain illegal files or graphics such as child pornography, or the computer itself can be an instrument used to commit cyber crime. Though computer investigations require a trained specialist, the legal rules governing search and seizure of criminal evidence generally apply here as well. In rare cases, warrantless computer searches may be authorized in exigent circumstances where a person is considered in imminent danger.

Second, law enforcement officials conduct computer surveillance of individual suspect computers or through networks. For instance, pen register and trap and trace devices can be surreptitiously installed on a computer to record IP addresses of the Web sites accessed. As authorized by the USA Patriot Act, police officials are permitted to use a sneak and peek warrant to enter the suspect's premises and covertly affix the tracking device.

Computer traffic can be tracked from a network using wiretapping methods such as packet sniffing software to locate and route certain information or evidence, as authorized by the court order. The most notorious of the black box–type sniffing programs was the FBI's Carnivore, later named DCS-1000. It was introduced in 2000 and was designed to monitor user e-mail and Internet traffic using a specific filter surveillance protocol. Amid a torrent of criticism, the FBI abandoned the program and has since opted to use commercial software and private vendors to conduct this type of monitoring.

One of the most difficult problems encountered in police computer surveillance or search is dealing with encrypted information. Key logger programs are used to circumvent encryption by recording keyboard user keystrokes. Originally, the device was manually installed to capture passwords so investigators could gain access to computer login codes or stored files. Since 2001, the FBI has utilized the Magic Lantern method that sends a Trojan horse virus to the target computer over the Internet and uses an imbedded key logger program to remotely record and transmit keystrokes. This enables the police to access the de-encryption information without making physical intrusion. Courts have authorized the use of key logger devices so long as they do not violate provisions of federal surveillance laws.[61]

Third, law enforcement officials may request computer user data from Internet Service Providers using Patriot Act NSLs in foreign intelligence and counterterrorism investigations or with a court-issued subpoena.

Dataveillance and Data Mining

After 9/11, authorities emphasized the need to obtain as much information as possible to identify potential criminal suspects, terrorists, and homeland security threats. New data mining models are designed to collect information from three sources—biographic, transaction, and biometric. This approach combines electronic and physical surveillance with "dataveillance," which Roger Clarke describes as "the systematic use of personal data systems in the investigation or monitoring of . . . persons."[62] The strategy collects data in all three areas, which together constitute a complete profile of the person. It consists of a multipart method that monitors, collects, and analyzes information from many sources to assess a person's crime or terrorism risk.

Individual dossiers contain a wealth of biographical data including name, date of birth, physical descriptors, and identification numbers. They also hold biometric identifiers such as digital photograph, iris scan, and digital fingerprint, which can be easily stored, matched, and disseminated using computer programs. Last, transactional history shows employment status, credit history, use of government services, travel patterns, financial transactions, and consumer habits that when combined depict the person's identity and overall activities.

Much of the data is collected from electronic surveillance and documents obtained by government agencies or in collaboration with commercial sources. In what Peter Swire, a Clinton administration privacy counselor, refers to as the security-industrial complex, private data collection entrepreneurs have entered into agreements with government agencies to provide a cornucopia of consumer and transactional data from the everyday activities of ordinary citizens. Not only are marquis data collection companies such as Choice-Point, LexisNexis, and Equifax involved in these joint ventures, but the surveillance industry is also booming as technology firms offer advanced monitoring devices to interested government agencies.[63] With the exception of unlawful electronic communication interception, private companies are able to track and gather consumer and transaction information without the legal constraints imposed on government officials. Hence, law enforcement and other government agencies purchase personal information from data collection companies and avoid many of the Fourth Amendment or electronic surveillance legal obstacles they would encounter in a criminal investigation. In sum, the burgeoning personal data industry holds a reservoir of information that government dataveillance operations consider a highly prized commodity.

Data Mining Programs

A number of government programs in criminal justice, intelligence, and defense rely on data mining to collect information. Ultimately, the goal is to meld the data from the primary sources to create a composite of the person. For example, Department of Defense programs such as Total Information Awareness, involving all three data areas, and Iraqi Biometric Scan, which collects biographic and biometric data using the Automated Biometric Identification System, depend on the development of these profiles to analyze threats or catalog identities of known or suspected combatants, insurgents, or terrorists. Similarly, intelligence organizations such as the Central Intelligence Agency or National Security Agency utilize a variety of surveillance methods to acquire profile data on persons of interest.

In criminal justice, particularly after 9/11, intelligence and investigation functions depend on this comprehensive information approach. Government program applications like US-VISIT screening protocols, REAL ID cards, and the Automated Targeting System (ATS) all rely on multiple data sources. For instance, ATS was launched in the 1990s, automated in 2002, and originally designed to be a cargo screening tool for U.S. Customs and Border Protection to evaluate materials that may pose a threat to the nation. However, Homeland Security officials in 2006 modified the system to create a terrorist risk rating formula and perform screening of both inbound and outbound cargo, travelers, and conveyances. The model assigns a risk assessment score to all import and export merchandise and every vessel, vehicle, aircraft, train, or passenger, crew, and operator that enters or exits the United States. In its current form, ATS maintains a voluminous database, and its risk profiles and scores will be kept for 40 years unable to be inspected or reviewed. In spite of the past inaccuracies and flaws with counterterrorism threat profile regimes, this ambitious program to evaluate and catalog millions of people and pieces of merchandise illustrates the comprehensive goal of this generation of data gathering.[64]

A host of other technologies and strategies are being used to gather unprecedented amounts of information on persons with the view of channeling it into police intelligence fusion centers. In 2004, state and federal law enforcement planners began establishing regional criminal intelligence fusion centers. Currently there are 38 centers located around the nation. A Department of Homeland Security report states,

> A fusion center is an effective and efficient mechanism to exchange information and intelligence . . . to fight crime and terrorism by merging data from a variety of sources . . . The ultimate goal is to provide a mechanism through which government, law enforcement, public safety, and the private sector can come together with a common purpose and improve the ability to safeguard our homeland and prevent criminal activity.[65]

This approach gathers information from virtually every public and private sector entity including financial, health, education, retail, public record, travel, leisure, law enforcement, and courts. In fact, some fusion center information sources include partnerships with high-profile companies such as Fidelity Investments and Microsoft Corporation.[66]

Due to advancing technology, troves of personal information are getting easier to collect, store, and share while justice officials are working to take advantage of more powerful microprocessors, radio-frequency identification technology, unmanned surveillance, satellite location tracking, and nanotechnology.[67]

SURVEILLANCE AND PRIVACY EFFECTS

All told, the post-9/11 world is extremely unpredictable and dangerous, leading government officials to take extraordinary measures to protect the public from new crime and terrorism threats. At the same time, globalization effects contribute to increasing interdependence among societies and have transformed information into a valuable commodity. Advanced technology changed the way people communicate and manage their daily lives. This is true for criminals, crime fighters, and the public at large. Now more than ever, a person's identity, social life, work life, and transactional activities are digitized, divulged, and prone to be outsourced or transmitted around the physical and virtual world. Conversion of people's lives to electronic digital bytes has in many ways relegated anonymity and privacy to a secondary status after being upstaged by government's compelling need to detect, investigate, and prosecute adversaries at all costs. Due to unknown or elusive crime and terrorism threats, officials have extended their net of suspicion to include most members of society, even those once considered beyond reproach. This is evidenced by the ubiquity of official surveillance that monitors the public, and often private, activities of society. No longer is anyone immune from suspicion or scrutiny as police strive to anticipate and thwart the next move of unknown crime and terrorism threats.

To say that civil liberty and privacy interests are being affected by official countermeasures and millennial threats is an understatement. Yet, in spite of efforts by government officials, law makers, and courts to strike a satisfactory balance between public safety and privacy rights, widespread surveillance has rendered some aspects of individual privacy a casualty of the war on global crime and terrorism.

Chapter 8

NAVIGATING THE NEW PRIVACY PARADIGM

I n spite of general agreement that privacy rights exist, and perhaps are inviolate, harmonizing meaning and interpretation continues to be difficult. Nonetheless, many legal experts and courts agree that some personal activities fall within a zone of privacy that should be protected from government intrusion.[1] Clearly, the Framers knew there was a need for protection from unreasonable government searches. At the time, Fourth Amendment provisions were considered sufficient if they safeguarded persons and their possessions from improper official intrusion. Since then, however, privacy principles have been incorporated into search and seizure law. And because of changes in crime, technology, and society, it became necessary to regularly refine privacy safeguards. As a result, they continue to evolve as surveillance and search have a different meaning today than they did 200 years ago.

Many of these same forces exerted pressure on the equilibrium between individual privacy rights and crime control methods, leading to the emergence of a new privacy paradigm. There are several circumstances that caused this transformation. Changes in modern crime and terrorism have provided part of the impetus for conditions that directly affect the privacy–criminal justice relationship. Inasmuch as crime and criminals have changed, so have the methods of crime fighting. Combined with modifications in laws and police practices, these factors have impacted the state of privacy in America in noticeable ways.

TRANSFORMATION IN CONTEMPORARY CRIME

Whether motivated by power, jealousy, or greed, people have been committing crimes since the advent of communal life. Although there are always unexplained fluctuations in crime types and rates, the general nature of crime is understood by criminologists. Even though there are many theories proffered to explain the causes, few hypotheses reveal how criminal behavior is different today than in the past. If the irreducible determinants of criminality are so enduring, then what has changed to make the current circumstances dissimilar?

Two factors provide insight into the transformation of contemporary crime in America—globalization and technology. There is a two-fold explanation that attributes facets of the modern crime phenomenon to the effects of globalization. First, all of the current interdependency witnessed in commerce, finance, and information sharing stems, in part, from what Thomas L. Friedman calls the "flattening of the world."[2] A natural by-product of this connectivity is a shrinking social distance between people in the physical and virtual world. Whether face-to-face or through the Internet, people are closer now than ever. The postmodern world has brought diverse cultures, norms, politics, and religions in close proximity. And pursuit of economic prosperity has fueled substantial global migration that brings native and diaspora populations near one another in an unprecedented way. On the one hand, such closeness fosters acceptance or tolerance among diverse peoples, while on the other it breeds enmity and conflict.

For example, at the root of radical Islamist disdain for Western societies is a clash between political-cultural ideologies. Western political models focus on secularism and capitalism, while Islamist fundamentalists advocate a puritanical theocracy that rejects corrupt Western values and emphasizes a self-described righteousness. Much of the contact between Muslim and Western cultures today is through migration bound for Western countries or electronic media exposure.[3]

A second part of the globalization equation is the explosive growth of advanced technology, particularly innovations in telecommunication. Technologies have revolutionized the way people around the world communicate, share information, and conduct business. They are a vital component in the operation of global finance, business, and government systems. Computing and electronic communication devices have become indispensable tools in the everyday lives of many people worldwide. Their widespread use provides benefits but also makes users more vulnerable to criminal victimization.

This generation of criminals is also a beneficiary of the technology revolution. In the world of criminals and terrorists, technology has two primary functions. First, computing, telecommunications, and global electronic networks are criminal facilitators used to promote nefarious objectives. Criminal actors take advantage of cellular telephony, electronic messaging, e-purchasing, remote banking, and dissemination of information and propaganda to direct criminal and terrorist enterprises.[4] They use these devices no differently than law-abiding citizens, aside from being utilized for illicit purposes.

Second, technologies are criminal instruments that become a means to commit cybercrime, identity theft, fraud, unlawful cloning, and other crimes. The crimes can be perpetrated from remote foreign locations, which not only extends the reach of the criminal but complicates police investigation and prosecution. Together, these factors enable criminals and terrorists to have unprecedented global access through the use of technology. The proliferation of telecommunications allows criminals to be more effective, and in some cases, transform local crime into transnational enterprises. This occurs not only with more sophisticated organized crime networks but through connections to local crime. Even some hometown drug peddlers obtain their contraband from foreign sources. For instance, all cocaine substances originate in the Andean mountain regions of Latin America since that is the only place where the coca plant will grow. Hence, every cocaine seller in the world is ultimately linked to transnational drug networks. Likewise, the nineteen 9/11 terrorists carried passports from several countries, planned their attacks in Germany, and carried them out in the United States. An increasing amount of the crime and terrorism that threatens America has a transnational dimension.

CRIMINAL JUSTICE RESPONSE TO CHANGING THREATS

Units of the criminal justice system are charged with protecting society from crime and terrorism. This is a long-standing obligation; however, in recent years they have faced mounting challenges. Some are old problems with a new twist, while others were previously unknown. Whether it is HIV-infected prison inmates or global terrorism plots, contemporary criminal justice officials have been forced to alter their ideologies and operational methods. Though venerable best practices are still effective, new adversaries demand innovative responses.

On 9/11, an unfamiliar threat completely revised the interpretation of national security. Reg Whitaker explains, "Al Qaeda is a contemporary product of globalization: flexible, adaptable, diversified, transnational, de-centered, a network of networks."[5] Officials have been called upon to think outside of the box and devise effective measures to combat such global menaces as illicit drug trafficking, transnational organized crime, and Islamist terrorism. To make matters worse, some analysts suggest that these groups collaborate at different levels to further their own objectives.[6] The situation called for sweeping changes. Some had already begun decades earlier but were accelerated by the events of 9/11.

Technology Adaptation

One of the first moves was to encourage justice agencies to utilize more technology. Its use in many criminal justice organizations has been virtually nonexistent or woefully inadequate. As the 9/11 Commission discovered, many intelligence and police organizations are territorial and adversarial with one another, not to mention being technologically primitive.[7] Criminal justice organizations are using more technology, and after 9/11, federal homeland security funds were available to assist with the cost and coordination. Meanwhile, police agencies shifted their ideology to a homeland security perspective with increasing emphasis on intelligence gathering and sharing.

Technology became a force multiplier as law enforcement agencies, courts, and correctional organizations relied more on computerized record keeping and electronic communication, offender monitoring, and surveillance to perform routine functions. Information became a valuable commodity that is shared with other agencies through networks, fusion centers, and multiagency task forces all in an effort to avert the intelligence failure that allowed the 9/11 terrorist attacks to occur. Though technology use by itself is not a panacea, it gave information discovery a new appeal in the functions of criminal justice. Science and technology were viewed as remedies for some of the vexing problems presented by sophisticated criminals and hidden threats. Even though science and crime fighting have a time-honored relationship, the current testing, monitoring, and surveillance capabilities are the most advanced in history. For criminal investigators, technology became a frontline crime-fighting tool. Its use has spread to many facets of crime control and offender management.

Threat Adaptation

By the 1960s, drug abuse joined the list of rising social and criminal hazards. Near the end of the century, technology and transnational crimes followed, only to be surpassed by global terrorism on 9/11. It is not unprecedented for groups or crimes to be ranked as greater threats. For instance, during the Cold War, Soviet espionage was classified by the FBI as a high-priority hazard. In every case, threat assessments focus on the named danger and often spawn anticrime campaigns as in the war on drugs in the 1970s.

The post-9/11 circumstances differ because public safety threats stem from several complex and unpredictable types of crime and terrorism. One of these imminent perils is Islamist terrorism, which by its nature, involves highly committed militants willing to take extreme measures to carry out attacks. Never before had American police been asked to devise countermeasures for suicide bombing as part of routine crime control. Before 9/11, emergency response was designed to react to natural disasters, industrial accidents, and traffic crashes. Ordinarily, first responders were not trained for anthrax, dirty bombs, or terrorist attacks on public transportation. Police tactical response teams, before 9/11, were prepared to deal with hostage situations and an occasional high-risk drug raid, not terrorists per se. Airport security measures did not include see-through x-ray scan and biometric identification before 9/11; that has all changed.

Criminal justice officials have been obliged to adapt threat assessments to include all of these risks. Given the events of 9/11 and the method of operation of covert terrorists, police have been forced to change the way they view public safety. For law enforcement, stereotypical profiles of criminal suspects alone are no longer effective because they are too narrow, if not overly presumptive. In an age of homeland security–centric approaches, a more encompassing perspective of crime risk is needed. Hence, officials widened their net of suspicion to include both traditional and nontraditional suspects. From that viewpoint, everyone is a potential crime or terrorism threat—from gangsters to airline passengers. Combined, all of these challenges were not only significantly amplified but became urgent matters on 9/11.

EMERGENCE OF THE NEW PRIVACY PARADIGM

Over 100 years ago legal commentators warned of the risks that emerging technology posed to individual privacy. For years, today's technological wonders existed only in the imagination of futuristic fiction writers such as H. G. Wells or George Lucas. Yet, the age of through-the-wall and backscatter x-ray probes, brain fingerprinting, thermal imaging, and satellite tracking are no longer the work of storytellers but actual surveillance and investigative tools used to combat crime and terrorism. Technology continues to impact the contours of personal privacy and has prompted the jurisprudence to change in response. Police eavesdropping in the 1920s and the use of a warrantless listening device in the 1960s led to momentous shifts in privacy law. With the 1968 *Katz* expectation of privacy doctrine came a different perspective on protection from unreasonable police search. In 1934 Congress began enacting surveillance statutes; however, since 9/11 a flood of new surveillance-centered legislation has been passed and that pattern continues to date.

It is one thing when people voluntarily divulge personal information by posting it on MySpace or YouTube, but it is an altogether different matter if law enforcement officials eavesdrop on private activities without a person's consent. The current world order has ushered in a new privacy paradigm. Privacy boundaries are being redrawn as courts and lawmakers alter the delicate balance between government powers and civil liberties in response to compelling public safety needs.

This is most evident in the functions of criminal justice. For a long time courts have signaled that persons accused of crime had diminished privacy rights. In the privacy–criminal justice relationship, the Fourth Amendment is the guidepost for lawful government surveillance, search, and seizure practices. The Supreme Court in the 1960s, however, substantially revised interpretation of the Amendment's fundamental tenets by creating additional exceptions to the original probable cause and warrant requirements. What followed was a pattern of revisionist interpretation of privacy and search and seizure law. A pivotal moment came when the Court established the special needs beyond law enforcement exception for warrantless, suspicionless school searches. As it turned out, that rationale has since been utilized by courts to justify a growing number of warrantless, suspicionless government drug testing, surveillance, and search activities.

Equipped with a widening net of suspicion, enhanced surveillance powers, and sophisticated eavesdropping technology, officials have adopted a total information awareness approach to crime fighting and counterterrorism. This modality has two critical prongs. First, dataveillance is part of the new strategy for ensuring public safety. Government officials, either unilaterally or in concert with private data management companies, have developed a voracious appetite for biographical, biometric, and transactional information on persons to assess their threat risk. Second, once obtained, the data must be analyzed if used effectively to prevent and investigate crime and terrorism. Thus, the need to collect, analyze, and disseminate volumes of information has created a neosecurity surveillance complex as a component of crime control. The trendy police lexicon for these functions is fusion center and intelligence-led policing, which promote an analysis-based solution to the challenge of translating raw information into usable intelligence that can be shared among agencies and applied in combating crime.[8]

The security surveillance complex has created a cottage industry for police analysts and surveillance-related devices. Law enforcement agencies are expanding their ranks of intelligence specialists who are responsible for analyzing and managing the flow of crime-related information. At the same time, the surveillance and data management industry is growing exponentially as the government demand for computer software and data mining, scanning, and monitoring gadgets steadily increases.

Each of these conditions has contributed to a transformation in the meaning of privacy right, and scope of its protection, in the midst of a technological and informational revolution.

FATE OF THE PRIVACY–CRIMINAL JUSTICE RELATIONSHIP

Clearly, shifting crime, technology, surveillance-centered crime control, and privacy interpretation are driving the transformation to a new privacy paradigm. The question is what does this portend for the future of individual privacy rights? Monitoring technology will become more pervasive in criminal justice functions. Not only is it an effective force multiplier for justice agencies, but it is a practical tool to enhance public and institutional safety. With correctional institutions increasingly congested, more tracking technology will be used to monitor and locate larger numbers of pretrial defendants or convicted offenders released in the community.

A growing array of surveillance, detection, recognition, and identification technologies are going to be used by police to prevent and investigate crimes, particularly as they become more available, affordable, and portable. Many agencies are using these devices to augment traditional law enforcement tasks, enhance personnel accountability, and promote safety. Identifying potential suspects and threats will remain a high priority for police given the dynamic and unpredictable nature of contemporary crime and terrorism. Therefore, surveillance strategies will become even more prominent in future preventive law enforcement. Due to the proliferation and vulnerability of electronic data in today's society, it is imperative that officials have the capability to conduct investigations in a digital environment.

Rapid advances in computing and telecommunications have given justice officials more intrusive tools to gather personal data on individuals and their activities. As public use of telecommunications increases, their susceptibility to cyber victimization and police surveillance grows in kind. The more persons store biographical, business, or biometric information in electronic records, microchips, or transmit data through virtual space, the greater likelihood of interception by government officials and criminal hackers. The trend toward more law enforcement information-oriented surveillance and data mining is not going to abate.

Likewise, new scanning, probing, tracking, identification, and verification technology is being developed at a rapid pace. And more powerful and intrusive surveillance technology is forthcoming. For example, Hitachi Corporation scientists recently developed a finger vein authentication program that maps the vascular pattern in the hand for identity verification. They claim the new technology is less intrusive than similar mapping protocols, while substantiating individual traits that cannot be fraudulently cloned.[9] Simply, the prognosis for individual anonymity is poor, and the expectation of privacy relative to criminal justice processes stands to be diminished further. At the same time, the nature of security threats will remain unpredictable and in a constant state of change.

For instance, some experts posit that radical Islamism will eventually wane, which may reduce the risk of terrorism, and yet, other threats will emerge.[10] Regardless of the menace, American police face one of the most fluid crime and crime-fighting conditions in their history. It is an understatement to say the task of protecting a large diverse population in an open democracy, while abiding by often vague guidelines in the enforcement of criminal law, is daunting. This same duty extends to justice components charged with prosecuting and managing criminal offenders. They too must effectively perform their function while ensuring constitutional and privacy protections. In spite of the challenges, assuring public safety is a fundamental responsibility of government; however, it is also bound to protect civil liberties.

For many years, writers have offered menacing forecasts predicting a dystopic society fraught with ubiquitous surveillance that leads to a complete loss of anonymity.[11] Such prognostications have contributed to popular culture ideas such as Orwell's Big Brother or M. G. Michael and K. Michael's überveillance, which describe an "always with you" depiction of government watching in a manner that has a chilling effect on personal privacy.[12] David Brin argues for more transparency, in the age of information, as his remedy for the stalemate between surveillance and privacy advocates.[13] Regardless of whether one subscribes to the loss-of-privacy or compromising-public-safety perspective, government's culture of surveillance will only proliferate so long as data mining and monitoring are viewed as effective crime control measures. All indications point in that direction. For some, allowing law enforcement to have greater access to personal information is an acceptable trade-off to keep society safe, manage criminals, and maintain the integrity of criminal justice personnel, whereas for others, the ubiquity and intrusiveness of official surveillance are intolerable invasions of privacy that offend democratic core values.

There are several undeniable truths in the discourse. First, the globalization and advanced technology effects witnessed in the beginning of the twenty-first century will grow at an astonishing rate. Second, both legitimate and illegitimate actors are going to remain beneficiaries of the information age, which has revolutionized business, personal, and criminal transactions. Third, contemporary crime and terrorism will be persistent long-term public threats and a challenge for crime fighters. Fourth, in administering criminal justice, the system will gradually, yet unevenly, adapt to new public safety models, technologies, and crime hazards. These modifications will result in the progressive expansion of the net of suspicion, use of surveillance technology, and erosion of individual expectation of privacy. In the new privacy paradigm, government officials have more private information on persons than ever in history.

It has never been more important to hold criminal justice officials accountable for the safe and lawful collection, handling, and maintenance of private data, not to mention their databases swollen with personal information. At the same time, a right to privacy will undergo perpetual reevaluation as courts and lawmakers struggle to find a satisfactory balance between public safety and civil liberties in a rapidly changing world. The last bastion of defense is the court whose responsibility it is to ensure a proper equilibrium between official surveillance authority and individual privacy rights in the administration of criminal justice.

If contemporary history is an accurate guide, privacy rights will continue to diminish, but not evaporate, for those affected by criminal justice processes. Perhaps suspects of all kinds will be *under a watchful eye* in the surveillance-rich world to come.

NOTES

FOREWORD

1. Henry Black, *Black's Law Dictionary,* abridged 6th ed. (St. Paul, MN: West Publishing, 1991), 829.

2. *Griswold v. Connecticut,* 381 U.S. 479 (1965).

3. Id.

INTRODUCTION

1. *Olmstead v. United States,* 277 U.S. 438 (1928).

2. *Winston v. Lee,* 470 U.S. 753 (1985).

3. Daniel Solove, "A Taxonomy of Privacy," *University of Pennsylvania Law Review* 154 (2006): 477.

4. Samuel D. Warren and Louis D. Brandeis, "The Right to Privacy," *Harvard Law Review* 4 (1890): 193.

5. Electronic Privacy Information Center, *Privacy & Human Rights: An International Survey of Privacy Laws and Developments* (Washington, DC: Electronic Information Privacy Center and Privacy International, 2006).

6. Barrington Moore, *Privacy: Studies in Social and Cultural History* (New York: Pantheon Books, 1984).

7. William Blackstone, *Ehrlich's Blackstone* (San Carlos, CA: Nourse Publishing, 1959).

8. Craig R. Ducat, *Constitutional Interpretation,* 8th ed. (Belmont, CA: Thomson/West, 2004).

9. Robert Allen Rutland, *The Birth of the Bill of Rights 1776–1791* (New York: Collier Books, 1962).

10. Alan F. Westin, *Privacy and Freedom* (New York: Atheneum, 1967).

11. Robert C. Post, "The Social Foundations of Privacy: Community and Self in the Common Law Tort," *California Law Review* 77 (1989): 957.

12. Daniel J. Solove, Marc Rotenberg, and Paul M. Schwartz, *Information Privacy Law,* 2nd ed. (New York: Aspen Publishers, 2006), 39.

13. John C. Domino, *Civil Rights and Liberties in the 21st Century,* 2nd ed. (New York: Longman, 2003), 1.

14. Carla Hall, "Restraining Order against Pedophile OK'd," *Los Angeles Times,* August 4, 2007, http://articles.latimes.com/2007/aug/04/local/me-mcclellan4 (accessed August 28, 2007); Richard Winton, "Avowed Pedophile Released; City Says Court Order Was Flawed," *Los Angeles Times,* August 22, 2007, http://articles.latimes.com/2007/aug/22/local/me-mcclellan22 (accessed August 28, 2007).

15. David F. Musto, *The American Disease: Origins of Narcotic Control,* 3rd ed. (New York: Oxford University Press, 1999).

16. President's Commission on Law Enforcement and Administration of Justice, *The Challenge of Crime in a Free Society* (Washington, DC: U.S. Government Printing Office, 1967).

17. Ted Gest, *Crime & Politics: Big Government's Erratic Campaign for Law and Order* (New York: Oxford University Press, 2001).

18. David Lyon, *Surveillance Society: Monitoring Everyday Life* (Buckingham, UK: Open University Press, 2001); William Bloss, "Escalating U.S. Police Surveillance after 9/11: An Examination of Causes and Effects," *Surveillance and Society* 4 (2007): 208.

19. Louise Shelley, "The Globalization of Crime," in *Introduction to International Criminal Justice,* ed. Mangai Natarajan (Boston: McGraw-Hill Publishing, 2005), 3–10.

20. George Orwell, *Nineteen Eighty-Four, A Novel* (New York: Harcourt, Brace, 1949).

21. Protect America Act of 2007, Public Law 110-55, 121 Stat. 552; Foreign Intelligence Surveillance Act of 1978, 50 U.S.C. § 1801 et seq; Elliot D. Cohen, "Why Haven't the Mainstream Corporate Media Covered the AT&T/NSA Domestic Spying Program?" (2007), www.buzzflash.com/articles/contributors/1232 (accessed September 10, 2007).

22. Michael D. Lyman, *Criminal Investigation: The Art and Science,* 5th ed. (Upper Saddle River, NJ: Pearson/Prentice-Hall, 2007).

23. "Biometrics History," The Biometric Consortium (2006), http://www.biometrics.gov/documents/biohistory.pdf (accessed July 5, 2007).

24. Richard Saferstein, *Criminalistics: An Introduction to Forensic Science,* 9th ed. (Upper Saddle River, NJ: Pearson/Prentice-Hall, 2007).

25. Christian Parenti, *The Soft Cage: Surveillance in America from Slavery to the War on Terror* (New York: Basic Books, 2003), 120.

26. Erich Taylor, "A New Wave of Police Interrogation? Brain Fingerprinting, the Constitutional Privilege against Self-Incrimination and Hearsay Jurisprudence," *University of Illinois Journal of Law, Technology & Policy* Fall (2006): 287; Lawrence A. Farwell, "The Role of Brain Fingerprinting in Criminal Proceedings," (2005), http://brainwavescience.com (accessed July 17, 2007).

27. Walter Laqueur, *The New Terrorism: Fanaticism and the Arms of Mass Destruction* (Oxford, UK: Oxford University Press, 1999).

28. Gerald L. Posner, *Why America Slept: The Failure to Prevent 9/11* (New York: Random House, 2003).

29. William L. Prosser, "Privacy," *California Law Review* 48 (1960): 383.

30. *Skinner v. Railway Labor Executives' Ass'n,* 489 U.S. 602 (1989).

31. *Olmstead v. United States.*

32. David Hume, *Enquiries Concerning the Human Understanding and Concerning the Principles of Morals* (Oxford, UK: Clarendon Press, 1936), 109.

33. James Swenson, *On Jean-Jacques Rousseau: Considered One of the First Authors of the Revolution* (Stanford, CA: Stanford University Press, 2000).

34. Jeffrey Rosen, *The Unwanted Gaze: The Destruction of Privacy in America* (New York: Random House, 2000).

35. Robert O'Harrow, Jr., *No Place to Hide* (New York: Free Press, 2005).

36. Roger Clarke, "Biometrics and Privacy" (2001), www.rogerclarke.com/DV/Biometrics.html (accessed March 3, 2007).

37. Michelle Lirtzman, "Surveillance Cameras Win Broad Support," *ABC News,* July 29, 2007, www.abcnews.go.com/US/story?id=3422372&page=1 (accessed August 4, 2007).

CHAPTER 1

1. *Katz v. United States,* 389 U.S. 347 (1967).

2. Richard Hixson, *Privacy in a Public Society: Human Rights in Conflict* (New York: Oxford University Press, 1987).

3. Philip L. Reichel, *Comparative Criminal Justice Systems: A Topical Approach,* 5th ed. (Upper Saddle River, NJ: Pearson, 2008).

4. John Hamilton Baker, *An Introduction to English Legal History,* 3rd ed. (London: Butterworths, 1990).

5. Page Keeton and William Lloyd Prosser, *Prosser and Keeton on the Law of Torts,* 5th ed. (St. Paul, MN: West Publishing, 1984).

6. William L. Prosser, *Handbook of the Law of Torts,* 4th ed. (St. Paul, MN: West Publishing, 1971).

7. William Searle Holdsworth, *A History of English Law,* 2nd ed. (New York: Macmillan, 1937), 311.

8. Baker, *An Introduction to English Legal History.*

9. Lee Epstein and Thomas G. Walker, *Constitutional Law for a Changing America: Rights, Liberties, and Justice* (Washington, DC: CQ Press, 2004), 101.

10. U.S. Constitution, Amendment IV.

11. *United States v. Lefkowitz,* 285 U.S. 452 (1932).

12. *Stanley v. Georgia,* 394 U.S. 557 (1969).

13. U.S. Constitution, Amendment V.

14. Id.

15. U.S. Constitution, Amendment XIV.

16. John H. F. Shattuck, *Rights of Privacy* (Skokie, IL: National Textbook Co., 1977), iii.

17. *Olmstead v. United States.*

18. *Griswold v. Connecticut.*

19. Ducat, *Constitutional Interpretation,* 707.

20. Thomas McIntyre Cooley, *Torts,* 2nd ed. (Chicago: Callahan, 1881), 91.

21. Warren and Brandeis, "The Right to Privacy," 193.

22. Id., 193, 194.

23. *Union Pacific Railway Co. v. Botsford,* 141 U.S. 250 (1891).

24. Michael A. Weinstein, "The Uses of Privacy in the Good Life," in *Privacy,* ed. Roland Pennock and John Chapman (New York: Atherton Press, 1971), 92–109, 94.

25. Charles Fried, *An Anatomy of Values: Problem of Personal and Social Choice* (Cambridge, MA: Harvard Press, 1970), 140.

26. Westin, *Privacy and Freedom,* 7.

27. David M. O'Brien, *Privacy, Law, and Public Policy* (New York: Praeger, 1979), 5.

28. Prosser, "Privacy," 383, 389.

29. Robert Allen Rutland, *The Birth of the Bill of Rights 1776–1791* (Chapel Hill: North Carolina Press, 1955).

30. *Olmstead v. United States.*

31. Epstein and Walker, *Constitutional Law for a Changing America,* 516.

32. *Katz v. United States.*

33. William S. McAninch, "Unreasonable Expectations: The Supreme Court and the Fourth Amendment," *Stetson Law Review* 20 (1991): 435.

34. Brian J. Serr, "Great Expectations of Privacy: A New Model for Fourth Amendment Protection," *Minnesota Law Review* 73 (1989): 583.

35. *California v. Ciraolo,* 476 U.S. 207 (1986).

36. *California v. Greenwood,* 486 U.S. 35 (1988).

37. *Oliver v. United States,* 466 U.S. 170 (1984).

38. Gerald Reamey, "When 'Special Needs' Meet Probable Cause: Denying the Devil Benefits of Law," *Hastings Constitutional Law Quarterly* 19 (1992): 295.

39. Rolando V. del Carmen, *Criminal Procedure: Law and Practice,* 7th ed. (Belmont, CA: Wadsworth, 2007), 172.

40. *Winston v. Lee.*

41. *United States v. Martinez-Fuerte,* 428 U.S. 543 (1976).

42. Thomas J. Gardner and Terry M. Anderson, *Criminal Law,* 9th ed. (Belmont, CA: Thomson Publishing, 2006).

43. *Ferguson v. City of Charleston,* 532 U.S. 67 (2001).

44. Id.

45. *Schmerber v. California,* 384 U.S. 757 (1966).

46. Moore, *Privacy: Studies in Social and Cultural History.*

47. *Plessy v. Ferguson,* 163 U.S. 537 (1896). The reasonableness standard used in this case is also known as the "rational basis test."

48. Henry Black, *Black's Law Dictionary,* abridged 5th ed. (St. Paul, MN: West Publishing, 1983).

49. *Maryland v. Pringle,* 540 U.S. 366 (2003).

50. *Cupp v. Murphy,* 412 U.S. 291 (1973).

51. *O'Connor v. Ortega,* 480 U.S. 709 (1987).

52. *Terry v. Ohio,* 392 U.S. 1 (1968).

53. *National Treasury Employees Union v. Von Raab,* 489 U.S. 656 (1989).

54. O'Harrow, Jr., *No Place to Hide.*

55. Nancy Chang, "How Democracy Dies: The War on Our Civil Liberties," in *Lost Liberties: Ashcroft and the Assault on Personal Freedom,* ed. Cynthia Brown (New York: The New Press, 2003), 33–51.

56. John B. Mitchell, "What Went Wrong with the Warren Court's Conception of the Fourth Amendment?" *New England Law Review* 27 (1992): 35, 37.

CHAPTER 2

1. *United States v. Ross,* 456 U.S. 798 (1982).

2. Id.

3. United States Constitution, Amendment IV.

4. John C. Klotter, Jacqueline R. Kanovitz, and Michael I. Kanovitz, *Constitutional Law,* 8th ed. (Cincinnati, OH: Anderson Publishing, 1999).

5. Dorothy Glancy, "Invention of the Right to Privacy," *Arizona Law Review* 21 (1979): 1.

6. Andrew C. McLaughlin, *A Constitutional History of the United States* (New York: Appleton-Century-Crofts, 1935).

7. *Kyllo v. United States,* 533 U.S. 27 (2001).

8. James R. Acker and David C. Brody, *Criminal Procedure: A Contemporary Perspective,* 2nd ed. (Sudbury, MA: Jones and Bartlett Publishers, 2004), 47.

9. *Texas v. Brown,* 460 U.S. 730 (1983).

10. U.S. Constitution, Amendment IV.

11. Id.

12. Ducat, *Constitutional Interpretation,* 745.

13. *Terry v. Ohio.*

14. U.S. Constitution, Amendment IV.

15. *Steele v. United States,* 267 U.S. 498 (1925).

16. *United States v. Rabinowitz,* 339 U.S. 56 (1950).

17. *Coolidge v. New Hampshire,* 403 U.S. 443 (1971).

18. Black, *Black's Law Dictionary,* abridged 5th ed., 627.

19. *Draper v. United States,* 358 U.S. 307 (1959).

20. *Illinois v. Gates,* 462 U.S. 213 (1983).

21. *Spinelli v. United States,* 393 U.S. 410 (1969); *Aguilar v. Texas,* 378 U.S. 108 (1964).

22. *Illinois v. Gates.*

23. *Wilson v. Arkansas,* 514 U.S. 927 (1995).

24. *United States v. Banks,* 540 U.S. 31 (2003).

25. del Carmen, *Criminal Procedure,* 235.

26. Michael Lyman and Gary W. Potter, *Drugs and Society,* 4th ed. (Cincinnati, OH: Anderson/Lexis-Nexis, 2003).

27. *Groh v. Ramirez et al.*, 540 U.S. 551 (2004).

28. *Horton v. California*, 496 U.S. 128 (1990).

29. Klotter, Kanovitz, and Kanovitz, *Constitutional Law.*

30. *Camara v. Municipal Court*, 387 U.S. 523 (1967).

31. Id.

32. Lynn S. Searle, "The Administrative Search from Dewey to Burger: Dismantling the Fourth Amendment," *Hastings Constitutional Law Quarterly* 16 (1989): 261.

33. *See v. City of Seattle*, 387 U.S. 541 (1967).

34. *Colonnade Catering Corp. v. United States*, 397 U.S. 72 (1970).

35. *United States v. Biswell*, 406 U.S. 311 (1972).

36. *Marshall v. Barlow's, Inc.*, 436 U.S. 307 (1978); *Michigan v. Clifford*, 464 U.S. 287 (1984).

37. *New York v. Burger*, 482 U.S. 691 (1987).

38. Id.

39. *Terry v. Ohio.*

40. Id.

41. Michael S. Vaughn and Rolando V. del Carmen, " 'Special Needs' in Criminal Justice: An Evolving Exception to the Fourth Amendment Warrant and Probable Cause Requirements," *George Mason Civil Rights Law Journal* 3 (1993): 203.

42. Reamey, "When 'Special Needs' Meet Probable Cause," 295.

43. *Ferguson v. City of Charleston.*

44. *California v. Greenwood.*

45. *Camara v. Municipal Court.*

46. *New Jersey v. T.L.O.*, 469 U.S. 325 (1985).

47. Id.

48. Yale Kamisar, Wayne R. LaFave, Jerold H. Israel, and Nancy J. King, *Modern Criminal Procedure*, 11th ed. (St. Paul, MN: Thomson/West, 2005).

49. *Bumper v. North Carolina*, 391 U.S. 543 (1968).

50. *Illinois v. Rodriguez*, 497 U.S. 177 (1990).

51. *Florida v. Jimeno*, 500 U.S. 248 (1991).

52. *Chimel v. California*, 395 U.S. 752 (1969).

53. *United States v. Chadwick*, 433 U.S. 1 (1977).

54. Id.

55. *Colorado v. Bertine*, 479 U.S. 367 (1987).

56. Black, *Black's Law Dictionary*, abridged 5th ed., 297.

57. *Johnson v. United States*, 333 U.S. 10 (1948).

58. *Warden v. Hayden*, 387 U.S. 294 (1967).

59. *Mincey v. Arizona*, 437 U.S. 385 (1978).

60. *Flippo v. West Virginia*, 528 U.S. 11 (1999). (No "murder scene" exception).

61. *Cupp v. Murphy.*

62. William P. Bloss, "Automobile Searches," in *Criminal Justice* Vol. I, ed. Phyllis Gerstenfeld (Pasadena, CA: Salem Press, 2005), 56–58.

63. *Carroll v. United States*, 267 U.S. 132 (1925).

64. Acker and Brody, *Criminal Procedure,* 200.

65. *Wyoming v. Houghton,* 526 U.S. 295 (1999).

66. *Horton v. California.*

67. Id.

68. *Arizona v. Hicks,* 480 U.S. 321 (1987).

69. *United States v. Knotts,* 460 U.S. 276 (1983).

CHAPTER 3

1. *Seattle Times,* "Green River Killings," November 19, 2004, http://seattle times.nwsource.com/html/greenriverkillings/; Superior Court of Washington for King County, *State of Washington v. Gary Leon Ridgway,* No. 01-1-10270-9 SEA, Prosecutor's Summary of Evidence (2003) (accessed November 14, 2007).

2. Black, *Black's Law Dictionary,* abridged 5th ed., 628.

3. *Ehrlich's Blackstone.*

4. Thomas J. Gardner and Terry M. Anderson, *Criminal Evidence: Principles and Cases,* 6th ed. (Belmont, CA: Thomson-Wadsworth, 2007).

5. *Federal Rules of Evidence,* "Rule 607" (Washington, DC: Government Printing Office, 2004).

6. Clifford L. Linedecker, *O. J. A to Z: The Complete Handbook of the Trial of the Century* (New York: St. Martin's Griffin, 1995).

7. Vincent Bugliosi, *Outrage: The Five Reasons Why O. J. Simpson Got Away with Murder* (New York: W. W. Norton & Company, 1996).

8. Henry J. Reske, "Verdict on Simpson Trial: Observers Say Prosecution Lost the Case over a Bloody Glove, Racist Cop," *ABA Journal* 81 (1995): 48.

9. Black, *Black's Law Dictionary,* abridged 5th ed., 341.

10. Saferstein, *Criminalistics: An Introduction to Forensic Science.*

11. Patrick Mcgreevy, "LAPD Still at Risk of Scandal Despite Reform, Panel Says," *Los Angeles Times,* July 12, 2006, http://articles.latimes.com/2006/jul/12/local/me-rampart12 (accessed November 18, 2007).

12. CNN.com, "First Officers Enter Pleas in LAPD's Rampart Division Scandal," May 16, 2000, http://archives.cnn.com/2000/LAW/05/16/lapd.corruption/index.html (accessed November 18, 2007).

13. Renford Reese, "The Multiple Causes of the LAPD Rampart Scandal," *Journal of Interdisciplinary Studies* 16 (2003): 85.

14. Susan Bandes, "Tracing the Pattern of No Pattern: Stories of Police Brutality," *Loyola of Los Angeles Law Review* 34 (2001): 665.

15. William P. Bloss, "Police Misconduct after the Rodney King Incident," in *The Encyclopedia of Police Science,* 3rd ed., ed. Jack Greene (London: Routledge, 2006), 964–68.

16. *Weeks v. United States,* 232 U.S. 383 (1914).

17. *Mapp v. Ohio,* 367 U.S. 643 (1961).

18. *Silverthorne Lumber Company v. United States,* 251 U.S. 385 (1920).

19. *United States v. Leon,* 468 U.S. 897 (1984); *Arizona v. Evans,* 514 U.S. 1 (1995).

20. *Nix v. Williams,* 467 U.S. 431 (1984); Robert M. Bloom, "Inevitable Discovery: An Exception beyond the Fruits," *American Journal of Criminal Law* 20 (1992): 79.

21. *Wong Sun v. United States,* 371 U.S. 471 (1963); *Taylor v. Alabama,* 457 U.S. 687 (1982).

22. *Murray v. United States,* 487 U.S. 533 (1988).

23. *Miranda v. Arizona,* 384 U.S. 436 (1966).

24. *United States v. Patane,* 542 U.S. 630 (2004).

25. *Roper v. Simmons,* 543 U.S. 551 (2005).

26. Orwell, *Nineteen Eighty-Four: A Novel.*

27. Sue Titus Reid, *Criminal Law,* 7th ed. (Los Angeles: Roxbury Publishing, 2007), 290.

28. Warren and Brandeis, "The Right to Privacy," 193.

29. Amy Beeman, "Chicago Suburb Outlaws 'Saggy Pants,'" *ncbuy.com,* July 22, 2008, www.ncbuy.com/news/2008-07-22/1016525.html (accessed July 26, 2008).

30. Id.

31. Thomas J. Gardner and Terry M. Anderson, *Criminal Law,* 10th ed. (Belmont, CA: Wadsworth, 2009), 204.

32. *Speiser v. Randall,* 357 U.S. 513 (1958).

33. *Schenck v. United States,* 249 U.S. 47 (1919).

34. *Cohen v. California,* 403 U.S. 15 (1971); *Texas v. Johnson,* 491 U.S. 397 (1989).

35. Roy R. Roberg, Kenneth J. Novak, and Gary W. Cordner, *Police and Society,* 4th ed. (New York: Oxford University Press, 2009).

36. George L. Kelling, *The Kansas City Preventive Patrol Experiment: A Summary Report* (Washington, DC: The Police Foundation, 1974).

37. Robert C. Trojanowicz, Victor E. Kappeler, and Larry K. Gaines, *Community Policing: A Contemporary Perspective,* 3rd ed. (Cincinnati, OH: Anderson, 2002).

38. *United States v. Mendenhall,* 446 U.S. 544 (1980).

39. *Florida v. Bostick,* 501 U.S. 429 (1991).

40. *Hiibel v. Sixth Judicial District Court of Nevada,* 542 U.S. 177 (2004).

41. Id.

42. *Illinois v. Wardlow,* 528 U.S. 119 (2000).

43. *California v. Hodari D.,* 499 U.S. 621 (1991).

44. del Carmen, *Criminal Procedure: Law and Practice,* 142.

45. *Minnesota v. Dickerson,* 508 U.S. 366 (1993).

46. John M. Memory and Randall Aragon, *Patrol Officer Problem Solving and Solutions* (Durham, NC: Carolina Academic Press, 2001).

47. *Delaware v. Prouse,* 440 U.S. 648 (1979).

48. *Whren v. United States,* 517 U.S. 806 (1996).

49. Id.

50. *United States v. Arvizu*, 534 U.S. 266 (2002).

51. *United States v. Hunnicutt*, 135 F.3d 1345 (10th Cir. 1998).

52. *United States v. Knotts*.

53. *United States v. Cortez*, 449 U.S. 411 (1981).

54. *Cardwell v. Lewis*, 417 U.S. 583 (1974).

55. Michael S. Scott, Nina J. Emerson, Louis B. Antonalli, and Joel B. Plant, "Drunk Driving," *Problem-Oriented Guide for Police, Problem-Specific Guides Series, No. 36* (Washington, DC: Office of Community-Oriented Policing Services, 2006).

56. Mary F. Gallagher, "Civil Libertarians Wince at New Device That 'Shines Light' on Drunken Drivers," *New Jersey Law Journal* 161 (2000): 6.

57. National Highway Traffic Safety Administration, *Standardized Field Sobriety Testing: Management Training System* (Washington, DC: U.S. Department of Transportation, 2001), http://www.nhtsa.dot.gov/people/injury/alcohol/SFST/appendix _a.htm (accessed December 16, 2007).

58. Patrick T. Barone and Jeffery S. Crampton, "Do 'Standardized Field Sobriety Tests' Reliably Predict Intoxication?" *Michigan Bar Journal* 84 (2005): 23.

59. *Michigan Department of State Police v. Sitz*, 496 U.S. 444 (1990).

60. Kim Han, "The Technological Sniffing Out of Constitutional Rights: Assessing the Constitutionality of the Passive Alcohol Sensor III," *Journal of Law and Policy* 9 (2001): 835.

61. John B. Mancke, "DUI Field Sobriety Tests: Have the Courts Missed a Step?" *Pennsylvania Bar Association Quarterly* 73 (2002): 117–32.

62. Gallagher, "Civil Libertarians Wince at New Device That 'Shines Light' on Drunken Drivers," 6, 8.

63. South Carolina Code of Laws (Unannotated) 2007. § 56-5-2930 Operating Motor Vehicle while under Influence; § 56-5-2933 Driving with an Unlawful Alcohol Concentration, http://www.scstatehouse.net/code/t56c005.htm (accessed December 10, 2007); *South Dakota v. Neville*, 459 U.S. 553 (1983).

64. *Schmerber v. California*.

65. Federal Bureau of Investigation, *Law Enforcement Officers Killed and Assaulted* (Washington, DC: Department of Justice, 2006), http://www.fbi.gov /ucr/killed/2006/table19.html (accessed January 11, 2008).

66. Illya D. Lichtenberg and Alisa Smith, "How Dangerous Are Routine Police-Citizen Traffic Stops? A Research Note," *Journal of Criminal Justice* 29 (2001): 419.

67. *Pennsylvania v. Mimms*, 434 U.S. 106 (1977); *Maryland v. Wilson*, 519 U.S. 408 (1997).

68. *Chimel v. California; Michigan v. Long*, 463 U.S. 1032 (1983).

69. *United States v. Mankani*, 738 F.2d 538 (2nd Cir. 1984).

70. *Whren v. United States*.

71. *New York v. Class*, 475 U.S. 106 (1986).

72. *Illinois v. Caballes*, 543 U.S. 405 (2005).

73. Id.

74. Id.

75. *Brendlin v. California*, 551 U.S.__(2007); 127 S.Ct. 2400 (2007).

76. *Schneckloth v. Bustamonte,* 412 U.S. 218 (1973).

77. *United States v. Ross; Wyoming v. Houghton.*

78. *Whren v. United States.*

79. *Maryland v. Pringle.*

80. *Atwater v. City of Lago Vista,* 532 U.S. 318 (2001).

81. *Michigan Department of State Police v. Sitz.*

82. *Almeida-Sanchez v. United States,* 413 U.S. 266 (1973); *United States v. Ortiz,* 422 U.S. 891 (1975).

83. *United States v. Martinez-Fuerte.*

84. *City of Indianapolis v. Edmond,* 531 U.S. 32 (2000).

85. Id.

86. *Illinois v. Lidster,* 540 U.S. 419 (2004).

87. Carrie Loewenthal, "U.S. to Welcome Record Number of International Visitors in 2007: Upward Trend to Continue, Commerce Secretary Gutierrez Predicts," *America.gov,* (2007), http://www.america.gov/st/washfile-english/2007/March/20070303174902lnkais0.2752497.html (accessed January 7, 2008).

88. Jeffrey S. Passel, *Size and Characteristics of the Unauthorized Migrant Population in the U.S.* (Washington, DC: Pew Hispanic Center, 2006), http://pewhispanic.org/reports/report.php?ReportID=61 (accessed January 7, 2008).

89. *United States v. Mendenhall; Florida v. Bostick.*

90. *United States v. Ramsey,* 431 U.S. 606 (1977).

91. *United States v. Montoya de Hernandez,* 473 U.S. 531 (1985).

92. *United States v. Flores-Montano,* 541 U.S. 149 (2004).

93. Id.

94. *Almeida-Sanchez v. United States.*

95. *United States v. Brignoni-Ponce,* 422 U.S. 873 (1975).

96. Lirtzman, "Surveillance Cameras Win Broad Support."

97. Orin S. Kerr, "The Fourth Amendment and New Technologies: Constitutional Myths and the Case for Caution," *Michigan Law Review* 102 (2004): 801.

98. *United States v. Knotts,* 460 U.S. 276 (1983).

99. *United States v. Karo,* 468 U.S. 705 (1984); *Kyllo v. United States.*

100. *Kyllo v. United States.*

101. *California v. Ciraolo.*

102. *Davis v. Mississippi,* 394 U.S. 721 (1969).

103. Kamisar et al., *Modern Criminal Procedure,* 786.

104. *Hayes v. Florida,* 470 U.S. 811 (1985); Kamisar et al., *Modern Criminal Procedure,* 786.

105. Local6.com, "Police Swabbing Mouths during Traffic Stops in Serial Killer Hunt," February 7, 2008, http://www.local6.com/print/15232197/detail.html; Beach Patrol Swabs Mouths in Hunt for Serial Killer: DNA Taken from Men at Sex Stings, February 20, 2008, http://www.local6.com/print/15361564/detail.html (accessed February 26, 2008).

106. Samuel Walker and Michael Harrington, "Police DNA 'Sweeps': A Proposed Model Policy on Police Requests for DNA Samples," *Police Professionalism Initiative,*

University of Nebraska at Omaha, (2005), 3–4, http://www.unomaha.edu/criminal-justice/PDF/dnamodelpolicyfinal.pdf. (accessed November 29, 2007).

107. *Kohler v. Englade,* 470 F.3d 1104 (5th Cir. 2006).

108. David Kaye, "Who Needs Special Needs?: On the Constitutionality of Collecting DNA and Other Biometric Data from Arrestees," *Journal of Law, Medicine & Ethics* 34 (2006): 188.

109. *Uniform Crime Reports* (Washington, DC: Federal Bureau of Investigation, 2006), http://www.fbi.gov/ucr/cius2006/arrests/ (accessed January 14, 2008).

110. Larry E. Holtz, *Contemporary Criminal Procedure: Court Decisions for Law Enforcement* (Longwood, FL: Gould Publications, 2004).

111. *United States v. Drayton,* 536 U.S. 194 (2002).

112. *California v. Hodari D.*

113. Victor E. Kappeler, *Critical Issues in Police Civil Liability,* 4th ed. (Long Grove, IL: Waveland, 2006).

114. *Vale v. Louisiana,* 399 U.S. 30 (1970).

115. *New York v. Belton,* 453 U.S. 454 (1981).

116. Id.

117. *Thornton v. United States,* 541 U.S. 615 (2004).

118. *Maryland v. Buie,* 494 U.S. 325 (1990).

119. *Illinois v. McArthur,* 531 U.S. 326 (2001).

120. *Schmerber v. California.*

121. *Winston v. Lee.*

122. Ronald J. Bacigal, "Dodging a Bullet, but Opening Old Wounds in Fourth Amendment Jurisprudence," *Seton Hall Law Review* 16 (1986): 597.

123. *Schmerber v. California; Bell v. Wolfish,* 441 U.S. 520 (1979).

124. *People v. Hall,* 10 NY3d 303 (NY Ct. of Appeals 2008).

125. Amy Luria, "Showup Identifications: A Comprehensive Overview of the Problems and a Discussion of Necessary Changes," *Nebraska Law Review* 86 (2008): 515.

126. Margery Malkin Koosed, "The Proposed Innocence Protection Act Won't—Unless It Also Curbs Mistaken Eyewitness Identifications," *Ohio State Law Journal* 63 (2002): 263.

127. Richard A. Wise, Kirsten A. Dauphinais, and Martin A. Safer, "A Tripartite Solution to Eyewitness Error," *Journal of Criminal Law and Criminology* 97 (2007): 807.

128. *Neil v. Biggers,* 409 U.S. 188 (1972).

129. *Stovall v. Denno,* 388 U.S. 293 (1967).

130. Gardner and Anderson, *Criminal Evidence,* 266.

131. *Manson v. Brathwaite,* 432 U.S. 98 (1977).

132. *Kirby v. Illinois,* 406 U.S. 682 (1972); *United States v. Wade,* 388 U.S. 218 (1967).

133. *United States v. Dionisio,* 410 U.S. 1 (1973).

134. *Gilbert v. California,* 388 U.S. 263 (1967).

135. *United States v. Gray,* 958 F.2d 9 (1st Cir. 1992); *Maryland v. Buie.*

136. Cliff Roberson, *Criminal Procedure Today: Issues and Cases,* 2nd ed. (Upper Saddle River, NJ: Prentice-Hall, 2003), 294.

137. *United States v. Dionisio.*

138. Saferstein, *Criminalistics.*

139. DNA Fingerprint Act 2005 (Title X Pub. Law 109–162); President's DNA Initiative, (2008), http://www.dna.gov/ (accessed February 8, 2008).

140. *United States v. Sczubelek,* 402 F.3d 175 (3rd Cir. 2005).

141. Kaye, "Who Needs Special Needs?" 188, 195.

142. *Rochin v. California,* 342 U.S. 165 (1952).

143. *Breithaupt v. Abram,* 352 U.S. 432 (1957).

144. *Schmerber v. California.*

145. *Winston v. Lee.*

146. *Miranda v. Arizona.*

147. U.S. Constitution, Amendment V.

148. *California v. Beheler,* 463 U.S. 1121 (1983).

149. *Pennsylvania v. Muniz,* 496 U.S. 582 (1990).

150. *Rhode Island v. Innis,* 446 U.S. 291 (1980).

151. *North Carolina v. Butler,* 441 U.S. 369 (1979).

152. *Rogers v. Richmond,* 365 U.S. 534 (1961).

153. *Brown v. Mississippi,* 297 U.S. 278 (1936); *Townsend v. Sain,* 372 U.S. 293 (1963); Catherine Hancock, "Due Process before Miranda," *Tulane Law Review* 70 (1996): 2195.

154. *Berkemer v. McCarty,* 468 U.S. 420 (1984).

155. *New York v. Quarles,* 467 U.S. 649 (1984).

156. *Illinois v. Perkins,* 496 U.S. 292 (1990).

157. *United States v. White,* 401 U.S. 745 (1971).

158. Federal Bureau of Investigation, *Crime in the United States,* (2006), http://www.fbi.gov/ucr/cius2006/offenses/clearances/index.html (accessed January 6, 2008).

159. Id.

160. *Hudson v. Palmer,* 468 U.S. 517 (1984).

161. *Bell v. Wolfish.*

162. Id.

163. John W. Palmer, *Constitutional Rights of Prisoners,* 8th ed. (Cincinnati, OH: Anderson/Lexis-Nexis, 2006), 43.

164. *Illinois v. Lafayette,* 462 U.S. 640 (1983).

165. *Albright v. Oliver,* 510 U.S. 266 (1994).

166. Kamisar et al., *Modern Criminal Procedure,* 1035–36.

167. Frank Schmalleger, *Criminal Law Today: An Introduction with Capstone Cases,* 3rd ed. (Upper Saddle River, NJ: Pearson/Prentice-Hall, 2006), 13.

168. *Gerstein v. Pugh,* 420 U.S. 103 (1975).

169. Not all jurisdictions use the terminology "first hearing." It is also known as preliminary, initial, probable cause, or bindover hearing depending on the locale.

170. U.S. Constitution, Amendment VIII.

171. Roberson, *Criminal Procedure Today,* 315.

172. Pretrial Services Resource Center, *The Supervised Release Primer.* (Washington, DC: Pretrial Services Resource Center, 1999), http://www.pretrial.org/Docs/Documents/supervised%20release%20primer.pdf (accessed September 14, 2007).

173. Bureau of Justice Statistics, *Pretrial Release of Felony Defendants in State Courts,* (2007), http://www.ojp.usdoj.gov/bjs/pub/pdf/prfdsc.pdf (accessed January 26, 2008).

174. Kamisar et al., *Modern Criminal Procedure,* 971–72.

175. Bail Reform Act of 1984, 18 U.S.C. § 3142.

176. *United States v. Salerno,* 481 U.S. 739 (1987).

177. James Austin, Barry Krisberg, and Paul Litsky, "The Effectiveness of Supervised Pretrial Release," *Crime and Delinquency* 31 (1985): 519.

178. Bureau of Justice Statistics, *Pretrial Release of Felony Defendants in State Courts.*

179. Marisol Bello, "Detroit Mayor Jailed for Violating Bond," *USA Today,* August 8, 2008, www.usatoday.com/printedition/news/20080808/a_mayor08.art.htm (accessed August 10, 2008).

180. Ann H. Crowe, Linda Sydney, Pat Bancroft, and Beverly Lawrence, *Offender Supervision with Electronic Technology: A User's Guide* (Lexington, KY: American Probation and Parole Association, 2002).

181. *Thornton v. United States.*

182. Andrew J. Smith, "Unconstitutional Conditional Release: A Pyrrhic Victory for Arrestees' Privacy Rights under *United States v. Scott,*" *William and Mary Law Review* 48 (2007): 2365, 2367.

183. Pretrial Services Resource Center, *The Supervised Release Primer.*

184. D. Alan Henry and John Clark, "Pretrial Drug Testing: An Overview of Issues and Practices," *Bureau of Justice Assistance Bulletin* (Washington, DC: U.S. Department of Justice, 1999).

185. John Clark and D. Alan Henry, *Pretrial Services Programming at the Start of the 21st Century: A Survey of Pretrial Service Programs* (Washington, DC: Bureau of Justice Assistance, 2003).

186. Bail Reform Act of 1984, 18 U.S.C. § 3142.

187. *United States v. Scott,* 450 F.3d 863 (9th Cir. 2006).

188. Smith, "Unconstitutional Conditional Release," 2365.

189. Melanie D. Wilson, "The Price of Pretrial Release: Can We Afford to Keep Our Fourth Amendment Rights?," *Iowa Law Review* 92 (2007): 159.

190. Ann H. Crowe, "Electronic Supervision: From Decision-Making to Implementation," *Corrections Today* 64 (2002): 130, 132.

191. South Carolina Code Annotated 2007, Home Detention Act § 24-13-1520, Definitions.

192. South Carolina Code Annotated 2007, Home Detention Act § 24-13-1580, Necessity of Written Consent to Electronic Home Detention; Other Residents' Knowledge.

193. *United States v. Gardner,* 523 F.Supp.2d 1025 (N. D. Cal. 2007).

194. Rolando V. del Carmen and Joseph Vaughn, "Legal Issues in the Use of Electronic Surveillance in Probation," *Federal Probation* 50 (1986): 60.

195. U.S. Constitution, Amendment V.

196. *United States v. Dionisio.*

197. *United States v. Mara,* 410 U.S. 19 (1973).

198. Kamisar et al., *Modern Criminal Procedure,* 822.

199. *In re Grand Jury Proceeding Involving Vickers,* 38 F.Supp.2d 159 (D.N.H. 1998).

200. *United States v. Calandra,* 414 U.S. 338 (1974).

201. *In re Grand Jury Proceedings (Danbom),* 827 F.2d 301 (8th Cir. 1987).

202. *Hoffman v. United States,* 341 U.S. 479 (1951).

203. *Murphy v. Waterfront Comm'n,* 378 U.S. 52 (1964).

204. *Couch v. United States,* 409 U.S. 322 (1973).

205. *Massiah v. United States,* 377 U.S. 201 (1964).

CHAPTER 4

1. *Massiah v. United States.*

2. Id.

3. *Brewer v. Williams,* 430 U.S. 387 (1977).

4. U.S. Constitution, Amendment VI.

5. *Gideon v. Wainwright,* 372 U.S. 335 (1963).

6. *Lefkowitz v. Turley,* 414 U.S. 70 (1973).

7. Gardner and Anderson, *Criminal Evidence: Principles and Cases.*

8. *Pointer v. Texas,* 380 U.S. 400 (1965); *Crawford v. Washington,* 541 U.S. 36 (2004).

9. *Chambers v. Mississippi,* 410 U.S. 284 (1973).

10. *Illinois v. Allen,* 397 U.S. 337 (1970).

11. *Coy v. Iowa,* 487 U.S. 1012 (1988).

12. Id.

13. *Maryland v. Craig,* 497 U.S. 836 (1990).

14. Id.

15. *United States v. Owens,* 484 U.S. 554 (1988); *Barnes v. Johnson,* 184 F3d. 816 (5th Cir. Texas 1999).

16. United States Code Service, "Federal Rules of Criminal Procedure, Title IV, USCS *Fed Rules Crim Proc R 16*," 2008.

17. *Rock v. Arkansas,* 483 U.S. 44 (1987).

18. *Griffin v. California,* 380 U.S. 609 (1965).

19. *United States v. Dionisio.*

20. *Brady v. Maryland,* 373 U.S. 83 (1963).

21. *United States v. Agurs,* 427 U.S. 97 (1976).

22. *United States v. Bagley,* 473 U.S. 667 (1985); *Kyles v. Whitley,* 514 U.S. 419 (1995).

23. *Banks v. Dretke,* 540 U.S. 668 (2004).

24. *Arizona v. Youngblood,* 488 U.S. 51 (1988).

25. *Illinois v. Fisher,* 540 U.S. 544 (2004).

26. *Strickler v. Greene,* 527 U.S. 263 (1999).

27. *Giglio v. United States,* 405 U.S. 150 (1972).

28. Lisa A. Regini, "Disclosing Officer Misconduct: A Constitutional Duty," *FBI Law Enforcement Bulletin* 65 (1996): 27, 31.

29. *United States v. Veras,* 51 F.3d 1365 (7th Cir. 1995).

30. Gabriel J. Chin and Scott C. Wells, "The 'Blue Wall of Silence' as Evidence of Bias and Motive to Lie: A New Approach to Police Perjury," *University of Pittsburgh Law Review* 59 (198): 233.

31. Jeff Noble, "Police Officer Truthfulness and the Brady Decision," *The Police Chief* 70 (2003): 92, 93.

32. *Wardius v. Oregon,* 412 U.S. 470 (1973).

33. FoxNews.com, "Timeline of Events in Duke LaCrosse 'Rape' Case," April 11, 2007, http://www.foxnews.com/story/0,2933,265386,00.html (accessed February 21, 2008).

34. Liza Porteus, "All Sex-Assault Charges against Duke Lacrosse Players Dropped: Players Glad Ordeal Is Over," *FoxNews.com,* April 11, 2007, http://www.foxnews.com/story/0,2933,265187,00.html (accessed February 21, 2008).

35. Id.

36. Id.

37. Robert Mosteller, "The Duke Lacrosse Case, Innocence, and False Identifications: A Fundamental Failure to 'Do Justice,'" *Fordham Law Review* 76 (2007): 1337.

38. Id.

39. *Strickler v. Greene.*

40. *Moore v. Illinois,* 434 U.S. 220 (1977).

41. *Riggins v. Nevada,* 504 U.S. 127 (1992).

42. Corpus Juris Secundum, "Prison Garb or Physical Restraints," 16C *C.J.S.* § 1640, 2008.

43. *Dawson v. Delaware,* 503 U.S. 159 (1992).

44. Roberson, *Criminal Procedure Today: Issues and Cases,* 440.

45. Harry E. Allen, Edward J. Latessa, Bruce S. Ponder, and Clifford E. Simonsen, *Corrections in America: An Introduction,* 11th ed. (Upper Saddle River, NJ: Pearson/Prentice-Hall, 2007).

46. Howard Abadinsky, *Probation and Parole,* 9th ed. (Upper Saddle River, NJ: Pearson/Prentice-Hall, 2006).

47. Allen et al., *Corrections in America: An Introduction,* 70–71.

48. United States Probation and Pretrial Services System, *Year-in-Review 2003,* (Washington, DC: Office of Probation and Pretrial Services, 2004), http://www.uscourts.gov/publications/year-in-review03-wlinks.pdf (accessed February 23, 2008).

49. Todd R. Clear, George F. Cole, and Michael D. Reisig, *American Corrections,* 7th ed. (Belmont, CA: Thomson, 2006), 199.

50. *Williams v. New York,* 337 U.S. 241 (1949).

51. Id.

52. *United States v. Tucker,* 404 U.S. 443 (1972).

53. *Gardner v. Florida,* 430 U.S. 349 (1977).

54. Kamisar et al., *Modern Criminal Procedure,* 1548.

55. Bureau of Justice Statistics, *Corrections Statistics Summary Findings* (Washington, DC: U.S. Department of Justice, 2008), http://www.ojp.usdoj.gov/bjs/correct.htm (accessed June 6, 2008).

56. International Centre for Prison Studies, *World Prison Brief* (2008), http://www.kcl.ac.uk/depsta/law/research/icps/worldbrief/wpb_stats.php?area=all&category=wb_poprate (accessed June 6, 2008).

57. James Byrne, "The Future of Intensive Probation Supervision," *Crime and Delinquency* 36 (1990): 6.

58. Abadinsky, *Probation and Parole.*

59. Lauren E. Glaze and Thomas P. Bonczar, *Probation and Parole in the United States, 2006* (Washington, DC: Bureau of Justice Statistics Bulletin, 2007), http://www.ojp.usdoj.gov/bjs/pub/pdf/ppus06.pdf (accessed May 2, 2008).

60. Id.

61. Id.

62. Rolando V. del Carmen, Maldine Beth Barnhill, Gene Bonham, Jr., Lance Hignite, and Todd Jermstad, *Civil Liabilities and Other Legal Issues for Probation/Parole Officers and Supervisors,* 3rd ed. (Washington, DC: National Institute of Corrections, 2001), 88. http://www.nicic.org/pubs/2001/017068.pdf (accessed April 27, 2008).

63. *State v. Kline,* 963 P.2d 697 (Or. App. 1998).

64. *Griffin v. Wisconsin,* 483 U.S. 868 (1987).

65. Id.

66. *United States v. Knights,* 534 U.S. 112 (2001).

67. Id.

68. *Samson v. California,* 547 U.S. 843 (2006).

69. Id.

70. Id.

71. Id.

72. Musto, *The American Disease: Origins of Narcotic Control.*

73. William P. Bloss, "Comparative European and American Drug Control Policy: An Examination of Efficacy and Contributing Factors," *European and International Research Group on Crime, Ethics, and Social Philosophy Quarterly Review* 2 (2005): 1, http://www.erces.com/journal/Journal.htm (accessed August 14, 2007).

74. Arrestee Drug Abuse Monitoring Program, *Drug and Alcohol Use and Related Matters among Arrestees, 2003* (Washington, DC: National Institute of Justice, 2003), http://www.ncjrs.gov/nij/adam/ADAM2003.pdf (accessed April 26, 2008).

75. Federal Bureau of Prisons, *Facts about the Bureau of Prisons* (Washington, DC: U.S. Department of Justice, 2008), http://www.bop.gov/news/quick.jsp#4 (accessed April 26, 2008).

76. Christopher J. Mumola and Thomas P. Bonczar, *Substance Abuse and Treatment of Adults on Probation 1995* (Washington, DC: Bureau of Justice Statistics,

1995), http://www.ojp.usdoj.gov/bjs/pub/pdf/satap95.pdf (accessed April 26, 2008).

77. National Institute of Justice Special Report, *Toward a Drugs and Crime Research Agenda for the 21st Century* (Washington, DC: National Institute of Justice, 2003), http://www.ncjrs.gov/pdffiles1/nij/194616.pdf (accessed April 26, 2008).

78. Todd R. Clear, Val B. Clear, and Anthony A. Braga, "Correctional Alternatives for Drug Offenders in an Era of Overcrowding," *The Prison Journal* 73 (1993): 178.

79. Bureau of Justice Statistics, *Participation of Adult Probationers in Special Supervision Programs* (Washington, DC: National Institute of Justice, 1997).

80. *United States v. Sczubelek.*

81. Electronic Information Privacy Center, *Privacy & Human Rights: An International Survey of Privacy Laws and Developments*, 158.

82. Tracey Maclin, "Is Obtaining an Arrestee's DNA a Valid Special Needs Search under the Fourth Amendment? What Should (and Will) the Supreme Court Do?" *Journal of Law, Medicine and Ethics* 33 (2005): 165.

83. Simon A. Cole and William C. Thompson, "Legal Issues Associated with DNA Evidence," in *Current Legal Issues in Criminal Justice*, ed. Craig Hemmens (Los Angeles: Roxbury Publishing, 2007), 135–49, 143.

84. *United States v. Kincade*, 379 F.3d 813 (9th Cir. 2004).

85. Id.

86. Yale Kamisar et al., *Basic Criminal Procedure*, 12th ed. (St. Paul, MN: Thomson/West, 2008), 447–49.

87. Crowe, "Electronic Supervision: From Decision-Making to Implementation," 130, 132.

88. Robert Stanz and Richard Tewksbury, "Predictors of Success and Recidivism in a Home Incarceration Program," *The Prison Journal* 80 (2000): 326; Mary Finn and Suzanne Muirhead-Steves, "The Effectiveness of Electronic Monitoring with Violent Male Parolees," *Justice Quarterly* 18 (2002): 293.

89. Crowe et al., *Offender Supervision with Electronic Technology: A User's Guide.*

90. Frances P. Reddington and Betsy Wright Kreisel, *Sexual Assault: The Victims, the Perpetrators, and the Criminal Justice System* (Durham, NC: Carolina Academic Press, 2005).

91. Bruce J. Winick and John Q. LaFond, *Protecting Society from Sexually Dangerous Offenders: Law, Justice, and Therapy* (Washington, DC: American Psychological Association, 2003).

92. *Kansas v. Hendricks*, 521 U.S. 346 (1997).

93. Id.

94. Cynthia A. King, "Fighting the Devil We Don't Know: Kansas v. Hendricks, A Case Study Exploring the Civilization of Criminal Punishment and Its Ineffectiveness in Preventing Child Sexual Abuse," *William and Mary Law Review* 40 (1999): 1427.

95. *Seling, Superintendent, Special Commitment Center v. Young*, 531 U.S. 250 (2001).

96. Adam Walsh Child Protection and Safety Act of 2006, 42 U.S.C. § 16901, Public Law 109-248.

97. Office of Sex Offender Sentencing, Monitoring, Apprehending, Registering, and Tracking, "Sex Offender Registration and Notification Act" (Washington, DC: Office of Justice Programs, U.S. Department of Justice, 2008), http://www.ojp.usdoj.gov/smart/guidelines.htm (accessed June 30, 2008).

98. United States Department of Justice (2008), *Dru Sjodin National Sex Offender Public Website,* http://www.nsopw.gov/(X(1)S(v5urm445krzwzoymcdmos-geu))/Core/Conditions.aspx?AspxAutoDetectCookieSupport=1.

99. Arthur J. Lurigio, Marylouise E. Jones, and Barbara E. Smith, "Child Sexual Abuse: Its Causes, Consequences, and Implications for Probation Practice," *Federal Probation* 69 (1995): 69.

100. National Law Enforcement and Correction Technology Center, "'Monitoring' the Sex Offender," *Tech Beat* (Washington, DC: National Institute of Justice, 2005), http://www.justnet.org/techbeat%20files/MonitorSexOffender.pdf (accessed May 4, 2008).

101. Kim English, Suzanne Pullen, and Linda Jones, *Managing Adult Sex Offenders in the Community—A Containment Approach* (Washington, DC: National Institute of Justice, 1997).

102. *Ex parte Renfro,* 999 S.W.2d 557 (Tex. App. Houston [14th Dist.] 1999); del Carmen et al., *Civil Liabilities and Other Legal Issues for Probation* 105, footnote 52.

103. del Carmen et al., *Civil Liabilities and Other Legal Issues for Probation,* 95–97.

104. *Connecticut Department of Public Safety et al. v. Doe, Individually and on Behalf of All Others Similarly Situated,* 538 U.S. 1 (2003).

105. *Minnesota v. Murphy,* 465 U.S. 420 (1984).

106. Id.

107. Leanne Fiftal Alarid, Paul Cromwell, and Rolando V. del Carmen, *Community-Based Corrections,* 7th ed. (Belmont, CA: Thomson, 2008).

108. Frank Schmalleger, *Criminal Justice: A Brief Introduction,* 7th ed. (Upper Saddle River, NJ: Pearson/Prentice-Hall, 2008), 369.

109. *Morrissey v. Brewer,* 408 U.S. 471 (1972).

110. *Gagnon v. Scarpelli,* 411 U.S. 778 (1973).

111. Byrne, "The Future of Intensive Probation Supervision," 6.

112. Glaze and Bonczar, *Probation and Parole in the United States, 2006.*

113. Bureau of Justice Statistics, *Corrections Statistics Summary Findings.*

114. Jack E. Call, "The Supreme Court and Prisoner's Rights," in *Correctional Contexts: Contemporary and Classical Readings,* 3rd ed., ed. Edward Latessa and Alexander Holsinger (Los Angeles: Roxbury Publishing, 2006), 209–24.

115. *Ruffin v. Commonwealth,* 62 Va. 790 (1871).

116. Ben M. Crouch and James W. Marquart, *An Appeal to Justice: Litigated Reform of Texas Prisons* (Austin: University of Texas Press, 1989).

117. Barbara Belbot, "Inmate Litigation and the Constitution," in *Current Legal Issues in Criminal Justice,* ed. Craig Hemmens (Los Angeles: Roxbury Publishing, 2007), 167–76.

118. S. Sidney Ulmer, "Government Litigants, Underdogs, and Civil Liberties in the Supreme Court: 1903–1968," *Journal of Politics* 47 (1985): 899.

119. *Monroe v. Pape,* 365 U.S. 167 (1961).

120. *Cooper v. Pate,* 378 U.S. 546 (1964); Ku Klux Klan Act of 1871, 42 U.S.C. § 1983 *et seq.*

121. Call, "The Supreme Court and Prisoner's Rights," 209–24, 219.

122. Rolando V. del Carmen, *Civil Liabilities in American Policing* (Englewood Cliffs, NJ: Brady, 1991).

123. *Turner v. Safley,* 482 U.S. 78 (1987).

124. Id.

125. *Bell v. Wolfish,* 441 U.S. 520 (1979).

126. Id.

127. Id.

128. *Hudson v. Palmer.*

129. Id.

130. *Bonner v. Coughlin,* 517 F.2d 1311 (7th Cir. 1975); *O'Connor v. Keller,* 510 F. Supp. 1359 (D. Md. 1981).

131. *Cornwell v. Dahlberg,* 963 F.2d 912 (6th Cir. 1992).

132. *Dawson v. Kendrick,* 527 F. Supp. 1252 (S.D.W.Va. 1981); *Canedy v. Boardman,* 16 F.3d 183 (7th Cir. 1994).

133. *Johnson v. Phelan,* 69 F.3d 144 (7th Cir. 1995).

134. *Whitley v. Albers,* 475 U.S. 312 (1986).

135. *Hudson v. McMillian,* 503 U.S. 1 (1992).

136. Id.

137. *Washington v. Harper,* 494 U.S. 210 (1990).

138. *Wolff v. McDonnell,* 418 U.S. 539 (1974).

139. U.S. Centers for Disease Control, "Persons Tested for HIV—United States 2006," *Morbidity and Mortality Weekly Report* 57 (2008): 845, http://www.cdc.gov/mmwr/preview/mmwrhtml/mm5731a1.htm (accessed July 12, 2008).

140. Laura Maruschak, *HIV in Prisons, 2006* (Washington, DC: Bureau of Justice Statistics, 2006), http://www.ojp.gov/bjs/pub/pdf/hivp06.pdf (accessed July 12, 2008).

141. Kathleen Knepper, "Responsibility of Correctional Officials in Responding to the Incidence of the HIV Virus in Jails and Prisons," *New England Journal on Criminal and Civil Confinement* 21 (1995): 45.

142. *Doe v. Borough of Barrington,* 729 F. Supp. 376 (D.N.J. 1990).

143. Karen E. Zuck, "HIV and Medical Privacy: Government Infringement on Prisoners' Constitutional Rights," *University of Pennsylvania Journal of Constitutional Law* 9 (2007): 1277.

144. *Doe v. Delie,* 257 F.3d 309 (3rd Cir. 2001).

145. *Camarillo v. McCarthy,* 998 F.2d 638 (9th Cir. 1993).

146. Robert D. Hanser, Jeffrey P. Rush, Scott M. Mire, and Attapol Kuanliang, "Liabilities Associated with HIV/AIDS in Jail Settings: Balancing Offender Legal Protections with Concerns for Public Safety," *Southern University Law Review* 34 (2007): 1; *Sherman v. Jones,* 258 F. Supp.2d 440 (E.D. Va. 2003).

147. Palmer, *Constitutional Rights of Prisoners.*

CHAPTER 5

1. *Baron v. Meloni,* 556 F. Supp. 796 (W.D.N.Y. 1983).
2. Id.
3. Victor E. Kappeler, *Critical Issues in Police Civil Liability,* 2nd ed. (Prospect Heights, IL: Waveland Press, 1997).
4. *O'Connor v. Ortega.*
5. Will Aitchison, *The Rights of Law Enforcement Officers,* 5th ed. (Portland, OR: LRIS Publications, 2004), 3.
6. Roberg, Novak, and Cordner, *Police and Society.*
7. Brian A. Reaves, "Census of State and Local Law Enforcement Agencies, 2004," *Bureau of Justice Statistics Bulletin* (2007), http://www.ojp.usdoj.gov/bjs/pub/pdf/csllea04.pdf; Brian A. Reaves, "Federal Law Enforcement Officers, 2004," *Bureau of Justice Statistics Bulletin* (2006), http://www.ojp.usdoj.gov/bjs/pub/pdf/fleo04.pdf (accessed January 4, 2008).
8. James Stephan, *Census of State and Federal Correctional Facilities, 2005* (2008), http://www.ojp.usdoj.gov/bjs/pub/pdf/csfcf05.pdf (accessed June 30, 2008).
9. *O'Connor v. Ortega.*
10. Id.
11. William P. Bloss, "Warrantless Search in the Law Enforcement Workplace: Court Interpretation of Employer Practices and Employee Privacy Rights under the *Ortega* Doctrine," *Police Quarterly* 1 (1998): 57.
12. *Garrity v. New Jersey,* 385 U.S. 493 (1967); *Foley v. Connelie,* 435 U.S. 291 (1978).
13. *United States v. Taketa,* 923 F.2d 665 (9th Cir. 1991).
14. *Shields v. Burge,* 874 F.2d 1201 (7th Cir. 1989).
15. *O'Connor v. Ortega.*
16. *Los Angeles Police Protective League v. Gates,* 907 F.2d 879 (9th Cir. 1990).
17. *Shields v. Burge.*
18. *Kirkpatrick v. City of Los Angeles,* 803 F.2d 485 (9th Cir. 1986); *McKenna v. City of Philadelphia,* 771 F. Supp. 124 (E. D. Pa. 1991); *Profitt v. District of Columbia,* 790 F. Supp. 304 (D.D.C. 1991).
19. *O'Connor v. Ortega.*
20. Electronic Privacy Information Center, *Privacy & Human Rights: An International Survey of Privacy Laws and Developments.*
21. *Thompson v. Johnson County Community College,* 930 F. Supp. 501 (D. Kan. 1996).
22. *Sacramento County Deputy Sheriffs' Assn. v. County of Sacramento,* 59 CalRprt.2d 834 (3rd Dist. 1996).
23. *United States v. Taketa.*
24. Electronic Communications Privacy Act of 1986, 18 U.S.C. § 2510.

25. *Hart v. Clearfield City,* 815 F. Supp. 1544 (D. Utah 1993).

26. *Angel v. Williams,* 12 F.3d 786 (8th Cir. 1993).

27. Sharlene A. McEvoy, "E-mail and Internet Monitoring and the Workplace: Do Employees Have a Right to Privacy?" *Communications and the Law* 24 (2002): 69.

28. Donald H. Nichols, "Window Peeping in the Workplace: A Look into Employee Privacy in a Technological Era," *William Mitchell Law Review* 27 (2001): 1587.

29. A. Michael Froomkin, "The Death of Privacy?" *Stanford Law Review* 52 (2000): 1461.

30. *United States v. Simmons,* 206 F.3d 392 (4th Cir. 2000).

31. *United States v. Slanina,* 283 F.3d 670 (5th Cir. 2002).

32. *Bohach v. City of Reno,* 932 F. Supp. 1232 (D. Nev. 1996).

33. *Quon v. Arch Wireless,* No. 07-55282, __F.3d__, WL2440559 (9th Cir. 2008).

34. Electronic Privacy Information Center, "Workplace Privacy" (2008), http://epic.org/privacy/workplace (accessed July 10, 2008).

35. Musto, *The American Disease: Origins of Narcotic Control.*

36. *National Treasury Employees Union v. Von Raab.*

37. *Policemen's Benevolent Association of New Jersey v. Washington Township,* 672 F. Supp. 779 (D.N.J. 1987).

38. *National Treasury Employees Union v. Von Raab.*

39. Id.

40. *O'Connor v. Police Commissioner of Boston,* 557 N.E. 2d 1146 (Mass. 1990).

41. *Loder v. City of Glendale et al.,* 59 Cal.Rptr.2d 696 (Cal. 1997).

42. *Guiney v. Roache,* 873 F.2d 1557 (1st Cir. 1989).

43. *Penny v. Kennedy,* 915 F.2d 1065 (6th Cir. 1990).

44. *Delaraba v. Nassau County Police Department,* 610 N.Y.S. 2d 928 (Ct. App. 1994).

45. *Byrne v. Massachusetts Bay Transportation Authority,* 196 F. Supp.2d 77 (D. Mass. 2002).

46. *Anchorage Police Department Employees Association v. Municipality of Anchorage,* 24 P.3d 547 (Alaska 2001).

47. Claudia San Miguel, "Drug Tests, the Fourth Amendment, and Supreme Court's Rationale for Warrantless and Suspicionless Searches," in *Current Legal Issues in Criminal Justice,* ed. Craig Hemmens (Los Angeles: Roxbury Publishing Company, 2007), 71–82.

48. Employee Polygraph Protection Act of 1988, 29 U.S.C. § 2001 et seq.

49. *Garrity v. New Jersey.*

50. *Gardner v. Broderick,* 392 U.S. 273 (1968).

51. Id.

52. Aitchison, *The Rights of Law Enforcement Officers.*

53. *Scott v. City of Dallas,* 876 F. Supp. 852 (N. D. Tex. 1995).

54. Rolando V. del Carmen, Che D. Williamson, William P. Bloss, and Jay Coons, *Civil Liabilities and Rights of Police Officers and Supervisors in Texas* (Huntsville, TX: Sam Houston State University Press, 2003), 211.

55. *Johnson v. City of Tarpon Springs,* 758 F. Supp. 1473 (M.D. Fla. 1991).

56. *Kallstrom v. City of Columbus,* 136 F.3d 1055 (6th Cir. 1998).

57. *Broderick v. Police Commissioner of Boston,* 330 N.E. 2d 199 (Mass. 1975).

58. Id.

59. *Pennsylvania State Police v. Pennsylvania State Troopers Assn.,* 634 A. 2d 730 (Pa. Cmwlth. 1993).

60. *Barry v. City of New York,* 712 F.2d 1554 (2nd Cir. 1983).

61. *O'Brien v. DiGrazia,* 544 F.2d 543 (1st Cir. 1976).

62. Americans with Disability Act of 1990, 42 U.S.C. § 12101; The Rehabilitation Act of 1973, 29 U.S.C. § 794.

63. Health Insurance Portability and Accountability Act of 1996, 45 C.F.R. § 160–64.

64. *Redmond v. City of Overland Park,* 672 F. Supp 473 (D. Kan. 1987); *Thompson v. City of Arlington,* 838 F. Supp. 1137 (N.D. Tex. 1993); *Gutierrez v. Lynch,* 826 F.2d 1534 (6th Cir. 1987).

65. *Roberts v. United States Jaycees,* 468 U.S. 609 (1984).

66. Erwin Griswold, "The Right to Be Let Alone," *Northwestern University Law Review* 55 (1960): 216.

67. *Bowers v. Hardwick,* 478 U.S. 186 (1986).

68. *Miller v. California,* 413 U.S. 15 (1973).

69. *Wilson v. Swing,* 463 F. Supp. 555 (M.D. N.C. 1978); *Smith v. Price,* 616 F.2d 1371 (5th Cir. 1980).

70. *Shawgo v. Spradlin,* 701 F.2d 470 (5th Cir. 1983).

71. *Oliverson v. West Valley City,* 875 F. Supp. 1465 (D. Utah 1995); *Mercure v. Van Buren Township,* 81 F. Supp.2d 814 (E.D. Mich. 2000).

72. *Shuman v. City of Philadelphia,* 470 F. Supp. 449 (E.D. Pa. 1979).

73. *Mercer v. City of Cedar Rapids,* 308 F.3d 840 (8th Cir. 2002).

74. *Swope v. Bratton,* 541 F. Supp. 99 (W.D. Ark. 1982); *Briggs v. North Muskegon Police Department,* 563 F. Supp. 585 (W.D. Mich. 1983); *Shuman v. City of Philadelphia,* 470 F. Supp. 449 (E.D. Pa. 1979).

75. *Kukla v. Village of Antioch,* 647 F. Supp. 799 (N.D. Ill. 1986); *Shawgo v. Spradlin.*

76. *Jackson v. Howell,* 577 F. Supp. 47 (W.D. Mich. 1983).

77. *Riveros v. City of Los Angeles,* 49 Cal.Rptr.2d 238 (Cal. App. 2 Dist. 1996).

78. *Wieland v. City of Arnold,* 100 F. Supp.2d 984 (E.D. Mo. 2000).

79. *Fugate v. Phoenix Civil Service Board,* 791 F.2d 736 (9th Cir. 1986).

80. *Baron v. Meloni.*

81. *Keeney v. Heath,* 57 F.3d 579 (7th Cir. 1995); *Akers v. McGinnis,* 352 F.3d 1030 (6th Cir. 2003).

82. *Reuters v. Skipper,* 4 F.3d 716 (9th Cir. 1993).

83. *Lawrence v. Texas,* 539 U.S. 558 (2003).

84. *Bowers v. Hardwick.*

85. *Padula v. Webster,* 822 F.2d 97 (D.C. Cir. 1987); *Endsley v. Naes,* 673 F. Supp. 1032 (D. Kan. 1987); *Todd v. Navarro,* 698 F. Supp. 871 (S.D. Fla. 1988); *Delahoussaye v. City of New Iberia,* 937 F.2d 144 (5th Cir. 1991).

86. *Lawrence v. Texas.*

87. Aitchison, *The Rights of Law Enforcement Officers,* 240.

88. Eric Surette, "Sodomy" *American Jurisprudence,* 2nd ed. 70C Am. Jur. 2d Sodomy § 7 (2008).

89. Dan Eggen, "Officials Say Justice Department Based Hires on Politics before Goodling Tenure," *Washington Post,* May 26, 2007, http://www.washingtonpost .com/wp-dyn/content/article/2007/05/25/AR2007052502124.html (accessed July 31, 2008).

90. Carrie Johnson, "Internal Justice Dept. Report Cites Illegal Hiring Practices," *Washington Post,* July 29, 2008, http://www.washingtonpost.com/wp-dyn/content/ article/2008/07/28/AR2008072801007.html (accessed July 31, 2008).

91. Fraternal Order of Police, 2008, http://www.grandlodgefop.org/ (accessed July 31, 2008).

92. *Mescall v. Rochford,* 655 F.2d 111 (7th Cir. 1981); *Latino Officer's Ass'n, New York v. The City of New York,* 196 F.3d 458 (2nd Cir. 1999).

93. Robin D. Barnes, "Blue by Day and White by Knight: Regulating the Political Affiliations of Law Enforcement and Military Personnel," *Iowa Law Review* 81 (1996): 1079.

94. *Elrod v. Burns,* 427 U.S. 347 (1976).

95. *Branti v. Finkel,* 445 U.S. 507 (1980).

96. *Jantzen v. Hawkins,* 188 F.3d 1247 (10th Cir. 1999); *Morris v. Crow,* 117 F.3d 449 (11th Cir. 1997); *Perry v. Larson,* 794 F.2d 279 (7th Cir. 1986).

97. *Heidman v. Wirsing,* 7 F.3d 659 (7th Cir. 1993); *Joyner v. Lancaster,* 815 F.2d 20 (4th Cir. 1987).

98. *Jones v. Dodson,* 727 F.2d 1329 (4th Cir. 1984).

99. *Jenkins v. Medford,* 119 F.3d 1156 (4th Cir. 1997); *McBee v. Jim Hogg County, Tex.,* 730 F.2d 1009 (5th Cir. 1984).

100. *Horstkoetter v. Department of Public Safety,* 159 F.3d 1265 (10th Cir. 1998).

101. *Krisher v. Sharpe,* 736 F.Supp. 1313 (E.D.Pa. 1991).

102. *Pickering v. Board of Education,* 391 U.S. 563 (1968).

103. *Connick v. Myers,* 461 U.S. 138 (1983).

104. Jody M. Litchford, "Police Discipline v. Free Speech: First Amendment Rights of Law Enforcement Personnel," *The Police Chief* 60 (1993): 8; *Delgado v. Jones,* 282 F.3d 511 (7th Cir. 2002).

105. *Rankin v. McPherson,* 483 U.S. 378 (1987).

106. *Mansoor v. County of Albemarle,* 124 F. Supp. 367 (W.D. Va. 2000); *Kessler v. City of Providence,* 167 F.Supp.2d 482 (D. Rhode Island 2001).

107. del Carmen et al., *Civil Liabilities and Rights of Police Officers and Supervisors in Texas,* 122; *O'Donnell v. Barry,* 148 F.3d 1126 (D.C. Cir. 1998).

108. *Myers v. City of Highland Village, Texas,* 269 F.Supp.2d 850 (E.D. Tex. 2003); *Beach v. City of Olathe, Kansas,* 185 F.Supp.2d 1229 (D. Kan. 2002).

109. Rosalie Berger Levinson, "Silencing Government Employee Whistle-blowers in the Name of Efficiency," *Ohio Northern University Law Review* 23 (1996): 17.

110. *Cochran v. City of Los Angeles,* 222 F.3d 1195 (9th Cir. 2000).

111. *Pappas v. Giuliani,* 290 F.3d 143 (2nd Cir. 2002).

112. *Kelley v. Johnson,* 425 U.S. 238 (1976).

113. Lisa P. Baker, "Regulating Matters of Appearance: Tattoos and Other Body Art," *FBI Law Enforcement Bulletin* 2 (2007): 25.

114. *Weaver v. Henderson,* 984 F.2d 11 (1st Cir. 1993).

115. *Fraternal Order of Police Newark Lodge No. 12 v. City of Newark,* 170 F.3d 359 (3rd Cir. 1999).

116. *Francis v. Keane,* 888 F. Supp. 568 (S.D.N.Y. 1995).

117. *Booth v. Maryland,* 327 F.3d 377 (4th Cir. 2003).

118. *Rathert v. Village of Peotone,* 903 F.2d 510 (7th Cir. 1990).

119. *Inturri v. City of Hartford, Conn.* 365 F. Supp.2d 240 (D. Conn. 2005).

120. *Riggs v. City of Fort Worth,* 229 F. Supp.2d 572 (N.D. Tex. 2002).

121. *Seabrook v. City of New York,* 210 F.3d 355 (2nd Cir. 2000); *Zalewski v. County of Sullivan, New York,* 180 F. Supp.2d 486 (S.D.N.Y. 2002).

122. Baker, "Regulating Matters of Appearance," 25.

123. U.S. Constitution, Amendment I.

124. Civil Rights Act of 1964, § 701 et seq., as amended, 42 U.S.C. A. § 2000e et seq.

125. *Rodriguez v. City of Chicago,* 156 F.3d 771 (7th Cir. 1998).

126. *Parrott v. District of Columbia,* WL 126020 (D.D.C. 1991), 58 Empl. Prac. Dec. P41,369.

127. *Ryan v. Department of Justice,* 950 F.2d 458 (7th Cir. 1991).

128. *Endres v. Indiana State Police,* 334 F.3d 618 (7th Cir. 2003).

129. *Daniels v. City of Arlington, Tex.,* 246 F.3d 500 (5th Cir. 2001).

130. *Venters v. City of Delphi,* 123 F.3d 956 (7th Cir. 1997).

131. *Balint v. Carson City, Nevada,* 180 F.3d 1047 (9th Cir. 1999).

132. William P. Bloss, "Protected Expression: Police Employee First Amendment Rights," in *Handbook of Police Administration,* ed. Jim Ruiz and Don Hummer (Boca Raton, FL: CRC Press, 2008), 105–18.

CHAPTER 6

1. CNN.com, "Kobe Bryant Must Stand Trial, Judge Rules," October 21, 2003, http://www.cnn.com/2003/LAW/10/20/bryant.hearing/index.html?iref=newssearch; Anthony J. Sebok, "Why Did Bryant's Accuser Become Uncooperative?" September 7, 2004, http://www.cnn.com/2004/LAW/09/07/sebok.bryant/index.html?iref=newssearch (accessed July 16, 2008).

2. Bureau of Justice Statistics, "The Nation's Two Crime Measures" (2004), http://www.ojp.usdoj.gov/bjs/pub/html/ntcm.htm (accessed July 19, 2008).

3. Id.

4. Bureau of Justice Statistics, "Criminal Victimization 2006" (2006), http://www.ojp.usdoj.gov/bjs/abstract/cv06.htm (accessed July 19, 2008).

5. Office of Justice Programs, U.S. Department of Justice, "Criminal Victimization, 2006," *Bureau of Justice Statistics Fact Sheet* (2007), http://www.ojp.usdoj.gov/bjs/pub/pdf/cv06fs.pdf (accessed July 19, 2008).

6. Callie Rennison, "Rape and Sexual Assault: Reporting to Police and Medical Attention, 1992–2000" (2002), www.ojp.gov/bjs/pub/pdf/rsarp00.pdf (accessed July 7, 2008).

7. The National Center for Victims of Crime, "Rights of Crime Victims" (2008), http://www.ncvc.org/ncvc (accessed August 14, 2008).

8. Paul G. Cassell, "Recognizing Victims in the Federal Rules of Criminal Procedure: Proposed Amendments in Light of the Crime Victims' Rights Act," *Brigham Young University Law Review* 2005 (2005): 835, 837.

9. Crime Victims' Rights Act of 2004, 18 U.S.C.A. § 3771 (a).

10. Deborah W. Denno, "Perspectives in Disclosing Rape Victims' Names," *Fordham Law Review* 61 (1993): 1113.

11. *The Florida Star v. B. J. F.,* 491 U.S. 524 (1989).

12. Id.

13. Florida Statutes, Fla.Stat, § 794.03 (1987).

14. *The Florida Star v. B. J. F.*

15. *Cox Broadcasting Corp. v. Cohn,* 420 U.S. 469 (1975).

16. *Globe Newspaper Co. v. Superior Court for Norfolk County,* 457 U.S. 596 (1982).

17. *Does I Thru XXIII v. Advanced Textile Corp.,* 214 F.3d 1058 (9th Cir. 2000).

18. Meg Garvin, "Protecting Victim Privacy: The Tool of Anonymous Pleading in Civil Cases," *NCVLI News* (Winter 2007–2008) 8, 10.

19. Daniel M. Murdock, "A Compelling State Interest: Constructing a Statutory Framework for Protecting the Identity of Rape Victims," *Alabama Law Review* 58 (2007) 1177, 1189.

20. Federal Rules of Evidence 412.

21. *People v. Bryant,* 94 P.3d 624 (Colo. 2004).

22. Id.

23. David E. Fialkow, "The Media's First Amendment Rights and Rape Victim's Right to Privacy: Where Does One Right End and the Other Begin?" *Suffolk University Law Review* 39 (2006): 745, 772.

24. Douglas E. Beloof, "Beyond Prosecution: Sexual Assault Victim's Rights in Theory and Practice Symposium: Enabling Rape Shield Procedures under Crime Victims' Constitutional Privacy Rights," *Suffolk University Law Review* 38 (2005): 291.

25. *Jaffee v. Redmond,* 518 U.S. 1 (1996).

26. Id.

27. "Privacy of Victims' Counseling Communications," *Legal Series Bulletin # 8, Office for Victims of Crime* (2002), 1.

28. "Identity Theft—Facts and Figures" (2008), http://www.ncjrs.gov/spotlight/ identity_theft/facts.html (accessed August 14, 2008).

29. Privacy Act of 1974, 5 U.S.C. § 552.

CHAPTER 7

1. CNN.com, "Police, School District Defend Drug Raid" (November 10, 2003), http://www.cnn.com/2003/US/South/11/07/school.raid/index.html?iref =newssearch (accessed July 20, 2008).

2. Id.

3. *Vernonia School District 47J v. Acton,* 515 U.S. 646 (1995).

4. *National Treasury Employees Union v. Von Raab.*

5. *Skinner v. Railway Labor Executives' Ass'n.*

6. Shelley, "The Globalization of Crime," 3–10.

7. United Nations Convention against Transnational Organized Crime (2000), http://www.unodc.org/unodc/en/treaties/CTOC/index.html (accessed November 14, 2007).

8. William P. Bloss, *Transnational Crime and Terrorism in a Global Context* (New York: McGraw-Hill Publishers, 2006).

9. The 9/11 Commission Report, *Final Report of the National Commission on Terrorist Attacks upon the United States: Executive Summary* (2004), http://www.9-11 commission.gov/report/911Report_Exec.pdf, 2 (accessed April 27, 2008).

10. Posner, *Why America Slept: The Failure to Prevent 9/11.*

11. Pat Milton, "FBI Worries about an Osama-Mobsters Link" (2006), http:// www.usatoday.com/news/washington/2006-10-01-terror-mob_x.htm (accessed February 17, 2007).

12. Rachel Ehrenfeld, *Funding Evil: How Terrorism Is Financed and How to Stop It* (Chicago: Bonus Books, 2003).

13. Jonathan R. White, *Terrorism and Homeland Security,* 5th ed. (Belmont, CA: Thomson, 2006).

14. David Cole, "The Course of Least Resistance: Repeating History in the War on Terrorism," in *Lost Liberties: Ashcroft and the Assault on Personal Freedoms,* ed. Cynthia Brown (New York: The New Press, 2003), 13–32.

15. Solove, Rotenberg, and Schwartz, *Information Privacy Law.*

16. The Freedom of Information Act of 1966, 5 U.S.C. § 552.

17. Privacy Act of 1974, 5 U.S.C. § 552.

18. *Dalia v. United States,* 441 U.S. 238 (1979).

19. Solove, Rotenberg, and Schwartz, *Information Privacy Law,* 272.

20. *Katz v. United States: Berger v. New York,* 388 U.S. 41 (1967).

21. Wire and Electronic Communications Interception and Interception of Oral Communications Act of 2002, 116 Stat. 2158, 18 U.S.C. § 2510–2520.

22. Electronic Communications Privacy Act of 1986, 18 U.S.C. § 2510.

23. Id.

24. Communications Assistance for Law Enforcement Act of 1994, 47 U.S.C. §1002.

25. William P. Bloss, "Transforming U.S. Police Surveillance in a New Privacy Paradigm," *Police Practice and Research: An International Journal* 10 (2008): 1.

26. John W. Whitehead and Steven H. Aden, "Forfeiting Enduring Freedom for Homeland Security: A Constitutional Analysis of the USA Patriot Act and the Justice Department's Anti-Terrorism Initiatives," *American University Law Review* 51 (2002): 1081.

27. Uniting and Strengthening America by Providing Appropriate Tools Required to Intercept and Obstruct Terrorism Act, Pub. Law 107-56, 115 Stat. 272.

28. Jim Ruiz and Kathleen H. Winters, "The USA Patriot Act: A Review of the Major Components," in *Current Legal Issues in Criminal Justice,* ed. Craig Hemmens (Los Angeles: Roxbury Publishing, 2007), 29–43.

29. Patricia Mell, "Big Brother at the Door: Balancing National Security with Privacy under the USA Patriot Act," *Denver University Law Review* 80 (2002): 375, 426.

30. Norman Abrams, *Anti-Terrorism and Criminal Enforcement,* 2nd ed. (St. Paul, MN: Thomson West, 2005).

31. Homeland Security Act of 2002, 6 U.S.C. § 222.

32. Intelligence Reform and Terrorism Prevention Act of 2004, Pub. Law 108-458.

33. The 9/11 Commission Report, *Final Report of the National Commission on Terrorist Attacks upon the United States: Executive Summary,* 21.

34. REAL ID Act of 2005, Pub. Law 109-13.

35. Electronic Privacy Information Center, "REAL ID Implementation Review: Few Benefits, Staggering Costs: Analysis of the Department of Homeland Security's National ID Program" (2008), http://epic.org/privacy/id-cards/epic_realid_0508 .pdf (accessed August 22, 2008).

36. Karl Koscher, Ari Juels, Tadayoshi Kohno, and Vjekoslav Brajkovic, "EPC RFID Tags in Security Applications: Passport Cards, Enhanced Drivers Licenses, and Beyond," RSA Laboratories and University of Washington (2008), http:// www.rsa.com/rsalabs/staff/bios/ajuels/publications/EPC_RFID/Gen2authentica-tion–22Oct08a.pdf (accessed October 23, 2008).

37. Christopher Slobogin, "Public Privacy: Camera Surveillance of Public Places and the Right to Anonymity," *Mississippi Law Journal* 72 (2002): 213.

38. *City of Indianapolis v. Edmond.*

39. Sewell Chan and Kareem Fahim, "New York Starts to Inspect Bags on the Subway," *New York Times,* July 22, 2005, http://www.nytimes.com/2005/07/22/ nyregion/22york.html (accessed July 17, 2008).

40. *MacWade v. Kelly,* 460 F.3d 260 (2nd Cir. 2006).

41. *New Jersey v. T.L.O.*

42. Bureau of Justice Statistics, "Indicators of School Crime and Safety, 2006" (2006), http://www.ojp.usdoj.gov/bjs/abstract/iscs06.htm (accessed July 24, 2008).

43. Christine Hauser and Anahad O'Connor, "Virginia Tech Shooting Leaves 33 Dead," *New York Times* (2007), http://www.nytimes.com/2007/04/16/us/16cnd-shooting.html?_r=1&oref=slogin (accessed August 24, 2008).

44. *Vernonia School District 47J v. Acton.*

45. Electronic Privacy Information Center, *Privacy & Human Rights: An International Survey of Privacy Laws and Developments*, 79.

46. *U.S. v. Hartwell*, 296 F.Supp.2d 596 (E. D. Pa. 2003).

47. *U.S. v. Edwards*, 498 F.2d 496 (2nd Cir. 1974).

48. Thomas Frank, "10 Airports Install Body Scanners: Devices Can Peer under Passengers' Clothes," *USA Today* (2008), http://www.usatoday.com/printedition/news/20080606/a_bodyscan06.art.htm (accessed July 10, 2008).

49. Electronic Privacy Information Center, *Secure Flight* (2007), http://epic.org/privacy/airtravel/secureflight.html (accessed July 30, 2008).

50. J. K. Petersen, *Understanding Surveillance Technologies: Spy Devices, Privacy, History & Applications*, 2nd ed. (Boca Raton, FL: Auerbach Publications, 2007).

51. The Biometric Consortium, "Biometrics History" (2006), http://biometrics.org/html/introduction.html (accessed February 2, 2008).

52. Saferstein, *Criminalistics: An Introduction to Forensic Science.*

53. The Biometric Consortium, "Face Recognition" (2006), http://www.biometrics.gov/Documents/facerec.pdf (accessed February 2, 2008).

54. Id.

55. Id.

56. Jonathan Karp and Laura Meckler, "Which Traveler's Have 'Hostile Intent'? Biometric Device May Have the Answer," *Wall Street Journal Online*, August 14, 2006, http://online.wsj.com/public/article/SB115551793796934752-2hgveyRtDDtssKo2VPmg6RAAa_w_20070813.html?mod=tff_main_tff_top (accessed May 14, 2007).

57. The Biometric Consortium, "Speaker Recognition" (2006), http://www.biometrics.gov/Documents/SpeakerRec.pdf (accessed February 2, 2008).

58. Sorin Draghici, "A Neural Network Based Artificial Vision System for Licence Plate Recognition," (1997), http://vortex.cs.wayne.edu/papers/ijns1997.pdf (accessed July 14, 2008).

59. Marcia Kramer, "NYPD's 'Operation Sentinel' to Track Everything" (2008), http://wcbstv.com/cbs2crew/operationa.sentinel.nypd.2.793133.html (accessed September 18, 2008).

60. Electronic Privacy Information Center, "Face Recognition" (2007), http://epic.org/privacy/facerecognition/ (accessed February 2, 2008).

61. *United States v. Scarpo*, 180 F. Supp.2d 572 (D.N.J. 2001).

62. Roger Clarke, "Introduction to Dataveillance and Information Privacy, and Definitions of Terms" (1997), http://www.rogerclarke.com (accessed March 14, 2008).

63. Robert O'Harrow, Jr., *No Place to Hide* (New York: Free Press, 2005), 9.

64. Electronic Privacy Information Center, "Automated Targeting System" (2008), http://epic.org/privacy/travel/ats/default.html (accessed July 14, 2008); Ellen Nakashima, "Collecting of Details on Travelers Documented: U.S. Effort

More Extensive Than Previously Known," September 22, 2007, http://www
.washingtonpost.com/wp-dyn/content/article/2007/09/21/AR2007092102347
.html (accessed February 5, 2008).

65. Department of Homeland Security, *Fusion Center Guidelines: Developing and Sharing Information and Intelligence in a New Era* (2006), http://www.iir
.com/global/products/fusion_center_executive_summary.pdf, 3–4 (accessed December 12, 2007).

66. Id.

67. Bloss, "Transforming U.S. Police Surveillance in a New Privacy Paradigm," 1.

CHAPTER 8

1. *Griswold v. Connecticut.*

2. Thomas L. Friedman, *The World Is Flat: A Brief History of the Twenty-First Century* (New York: Farrar, Straus, and Giroux, 2005).

3. William P. Bloss, "Culture Clash: Investigating the Nexus between Western-Muslim Ideological Dissonance and Islamist Terrorism," *European and International Research Group on Crime, Ethics, and Social Philosophy Online Quarterly Review* 5 (2008): 31, http://www.erces.com/journal/articles/actuel/v04.htm (accessed September 4, 2008).

4. See Margaret E. Beare, *Critical Reflections on Transnational Organized Crime, Money Laundering, and Corruption* (Toronto: University of Toronto Press, 2003).

5. Reg Whitaker, "After 9/11: A Surveillance State?" in *Lost Liberties: Ashcroft and the Assault on Personal Freedom,* ed. Cynthia Brown (New York: The New Press, 2003), 52–74, 53.

6. William P. Bloss, "Transforming Transnational Crime," in *Transnational Crime and Terrorism in a Global Context,* ed. William Bloss (New York: McGraw-Hill, 2006), 33–40.

7. The 9/11 Commission Report, *Final Report of the National Commission on Terrorist Attacks upon the United States: Executive Summary,* 2.

8. Marilyn Peterson, "Intelligence-Led Policing: The New Intelligence Architecture, *Bureau of Justice Assistance* (Washington, DC: U.S. Department of Justice, 2005).

9. Mike Harvey, "Why Veins Could Replace Fingerprints and Retinas as Most Secure Form of ID," *Times Online,* November 11, 2008, http://technology
.timesonline.co.uk/tol/news/tech_and_web/article5129384.ece (accessed November 11, 2008).

10. Walter Laqueur, "The Terrorism to Come," *Policy Review* 8 (2004): 49.

11. Aldous Huxley, *Brave New World* (New York: Harper & Row Publishers, 1946).

12. Orwell, *Nineteen Eighty-Four, A Novel;* M. G. Michael and K. Michael, "A Note on Überveillance" (2007), http://ro.uow.edu.au/infopapers/560 (accessed August 12, 2008).

13. David Brin, *The Transparent Society: Will Technology Force Us to Choose between Privacy and Freedom?* (Reading, MA: Addison-Wesley, 1998).

SELECT BIBLIOGRAPHY

Abadinsky, Howard. *Probation and Parole.* 9th ed. Upper Saddle River, NJ: Pearson/
   Prentice-Hall, 2006.
Abrams, Norman. *Anti-Terrorism and Criminal Enforcement.* 2nd ed. St. Paul, MN:
   Thomson West, 2005.
Acker, James R., and David C. Brody. *Criminal Procedure: A Contemporary Perspec-
   tive.* 2nd ed. Sudbury, MA: Jones and Bartlett Publishers, 2004.
Aguilar v. Texas, 378 U.S. 108 (1964).
Aitchison, Will. *The Rights of Law Enforcement Officers.* 5th ed. Portland, OR: LRIS
   Publications, 2004.
Alarid, Leanne Fiftal, Paul Cromwell, and Rolando V. del Carmen. *Community-
   Based Corrections.* 7th ed. Belmont, CA: Thomson, 2008.
Albright v. Oliver, 510 U.S. 266 (1994).
Allen, Harry E., Edward J. Latessa, Bruce S. Ponder, and Clifford E. Simonsen. *Cor-
   rections in America: An Introduction.* 11th ed. Upper Saddle River, NJ: Pearson/
   Prentice-Hall, 2007.
Almeida-Sanchez v. United States, 413 U.S. 266 (1973).
Arizona v. Evans, 514 U.S. 1 (1995).
Arizona v. Hicks, 480 U.S. 321 (1987).
Arizona v. Youngblood, 488 U.S. 51 (1988).
Ashcraft v. Tennessee, 322 U.S. 143 (1944).
Atwater v. City of Lago Vista, 532 U.S. 318 (2001).
Austin, James, Barry Krisberg, and Paul Litsky. "The Effectiveness of Supervised
   Pretrial Release." *Crime and Delinquency* 31 (1985): 519–37.
Bacigal, Ronald J. "Dodging a Bullet, but Opening Old Wounds in Fourth Amend-
   ment Jurisprudence." *Seton Hall Law Review* 16 (1986): 597–629.
Baker, John Hamilton. *An Introduction to English Legal History.* 3rd ed. Boston: But-
   terworth's, 1990.
Baker, Lisa A. "Regulating Matters of Appearance: Tattoos and Other Body Art."
   FBI Law Enforcement Bulletin, 2 (2007): 25–33.
Bandes, Susan. "Tracing the Pattern of No Pattern: Stories of Police Brutality."
   Loyola of Los Angeles Law Review 34 (2001): 665–80.
Banks v. Dretke, 540 U.S. 668 (2004).

Barnes, Robin D. "Blue by Day and White by Knight: Regulating the Political Affiliations of Law Enforcement and Military Personnel." *Iowa Law Review* 81 (1996): 1079–1172.

Barone, Patrick T., and Jeffery S. Crampton. "Do 'Standardized Field Sobriety Tests' Reliably Predict Intoxication." *Michigan Bar Journal* 84 (2005): 23–26.

Beare, Margaret E. *Critical Reflections on Transnational Organized Crime, Money Laundering, and Corruption.* Toronto: University of Toronto Press, 2003.

Belbot, Barbara. "Inmate Litigation and the Constitution." In *Current Legal Issues in Criminal Justice,* edited by Craig Hemmens, 167–76. Los Angeles: Roxbury Publishing, 2007.

Bell v. Wolfish, 441 U.S. 520 (1979).

Beloof, Douglas E. "Beyond Prosecution: Sexual Assault Victim's Rights in Theory and Practice Symposium: Enabling Rape Shield Procedures under Crime Victims' Constitutional Privacy Rights," *Suffolk University Law Review* 38 (2005): 291–301.

Berkemer v. McCarty, 468 U.S. 420 (1984).

Black, Henry. *Black's Law Dictionary.* Abridged 5th ed. St. Paul, MN: West Publishing, 1983.

Blackstone, William. *Ehrlich's Blackstone.* San Carlos, CA: Nourse Publishing Co., 1959.

Bloom, Robert M. "Inevitable Discovery: An Exception beyond the Fruits." *American Journal of Criminal Law* 20 (1992): 79–103.

Bloss, William. "Escalating U.S. Police Surveillance after 9/11: An Examination of Causes and Effects." *Surveillance and Society* 4 (2007): 208–28.

Bloss, William P. "Police Misconduct after the Rodney King Incident." In *The Encyclopedia of Police Science, 3rd Edition,* edited by Jack Greene, 964–68. London: Routledge, 2006.

———. "Privacy Issues Involving Law Enforcement Personnel: A Constitutional Analysis." Ph.D. diss., Sam Houston State University, 1996.

———. "Protected Expression: Police Employee First Amendment Rights." In *Handbook of Police Administration,* edited by Jim Ruiz and Don Hummer, 105–18, Boca Raton, FL: CRC Press, 2008.

———. *Transnational Crime and Terrorism in a Global Context.* New York: McGraw-Hill Publishers, 2006.

———. "Warrantless Search in the Law Enforcement Workplace: Court Interpretation of Employer Practices and Employee Privacy Rights Under the *Ortega* Doctrine," *Police Quarterly* 1 (1998): 57–70.

Board of Education of Independent School District No. 92 of Pottawatomie County v. Earls, 536 U.S. 822 (2002).

Bowers v. Hardwick, 478 U.S. 186 (1986).

Boyd v. United States, 116 U.S. 616 (1886).

Brady v. Maryland, 373 U.S. 83 (1963).

Branti v. Finkel, 445 U.S. 507 (1980).

Breithaupt v. Abram, 352 U.S. 432 (1957).

Brendlin v. California, 551 U.S.__(2007); 127 S.Ct. 2400 (2007).

Brewer v. Williams, 430 U.S. 387 (1977).

Brin, David. *The Transparent Society: Will Technology Force Us to Choose between Privacy and Freedom?* Reading, MA: Addison-Wesley, 1998.

Brown v. Mississippi, 297 U.S. 278 (1936).

Bugliosi, Vincent. *Outrage: The Five Reasons Why O.J. Simpson Got Away with Murder.* New York: W. W. Norton & Company, 1996.

Bumper v. North Carolina, 391 U.S. 543 (1968).

Byrne, James. "The Future of Intensive Probation Supervision." *Crime and Delinquency* 36 (1990): 6–42.

California v. Beheler, 463 U.S. 1121 (1983).

California v. Ciraolo, 476 U.S. 207 (1986).

California v. Greenwood, 486 U.S. 35 (1988).

California v. Hodari D., 499 U.S. 621 (1991).

Call, Jack E. "The Supreme Court and Prisoner's Rights." In *Correctional Contexts: Contemporary and Classical Readings,* 3rd ed., edited by Edward Latessa and Alexander Holsinger, 209–24. Los Angeles: Roxbury Publishing, 2006.

Camara v. Municipal Court, 387 U.S. 523 (1967).

Cardwell v. Lewis, 417 U.S. 583 (1974).

Carroll v. United States, 267 U.S. 132 (1925).

Cassell, Paul G. "Recognizing Victims in the Federal Rules of Criminal Procedure: Proposed Amendments in Light of the Crime Victims' Rights Act," *Brigham Young University Law Review* 2005 (2005): 835–51.

Chambers v. Florida, 309 U.S. 227 (1940).

Chambers v. Maroney, 399 U.S. 42 (1970).

Chambers v. Mississippi, 410 U.S. 284 (1973).

Chang, Nancy. "How Democracy Dies: The War on Our Civil Liberties." In *Lost Liberties: Ashcroft and the Assault on Personal Freedom,* edited by Cynthia Brown, 33–51. New York: The New Press, 2003.

Chimel v. California, 395 U.S. 752 (1969).

Chin, Gabriel J., and Scott C. Wells. " 'The Blue Wall of Silence' as Evidence of Bias and Motive to Lie: A New Approach to Police Perjury." *University of Pittsburgh Law Review* 59 (1998): 233–299.

City of Indianapolis v. Edmond, 531 U.S. 32 (2000).

Clear, Todd R., Val B. Clear, and Anthony A. Braga. "Correctional Alternatives for Drug Offenders in an Era of Overcrowding." *The Prison Journal* 73 (1993): 98.

Clear, Todd R., George F. Cole, and Michael D. Reisig. *American Corrections,* 7th ed. Belmont, CA: Thomson, 2006.

Cohen v. California, 403 U.S. 15 (1971).

Cole, David. "The Course of Least Resistance: Repeating History in the War on Terrorism." In *Lost Liberties: Ashcroft and the Assault on Personal Freedom,* edited by Cynthia Brown, 13–32. New York: The New Press, 2003.

Cole, Simon A., and William C. Thompson. "Legal Issues Associated with DNA Evidence." In *Current Legal Issues in Criminal Justice,* edited by Craig Hemmens, 135–49. Los Angeles: Roxbury Publishing, 2007.

Colonnade Catering Corp. v. United States, 397 U.S. 72 (1970).

Colorado v. Bannister, 449 U.S. 1 (1980).

Colorado v. Bertine, 479 U.S. 367 (1987).

Connecticut Department of Public Safety et al. v. Doe, Individually and on Behalf of All Others Similarly Situated, 538 U.S. 1 (2003).

Connick v. Myers, 461 U.S. 138 (1983).

Cooley, Thomas McIntyre. *Torts,* 2nd ed. Chicago: Callahan, 1881.

Coolidge v. New Hampshire, 403 U.S. 443 (1971).

Cooper v. Pate, 378 U.S. 546 (1964).

Cox Broadcasting Corp. v. Cohn, 420 U.S. 469 (1975).

Coy v. Iowa, 487 U.S. 1012 (1988).

Crawford v. Washington, 541 U.S. 36 (2004).

Crouch, Ben M., and James W. Marquart. *An Appeal to Justice: Litigated Reform of Texas Prisons.* Austin: University of Texas Press, 1989.

Crowe, Ann H. "Electronic Supervision: From Decision-Making to Implementation." *Corrections Today* 64 (2002): 130–33.

Crowe, Ann H., Linda Sydney, Pat Bancroft, and Beverly Lawrence. *Offender Supervision with Electronic Technology: A User's Guide.* Lexington, KY: American Probation and Parole Association, 2002.

Cupp v. Murphy, 412 U.S. 291 (1973).

Dalia v. United States, 441 U.S. 238 (1979).

Davis v. Mississippi, 394 U.S. 721 (1969).

Dawson v. Delaware, 503 U.S. 159 (1992).

Deck v. Missouri, 544 U.S. 6622 (2005).

Delaware v. Prouse, 440 U.S. 648 (1979).

del Carmen, Rolando V. *Civil Liabilities in American Policing.* Englewood Cliffs, NJ: Brady, 1991.

———. *Criminal Procedure: Law and Practice.* 7th ed. Belmont, CA: Wadsworth Publishing, 2007.

del Carmen, Rolando V., Maldine Beth Barnhill, Gene Bonham, Jr., Lance Hignite, and Todd Jermstad. *Civil Liabilities and Other Legal Issues for Probation/Parole Officer and Supervisors.* 3rd ed. Washington, DC: National Institute of Corrections, 2001. http://www.nicic.org/pubs/2001/017068.pdf.

del Carmen, Rolando V., and Joseph Vaughn. "Legal Issues in the Use of Electronic Surveillance in Probation." *Federal Probation* 50 (1986): 60–69.

del Carmen, Rolando V., Che D. Williamson, William P. Bloss, and Jay Coons. *Civil Liabilities and Rights of Police Officers and Supervisors in Texas.* Huntsville, TX: Sam Houston State University Press, 2003.

Denno, Deborah W. "Perspectives in Disclosing Rape Victims' Names," *Fordham Law Review* 61 (1993): 1113–31.

Domino, John C. *Civil Rights and Liberties in the 21st Century.* 2nd ed. New York: Longman, 2003.

Donovan v. Dewey, 452 U.S. 594 (1981).

Draper v. United States, 358 U.S. 307 (1959).

Ducat, Craig R. *Constitutional Interpretation.* 8th ed. Belmont, CA: Thomson/West, 2004.

Ehrenfeld, Rachel. *Funding Evil: How Terrorism Is Financed and How To Stop It.* Chicago: Bonus Books, 2003.

Elkins v. United States, 364 U.S. 206 (1960).

Elrod v. Burns, 427 U.S. 347 (1976).

Epstein, Lee, and Thomas G. Walker. *Constitutional Law for a Changing America: Rights, Liberties, and Justice.* Washington, DC: CQ Press, 2004.

Estelle v. Williams, 425 U.S. 501 (1976).

Federal Rules of Evidence. Washington, DC: Government Printing Office, 2004.

Ferguson v. City of Charleston, 532 U.S. 67 (2001).

Fialkow, David E. "The Media's First Amendment Rights and Rape Victim's Right to Privacy: Where Does One Right End and the Other Begin?" *Suffolk University Law Review* 39 (2006): 745–72.

Finn, Mary A., and Suzanne Muirhead-Steves. "The Effectiveness of Electronic Monitoring with Violent Male Parolees." *Justice Quarterly* 18 (2002): 293–313.

Flippo v. West Virginia, 528 U.S. 11 (1999).

Florida v. Bostick, 501 U.S. 429 (1991).

Florida v. Jimeno, 500 U.S. 248 (1991).

Foucault, Michel. *Discipline and Punishment: The Birth of the Prison.* New York: Pantheon Books, 1977.

Fried, Charles. *An Anatomy of Values: Problem of Personal and Social Choice.* Cambridge: Harvard Press, 1970.

Friedman, Thomas L. *The World Is Flat: A Brief History of the Twenty-First Century.* New York: Farrar, Straus, and Giroux, 2005.

Froomkin, A. Michael. "The Death of Privacy?" *Stanford Law Review* 52 (2000): 1461–550.

Gagnon v. Scarpelli, 411 U.S. 778 (1973).

Gallagher, Mary P. "Civil Libertarians Wince at New Device That 'Shines Light' on Drunken Drivers." *New Jersey Law Journal* 161 (2000): 6–9.

Gardner, Thomas J., and Terry M. Anderson. *Criminal Evidence: Principles and Cases.* 6th ed. Belmont, CA: Thomson-Wadsworth, 2007.

———. *Criminal Law.* 10th ed. Belmont, CA: Thomson-Wadsworth, 2009.

Gardner v. Broderick, 392 U.S. 273 (1968).

Gardner v. Florida, 430 U.S. 349 (1977).

Garrity v. New Jersey, 385 U.S. 493 (1967).

Gerstein v. Pugh, 420 U.S. 103 (1975).

Gest, Ted. *Crime & Politics: Big Government's Erratic Campaign for Law and Order.* New York: Oxford University Press, 2001.

Gideon v. Wainwright, 372 U.S. 335 (1963).

Giglio v. United States, 405 U.S. 105 (1972).

Gilbert v. California, 388 U.S. 263 (1967).

Glancy, Dorothy. "Invention of the Right to Privacy." *Arizona Law Review* 21 (1979): 1–43.

Globe Newspaper Co. v. Superior Court, 457 U.S. 596 (1982).

Griffin v. California, 380 U.S. 609 (1965).

Griffin v. Wisconsin, 483 U.S. 868 (1987).

Griswold, Erwin. "The Right to Be Let Alone." *Northwestern University Law Review,* 55 (1960): 216–31.

Griswold v. Connecticut, 381 479 (1965).

Groh v. Ramirez et al., 540 U.S. 551 (2004).

Han, Kim. "The Technological Sniffing Out of Constitutional Rights: Assessing the Constitutionality of the Passive Alcohol Sensor III." *Journal of Law and Policy* 9 (2001): 835–77.

Hancock, Catherine. "Due Process before Miranda." *Tulane Law Review* 70 (1996): 2195–237.

Hanser, Robert D., Jeffrey P. Rush, Scott M. Mire, and Attapol Kuanliang. "Liabilities Associated with HIV/AIDS in Jail Settings: Balancing Offender Legal Protections with Concerns for Public Safety." *Southern University Law Review* 34 (2007): 1–26.

Hayes v. Florida, 470 U.S. 811 (1985).

Hiibel v. Sixth Judicial District Court, 542 U.S. 177 (2004).

Hixson, Richard F.. *Privacy in a Public Society: Human Rights in Conflict.* New York: Oxford University Press, 1987.

Hoffman v. United States, 341 U.S. 479 (1951).

Holbrook v. Flynn, 475 U.S. 560 (1986).

Holdsworth, William Searle. *A History of English Law.* 2nd ed. New York: Macmillan, 1937.

Holtz, Larry E.. *Contemporary Criminal Procedure: Court Decisions for Law Enforcement.* Longwood, FL: Gould Publications, 2004.

Horton v. California, 496 U.S. 128 (1990).

Hudson v. McMillian, 503 U.S. 1 (1992).

Hudson v. Palmer, 468 U.S. 517 (1984).

Huxley, Aldous. *Brave New World.* New York: Harper & Row Publishers, 1946.

Illinois v. Allen, 397 U.S. 337 (1970).

Illinois v. Caballes, 543 U.S. 405 (2005).

Illinois v. Fisher, 540 U.S. 544 (2004).

Illinois v. Gates, 462 U.S. 213 (1983).

Illinois v. Krull, 480 U.S. 340 (1987).

Illinois v. Lidster, 540 U.S. 419 (2004).

Illinois v. Perkins, 496 U.S. 292 (1990).

Illinois v. Rodriguez, 497 U.S. 177 (1990).

Illinois v. Wardlow, 528 U.S. 119 (2000).

Jaffee v. Redmond, 518 U.S. 1 (1996).

Johnson v. U.S., 333 U.S. 10 (1948).

Kamisar, Yale, Wayne R. LaFave, Jerold H. Israel, and Nancy J. King. *Modern Criminal Procedure.* 11th ed. St. Paul, MN: Thomson/West, 2005.

Kamisar, Yale, Wayne R. LaFave, Jerold H. Israel, Nancy J. King, and Orin S. Kerr. *Modern Criminal Procedure*. 12th ed. St. Paul, MN: Thomson/West, 2008.

Kansas v. Hendricks, 521 U.S. 346 (1997).

Kappeler, Victor E. *Critical Issues in Police Civil Liability*. 4th ed. Long Grove, IL: Waveland, 2006.

Karmen, Andrew. *Crime Victims: An Introduction to Victimology*. 6th ed. Belmont, CA: Wadsworth Publishing, 2007.

Katz v. United States, 389 U.S. 347 (1967).

Kaye, David. "Who Needs Special Needs? On the Constitutionality of Collecting DNA and Other Biometric Data from Arrestees." *Journal of Law, Medicine & Ethics* 34 (2006): 188–95.

Keeton, Page W., and William Lloyd Prosser. *Prosser and Keeton on the Law of Torts*. 5th ed. St. Paul, MN: West Publishing, 1984.

Kelling, George L. *The Kansas City Preventive Patrol Experiment: A Summary Report*. Washington, DC: The Police Foundation, 1974.

Kerr, Orin S. "The Fourth Amendment and New Technologies: Constitutional Myths and the Case for Caution." *Michigan Law Review* 102 (2004): 801–88.

King, Cynthia A. "Fighting the Devil We Don't Know: Kansas v. Hendricks, A Case Study Exploring the Civilization of Criminal Punishment and Its Ineffectiveness in Preventing Child Sexual Abuse." *William and Mary Law Review* 40 (1999): 1427–69.

Kirby v. Illinois, 406 U.S. 682 (1972).

Klotter, John C., Jacqueline R. Kanovitz, and Michael I. Kanovitz. *Constitutional Law*. 8th ed. Cincinnati, OH: Anderson Publishing, 1999.

Knepper, Kathleen. "Responsibility of Correctional Officials in Responding to the Incidence of the HIV Virus in Jails and Prisons." *New England Journal on Criminal and Civil Confinement* 21 (1995): 45–70.

Koosed, Margery Malkin. "The Proposed Innocence Protection Act Won't—Unless It Also Curbs Mistaken Eyewitness Identifications." *Ohio State Law Journal* 63 (2002): 263–314.

Kyles v. Whitley, 514 U.S. 419 (1995).

Kyllo v. United States, 533 U.S. 27 (2001).

Laqueur, Walter. *The New Terrorism: Fanaticism and the Arms of Mass Destruction*. Oxford, UK: Oxford University Press, 1999.

Lawrence v. Texas, 539 U.S. 558 (2003).

Lee, Gregory D. *Practical Criminal Evidence*. Upper Saddle River, NJ: Pearson/ Prentice-Hall, 2007.

Lefkowitz v. Turley, 414 U.S. 70 (1973).

Levinson, Rosalie Berger. "Silencing Government Employee Whistleblowers in the Name of Efficiency." *Ohio Northern University Law Review* 23 (1996): 17–42.

Lichtenberg, Illya D., and Alisa Smith. "How Dangerous Are Routine Police-Citizen Traffic Stops? A Research Note." *Journal of Criminal Justice* 29 (2001): 419–28.

Linedecker, Clifford L. *O. J. A to Z: The Complete Handbook of the Trial of the Century*. New York: St. Martin's Griffin, 1995.

Litchford, Jody M. "Police Discipline v. Free Speech: First Amendment Rights of Law Enforcement Personnel." *The Police Chief* 60 (1993): 8–12.

Luria, Amy. "Showup Identifications: A Comprehensive Overview of the Problems and a Discussion of Necessary Changes." *Nebraska Law Review* 86 (2008): 515–51.

Lurigio, Arthur J., Marylouise E. Jones, and Barbara E. Smith. "Child Sexual Abuse: Its Causes, Consequences, and Implications for Probation Practice." *Federal Probation* 69 (1995): 69–77.

Lyman, Michael D. *Criminal Investigation: The Art and Science.* 5th ed. Upper Saddle River, NJ: Prentice-Hall, 2007.

Lyman, Michael D., and Gary W. Potter. *Drugs and Society.* 4th ed. Cincinnati, OH: Anderson/Lexis-Nexis, 2003.

Lyon, David. *Surveillance Society: Monitoring Everyday Life.* Buckingham, UK: Open University Press, 2001.

MacDade v. Kelly, 460 F.3d 260 (2nd Cir. 2006).

Maclin, Tracey. "Is Obtaining an Arrestee's DNA a Valid Special Needs Search under the Fourth Amendment? What Should (and Will) the Supreme Court Do?" *Journal of Law, Medicine and Ethics* 33 (2005): 165–181.

Mancke, John B. "DUI Field Sobriety Tests: Have the Courts Missed a Step?" *Pennsylvania Bar Association Quarterly* 73 (2002): 117–32.

Manson v. Brathwaite, 432 U.S. 98 (1977).

Mapp v. Ohio, 467 U.S. 643 (1961).

Marshall v. Barlow's, Inc., 436 U.S. 307 (1970).

Maryland v. Buie, 494 U.S. 325 (1990).

Maryland v. Craig, 497 U.S. 836 (1990).

Maryland v. Garrison, 480 U.S. 79 (1987).

Maryland v. Pringle, 540 U.S. 366 (2003).

Maryland v. Wilson, 519 U.S. 408 (1997).

Massachusetts v. Sheppard, 468 U.S. 981 (1984).

Massiah v. United States, 377 U.S. 201 (1964).

McAninch, William Shepard. "Unreasonable Expectations: The Supreme Court and the Fourth Amendment." *Stetson Law Review* 20 (1991): 435–73.

McEvoy, Sharlene A. "E-mail and Internet Monitoring and the Workplace: Do Employees Have a Right to Privacy?" *Communications and the Law* 24 (2002): 69–84.

McLaughlin, Andrew Cunningham. *A Constitutional History of the United States.* New York: Appleton-Century-Crofts, 1935.

Mell, Patricia. "Big Brother at the Door: Balancing National Security with Privacy under the USA Patriot Act." *Denver University Law Review* 80 (2002): 375–427.

Memory, John M., and Randall Aragon. *Patrol Officer Problem Solving and Solutions.* Durham, NC: Carolina Academic Press, 2001.

Mempa v. Rhay, 389 U.S. 128 (1967).

Michigan Department of State Police v. Sitz, 496 U.S. 444 (1990).

Michigan v. Clifford, 464 U.S. 287 (1984).

Michigan v. Long, 463 U.S. 1032 (1983).

Miller v. California, 413 U.S. 15 (1973).

Mincey v. Arizona, 437 U.S. 385 (1978).

Minnesota v. Dickerson, 508 U.S. 366 (1993).

Minnesota v. Murphy, 465 U.S. 420 (1984).

Miranda v. Arizona, 384 U.S. 436 (1966).

Mitchell, John B. "What Went Wrong with the Warren Court's Conception of the Fourth Amendment?" *New England Law Review* 27 (1992): 35–59.

Monroe v. Pape. 365 U.S. 167 (1961).

Moore, Barrington. *Privacy: Studies in Social and Cultural History.* New York: Pantheon Books, 1984.

Moore v. Illinois, 434 U.S. 220 (1977).

Morrissey v. Brewer, 408 U.S. 471 (1972).

Mosteller, Robert P. "The Duke Lacrosse Case, Innocence, and False Identifications: A Fundamental Failure to 'Do Justice.'" *Fordham Law Review* 76 (2007): 1337–412.

Murdock, Daniel M. "A Compelling State Interest: Constructing a Statutory Framework for Protecting the Identity of Rape Victims." *Alabama Law Review* 58 (2007): 1177–98.

Murray v. United States, 487 U.S. 533 (1988).

Musto, David F. *The American Disease: Origins of Narcotic Control.* 3rd ed. New York: Oxford University Press, 1999.

National Treasury Employees Union v. Von Raab, 489 U.S. 656 (1989).

Neil v. Biggers, 409 U.S. 188 (1972).

New Jersey v. T.L.O., 469 U.S. 325 (1985).

New York v. Belton, 453 U.S. 454 (1981).

New York v. Burger, 482 U.S. 691 (1987).

New York v. Class, 475 U.S. 106 (1986).

New York v. Quarles, 467 U.S. 649 (1984).

Nix v. Williams, 467 U.S. 431 (1984).

Noble, Jeff. "Police Officer Truthfulness and the Brady Decision." *The Police Chief* 70 (2003): 92–101.

North Carolina v. Butler, 441 U.S. 369 (1979).

O'Brien, David M. *Privacy, Law, and Public Policy.* New York: Praeger, 1979.

O'Connor v. Ortega, 480 U.S. 709 (1987).

O'Harrow, Jr., Robert. *No Place to Hide.* New York: Free Press, 2005.

Oliver v. United States, 466 U.S. 170 (1984).

Olmstead v. U.S. 277 U.S. 438 (1928).

Orwell, George. *Nineteen Eighty-Four, A Novel.* New York: Harcourt, Brace & Co., 1949.

Palmer, John W. *Constitutional Rights of Prisoners,* 8th ed. Columbus, OH: Lexis Nexis, 2006.

Parenti, Christian. *The Soft Cage: Surveillance in America from Slavery to the War on Terror.* New York: Basic Books, 2003.

Pennsylvania v. Mimms, 434 U.S. 106 (1977).

Pennsylvania v. Muniz, 496 U.S. 582 (1990).

People v. Bryant, 94 P.3d 624 (Colo. 2004).

Petersen, J. K. *Understanding Surveillance Technologies: Spy, Devices, Privacy, History & Applications,* 2nd ed. Boca Raton, FL: Auerbach Publications, 2007.

Pickering v. Board of Education, 391 U.S. 563 (1967).

Plessy v. Ferguson, 163 U.S. 537 (1896).

Pointer v. Texas, 380 U.S. 400 (1965).

Posner, Gerald L. *Why America Slept: The Failure to Prevent 9/11.* New York: Random House, 2003.

Post, Robert C. "The Social Foundations of Privacy: Community and Self in the Common Law Tort." *California Law Review* 77 (1989): 957–1010.

President's Commission on Law Enforcement and Administration of Justice. *The Challenge of Crime in a Free Society.* Washington, DC: U.S. Government Printing Office, 1967.

Procunier v. Martinez, 416 U.S. 396 (1974).

Prosser, William L. *Handbook of the Law of Torts,* 4th ed. St. Paul, MN: West Publishing, 1971.

———. "Privacy." *California Law Review* 48 (1960): 383–430.

Rankin v. McPherson, 483 U.S. 378 (1987).

Reamey, Gerald S. "When 'Special Needs' Meet Probable Cause: Denying the Devil Benefits of Law." *Hastings Constitutional Law Quarterly* 19 (1992): 295–341.

Reddington, Frances P., and Betsy Wright Kreisel. *Sexual Assault: The Victims, the Perpetrators, and the Criminal Justice System.* Durham, NC: Carolina Academic Press, 2005.

Reese, Renford. "The Multiple Causes of the LAPD Rampart Scandal." *Journal of Interdisciplinary Studies* 16 (2003): 85–97.

Regini, Lisa A. "Disclosing Officer Misconduct: A Constitutional Duty." *FBI Law Enforcement Bulletin* 65 (1996): 27–32.

Reichel, Philip L. *Comparative Criminal Justice Systems: A Topical Approach,* 5th ed. Upper Saddle River, NJ: Pearson/Prentice-Hall, 2008.

Reid, Sue Titus. *Criminal Law,* 7th ed. Los Angeles, CA: Roxbury Publishing, 2007.

Reske, Henry J. "Verdict on Simpson Trial: Observers Say Prosecution Lost the Case over a Bloody Glove, Racist Cop." *ABA Journal* 81 (1995): 48–51.

Rhode Island v. Innis, 446 U.S. 291 (1980).

Riggins v. Nevada, 504 U.S. 127 (1992).

Roberg, Roy R., Kenneth J. Novak, and Gary W. Cordner. *Police and Society,* 4th ed. New York: Oxford University Press, 2009.

Roberson, Cliff. *Criminal Procedure Today,* 2nd ed. Upper Saddle River, NJ: Prentice-Hall, 2003.

Roberts v. United States Jaycees, 468 U.S. 609 (1984).

Rochin v. California, 342 U.S. 165 (1952).

Rock v. Arkansas, 483 U.S. 44 (1987).

Rogers v. Richmond, 365 U.S. 534 (1961).

Roper v. Simmons, 543 U.S. 551 (2005).

Rosen, Jeffrey. *The Unwanted Gaze: The Destruction of Privacy in America.* New York: Random House, 2000.

Ruffin v. Commonwealth, 62 Va. 790 (1871).

Ruiz, Jim, and Kathleen H. Winters. "The USA Patriot Act: A Review of the Major Components." In *Current Legal Issues in Criminal Justice,* edited by Craig Hemmens, 29–43. Los Angeles, CA: Roxbury Publishing, 2007.

Rutland, Robert Allen. *The Birth of the Bill of Rights 1776–1791.* New York: Collier Books, 1962.

Saferstein, Richard. *Criminalistics: An Introduction to Forensic Science,* 9th ed. Upper Saddle River, NJ: Pearson/Prentice-Hall, 2007.

Samaha, Joel. *Criminal Law,* 9th ed. Belmont, CA: Thomson/Wadsworth Publishing, 2008.

Samson v. California, 547 U.S. 843 (2006).

San Miguel, Claudia. "Drug Tests, the Fourth Amendment, and Supreme Court's Rationale for Warrantless and Suspicionless Searches." In *Current Legal Issues in Criminal Justice,* edited by Craig Hemmens, 71–82 (Los Angeles, CA: Roxbury Publishing Company, 2007).

Schenck v. United States, 249 U.S. 47 (1919).

Schmalleger, Frank. *Criminal Justice: A Brief Introduction,* 7th ed. Upper Saddle River, NJ: Pearson/Prentice-Hall, 2008.

———. *Criminal Law Today: An Introduction with Capstone Cases,* 3rd ed. Upper Saddle River, NJ: Pearson/Prentice-Hall, 2006.

Schmerber v. California, 384 U.S. 457 (1966).

Schneckloth v. Bustamonte, 412 U.S. U.S. 218 (1973).

Searle, Lynn S. "The Administrative Search from Dewey to Burger: Dismantling the Fourth Amendment." *Hastings Constitutional Law Quarterly* 16 (1989): 261–84.

See v. City of Seattle, 387 U.S. 541 (1967).

Seling, Superintendent, Special Commitment Center v. Young, 531 U.S. 250 (2001).

Serr, Brian J. "Great Expectations of Privacy: A New Model for Fourth Amendment Protection." *Minnesota Law Review* 73 (1989): 583–642.

Shattuck, John H. F. *Rights of Privacy.* Skokie, IL: National Textbook Co, 1977.

Silverthorne Lumber Company v. United States, 251 U.S. 385 (1920).

Skinner v. Railway Labor Executives Association, 489 U.S. 602 (1989).

Slobogin, Christopher. "Public Privacy: Camera Surveillance of Public Places and the Right to Anonymity." *Mississippi Law Journal* 72 (2002): 213–315.

Smith, Andrew J. "Unconstitutional Conditional Release: A Pyrrhic Victory for Arrestees' Privacy Rights under *United States v. Scott.*" *William and Mary Law Review* 48 (2007): 2365–99.

Smith, Christopher E., and Thomas R. Hensley. "Assessing the Conservatism of the Rehnquist Court." *Judicature* 77 (1993): 83–90.

Solove, Daniel. "A Taxonomy of Privacy." *University of Pennsylvania Law Review* 154 (2006): 477–591.

Solove, Daniel J., Marc Rotenberg, and Paul M. Schwartz. *Information Privacy Law.* New York: Aspen Publishers, 2006.

South Dakota v. Opperman, 428 U.S. 364 (1976).

Spano v. New York, 360 U.S. 315 (1959).

Speiser v. Randall, 357 U.S. 513 (1958).

Spinelli v. United States, 393 U.S. 410 (1969).

Stanley v. Georgia, 394 U.S. 557 (1969).

Stanz, Robert, and Richard Tewksbury. "Predictors of Success and Recidivism in a Home Incarceration Program." *The Prison Journal* 80 (2000): 326–46.

Steblay, Nancy M., Jennifer Dysart, Solomon Fulero, and R. C. L. Lindsay. "Eyewitness Accuracy Rates in Police Showup and Lineup Presentations: A Meta-Analytic Comparison." *Law and Human Behavior* 27 (2003): 523–40.

Steele v. United States, 267 U.S. 498 (1925).

Stovall v. Denno, 388 U.S. 293 (1967).

Strickler v. Greene, 527 U.S. 263 (1999).

Sykes, Gresham M. *The Society of Captives: A Study of a Maximum Security Prison.* Princeton, NJ: Princeton University Press, 1958.

Taylor, Erich. "A New Wave of Police Interrogation? 'Brain Fingerprinting,' the Constitutional Privilege Against Self-incrimination and Hearsay Jurisprudence." *University of Illinois Journal of Law, Technology & Policy* Fall (2006): 287–312.

Taylor v. Alabama, 457 U.S. 687 (1982).

Terry v. Ohio, 392 U.S. 1 (1968).

Texas v. Brown, 460 U.S. 730 (1983).

Texas v. Johnson, 491 U.S. 397 (1989).

The 9/11 Commission Report, *Final Report of the National Commission on Terrorist Attacks upon the United States: Executive Summary,* 2004, http://www.9-11 commission.gov/report/911Report_Exec.pdf.

Thornburgh v. Abbott, 490 U.S. 402 (1989).

Thornton v. United States, 541 U.S. 615 (2004).

Townsend v. Sain, 372 U.S. 293 (1963).

Travis, Lawrence F., and Robert H. Langworthy. *Policing in America: A Balance of Forces,* 4th ed. Upper Saddle River, NJ: Pearson/Prentice-Hall, 2008.

Trojanowicz, Robert C., Victor E. Kappeler, and Larry K. Gaines. *Community Policing: A Contemporary Perspective,* 3rd ed. Cincinnati, OH: Anderson, 2002.

Turner v. Safley, 482 U.S. 78 (1987).

Ulmer, S. Sidney. "Government Litigants, Underdogs, and Civil Liberties in the Supreme Court 1903–1968." *Journal of Politics* 47 (1985): 899–910.

Union Pacific Railway Co. v. Botsford, 141 U.S. 250 (1891).

United States v. Agurs, 427 U.S. 97 (1976).

United States v. Arvizu, 534 U.S. 266 (2002).

United States v. Bagley, 473 U.S. 667 (1985).

United States v. Banks, 540 U.S. 31 (2003).

United States v. Biswell, 406 U.S. 311 (1972).

United States v. Brignoni-Ponce, 422 U.S. 873 (1975).

United States v. Calandra, 414 U.S. 338 (1974).

United States v. Chadwick, 433 U.S. 1 (1977).

United States v. Cortez, 449 U.S. 411 (1981).

United States v. Dionisio, 410 U.S. 1 (1973).

United States v. Drayton, 536 U.S. 194 (2002).

United States v. Flores-Montano, 541 U.S. 149 (2004).

United States v. Karo, 468 U.S. 705 (1984).

United States v. Knights, 534 U.S. 112 (2001).

United States v. Knotts, 460 U.S. 276 (1983).

United States v. Lefkowitz, 285 U.S. 452 (1932).

United States v. Leon, 468 U.S. 897 (1984).

United States v. Mara, 410 U.S. 19 (1973).

United States v. Martinez-Fuerte, 428 U.S. 543 (1976).

United States v. Mendenhall, 446 U.S. 544 (1980).

United States v. Montoya de Hernandez, 473 U.S. 531 (1985).

United States v. Ortiz, 422 U.S. 891 (1975).

United States v. Owens, 484 U.S. 554 (1988).

United States v. Patane, 542 U.S. 630 (2004).

United States v. Rabinowitz, 339 U.S. 56 (1950).

United States v. Ramsey, 431 U.S. 606 (1977).

United States v. Ross, 456 U.S. 798 (1982).

United States v. Salerno, 481 U.S. 739 (1987).

United States v. Tucker, 404 U.S. 443 (1972).

United States v. Wade, 388 U.S. 218 (1967).

Vale v. Louisiana, 399 U.S. 30 (1970).

Vaughn, Michael S., and Rolando V. del Carmen. "'Special Needs' in Criminal Justice: An Evolving Exception to the Fourth Amendment Warrant and Probable Cause Requirements." *George Mason Civil Rights Law Journal* 3 (1993): 203–26.

Vernonia School District 47J v. Acton, 515 U.S. 646 (1995).

Walker, Samuel, and Michael Harrington. "Police DNA 'Sweeps': A Proposed Model Policy on Police Requests for DNA Samples." *Police Professionalism Initiative, University of Nebraska at Omaha* (2005), 1–19. http://www.unomaha.edu/criminaljustice/PDF/dnamodelpolicyfinal.pdf.

Warden v. Hayden, 387 U.S. 294 (1967).

Wardius v. Oregon, 412 U.S. 470 (1973).

Warren, Samuel D., and Louis D. Brandeis. "The Right to Privacy." *Harvard Law Review* 4 (1890): 193–220.

Washington v. Harper, 494 U.S. 210 (1990).

Weeks v. United States, 232 U.S. 383 (1914).

Weinstein, Michael A. "The Uses of Privacy in the Good Life." In *Privacy*, edited by Roland Pennock and John Chapman, 94–118. New York: Atherton Press, 1971.

Westin, Alan F. *Privacy and Freedom*. New York: Atheneum, 1967.

Whitaker, Reg. "After 9/11: A Surveillance State?" In *Lost Liberties: Ashcroft and the Assault on Personal Freedom*, edited by Cynthia Brown, 52–74. New York: The New Press, 2003.

White, Jonathon R. *Terrorism and Homeland Security*, 5th ed. Belmont, CA: Wadsworth Publishing, 2006.

Whitehead, John W., and Steven H. Aden. "Forfeiting Enduring Freedom for Homeland Security: A Constitutional Analysis of the USA Patriot Act and the Justice Department's Anti-Terrorism Initiatives," *American University Law Review* 51 (2002): 1081–133.

Whitley v. Albers, 475 U.S. 312 (1986).

Whren v. United States, 517 U.S. 806 (1996).

Williams v. New York, 337 U.S. 241 (1949).

Wilson, Melanie D. "The Price of Pretrial Release: Can We Afford to Keep Our Fourth Amendment Rights?" *Iowa Law Review* 92 (2007): 159–211.

Wilson v. Arkansas, 514 U.S. 927 (1995).

Winick, Bruce J., and John Q. LaFond. *Protecting Society from Sexually Dangerous Offenders: Law, Justice, and Therapy*. Washington, DC: American Psychological Association, 2003.

Winston v. Lee, 470 U.S. 753 (1985).

Wise, Richard A., Kirsten A. Dauphinais, and Martin A. Safer. "A Tripartite Solution to Eyewitness Error." *Journal of Criminal Law and Criminology* 97 (2007): 807–71.

Wolfe, Christopher. *Judicial Activism: Bulwark of Freedom or Precarious Security*. Lanham, MD: Rowman & Littlefield, 1997.

Wolf v. Colorado, 338 U.S. 25 (1949).

Wolff v. McDonnell, 418 U.S. 539 (1974).

Wong Sun v. United States, 371 U.S. 471 (1963).

Wyoming v. Houghton, 526 U.S. 295 (1999).

Zuck, Karen E. "HIV and Medical Privacy: Government Infringement on Prisoners' Constitutional Rights." *University of Pennsylvania Journal of Constitutional Law* 9 (2007): 1277–96.

INDEX

Adam Walsh Child Protection and Safety Act of 2006, 108. *See also* Sex offender

Administrative search, 21–23. *See also Camara v. Municipal Court*

Aguilar-Spinelli rule, 19–20

Airline passenger surveillance, 173; passenger name record, 174; Secure Flight program, 174; United States Visitor and Immigrant Status Indicator Technology (US-VISIT program), 175. *See also* Public space: public transportation search

Albright v. Oliver, 75

Anglo-American law: history of, 1–3; privacy rights in American law, 3–5

Antiterrorism laws, 167–71

Arrest: elements of, 61; number of, 60; related exigencies, 62–63; search incident to, 26–27

Attorney-client privilege, 89; privileged communication, 89; victim counseling, 156. *See also* Probation: self-incrimination privilege

Atwater v. City of Lago Vista, 53

At-will employment, 124; employee political association, 143

Automated Fingerprint Identification System (AFIS), 69, 176

Automated License Plate Recognition (ALPR), 178–79

Automated Targeting System (ATS), 182

Backscatter x-ray, 174, 189

Bail: Bail Reform Act of 1984, 80; categories of, 76; pretrial release, 76

Balancing of competing interests test, 11–12; employer regulation, 124, 148; inmate rights, 113; public safety, 121; value of, 12

Balint v. Carson City, Nevada, 148

Banks v. Dretke, 93

Baron v. Meloni, 123, 140

Bell v. Wolfish, 64, 75, 115

Berger v. New York, 165–66

Berkemer v. McCarty, 72

Bertillon, Alphonse, xix, 176

Big Brother, xviii, 39, 192. *See also* George Orwell

Bill of Rights, xiv–xv, 3

Biographical information, 175, 181–82, 190–92; identity, 183. *See also* REAL ID Act of 2005

Biometric, xxiv, 175–78; arrestee sample, 68; Automated Biometric System, 182; behavioral modalities, 177–78; grand jury subpoena of, 84–85; measuring technology, 175; physiological modalities, 176–77; probation and parole collection of, 105–6. *See also* DNA

Body fluid, 68–71; inmate HIV/AIDS, 119–20; warrantless collection of, 69. *See also Schmerber v. California*

Body geometry, 176–77

Bohach v. City of Reno, 130

Booking process, 74–75

Booth v. State of Maryland, 146

Border checkpoint, 55–57; search at, 55. *See also* Airline passenger surveillance

Bowers v. Hardwick, 141

Brady v. Maryland, 192

Brain scanning, xix

Brandeis, Louis, xiv, xxi, 4–5

Branti v. Finkel, 143

Breathalyzer™, 48

Breithaupt v. Abram, 70

Brendlin v. California, 52

Brennan, William, xiii, 66

Breyer, Stephen, 63

Broderick v. Police Commissioner of Boston, 136

Bryant, Kobe, 149, 155

California v. Ciraolo, 8, 58

California v. Greenwood, 8

California v. Hodari D., 44, 61

Camara v. Municipal Court, 22

Camarillo v. McCarthy, 120

Cardwell v. Lewis, 47

Carnivore program, 180

Carroll v. United States, 29, 52

Case disposition, 73–74; police criminal, 73

Chimel v. California, 26, 61

City of Indianapolis v. Edmond, 54, 171

Civil Rights Act of 1964, 147

Clark, Tom, 37

Closed circuit television (CCTV), 57–58, 171; workplace surveillance using, 128–29

Colonnade Catering Corp. v. United States, 22

Color of law, 113, 124

Combined DNA Index System (CODIS), 69, 176

Common law, xiv, 1–2

Communications Assistance for Law Enforcement Act of 1994 (CALEA), 167

Community-based corrections, 100–101

Computer surveillance, 179–80; law enforcement access to, 166–67. *See also* Communications Assistance for Law Enforcement Act of 1994; Electronic Communications Privacy Act of 1986; Patriot Act of 2001

Confrontation clause, 89–90; evidence of, 89; probation and parole revocation hearing, 111. *See also* Evidence: motion to suppress

Connecticut Department of Public Safety, et al. v. Doe, individually and on behalf of all others similarly situated, 109

Connick v. Myers, 144

Consent search, 26

Cooper v. Pate, 113–14

Couch v. United States, 86

Coy v. Iowa, 89

Crime measurement, 73, 150–51, 157

Crime victim: Crime Victims' Rights Act of 2004, 152; legal rights of, 151–52; personal data theft, 157–58; privacy rights of, 152–53; victimization in America, 151

Criminal justice, xxiv, xvii; President's Commission on Law Enforcement and Administration of Justice, xvii; social and political influences on, xvi; system, xv

Criminal justice personnel. *See* Personnel

Cruel and unusual punishment, 100

Cupp v. Murphy, 11, 28

Custodial interrogation. *See Miranda v. Arizona*

Dalia v. United States, 164

Data mining, 180–83, 192; programs, 181

Dataveillance, 180–81, 190

Davis v. Mississippi, 59

Dawson v. Delaware, 97

Day, William, 37

Delaware v. Prouse, 46, 54

Discovery, 90–91; *See also* Evidence

DNA, xix, 176; arrestee collection of, 68–69; grand jury subpoena of, 84–85; police identification sample collection of, 59; probation and parole collection of, 105–6. *See also* Biometric; Combined DNA Index System

Does I Thru XXIII v. Advanced Textile Corp., 154

Driving under the influence of alcohol or drug, 47–49; field sobriety test, 48–49. *See also* Breathalyzer™

Drug testing: employee, 131–32; pretrial release, 79; probation and parole, 105; public safety employee programs, 132–34

Electronic Communications Privacy Act of 1986, 129–30, 166

Electronic monitoring and supervision: prerelease, 81; probation and parole, 107

Electronic surveillance: federal laws, 164–65; methods, 175; recognition technology, 178–79. *See also* Closed circuit television; Communications Assistance for Law Enforcement Act of 1994; Electronic Communications Privacy Act of 1986; Patriot Act of 2001

Elrod v. Burns, 143

Employee Polygraph Protection Act of 1988, 134

Employee regulation. *See* Personnel

Employment relationship: classification, 124. *See also* At-will employment

Evidence: categories of, 33; collection of, 32; defendant access to exculpatory, 92–95; discovery rules, 90–91; exemplar, 35, 68, 84; impeaching, 32, 91; motion to suppress, 91–92; types of seizable, 34; use in trial for conviction, 32. *See also* Confrontation clause; *Miranda v. Arizona*

Exclusionary rule, 36–37; exceptions to, 37–38; Fruits of the Poisonous Tree Doctrine, 37. *See also Miranda v. Arizona; United States v. Patane*

Exigent search, 27–28, 62–63

Expectation of privacy, 1, 7–8, 171, 189, 191; hierarchy of, 9–10

Eye scanning, 177. *See also* Biometric

Facial analysis, 176, 179

Farwell, Lawrence, xix

Faulds, Henry, xix

Federal Communications Act of 1934, 164

Federal privacy law, 163

Ferguson v. City of Charleston, 10

Field sobriety test. *See* Driving under the influence of alcohol or drug

Fifth Amendment: due process, 4, 96; grand jury investigation, 83; self-incrimination, 34, 38, 85–86, 96, 110, 135. *See also Miranda v. Arizona*

First Amendment: employee appearance, 145–46; employee association, 138–39, 142; employee religious practice, 147–48; employee speech, 143–45; rights in public, 40

Florida v. Bostick, 42, 55

Florida Star v. B.J.F., 153–54

Foreign Intelligence Surveillance Act (FISA), 168

Fourth Amendment, 3; core principles, 17–18; criminal proceedings, 95–96; execution of search warrant, 20–21; probable cause, 19; privacy right, 16–17; warrant exceptions, 21–30; warrant requirements, 18–19. *See also* Search and seizure

Frankfurter, Felix, 70, 72

Fraternal Order of Police, 142

Fraternal Order of Police Newark Lodge No. 12 v. City of Newark, 145

Freedom of Information Act (FOIA), 163–64

Fruits of the Poisonous Tree Doctrine. *See* Exclusionary rule

Fugate v. Phoenix Civil Service Board, 140

Fusion center, 182, 190

Gagnon v. Scarpelli, 111

Gardner v. Broderick, 134

Gardner v. Florida, 99
Garrity v. New Jersey, 134, 136
Gerstein v. Pugh, 76
Gideon v. Wainwright, 88
Giglio v. United States, 93
Globalization effect, xvii, 160–61, 186–87
Goldberg, Arthur, 85
Grand jury, 83–86
Green River Killer, 31
Griffin v. Wisconsin, 103
Griswold v. Connecticut, 4

Handwriting analysis, 178
Harlan, John Marshall, II, 1, 8
Harrison Narcotics Act of 1914, 160
Hayes v. Florida, 59
Henry, Edward, xix
Hiibel v. Sixth Judicial District Court of Nevada, 43
HIV/AIDS, 119–20
Hoffman v. United States, 85
Holmes, Oliver Wendell, 40
Homeland Security Act of 2002, 169
Horton v. California, 29
Hudson v. McMillian, 118
Hudson v. Palmer, 74, 116
Hume, David, xxiii

Identification detention, 58–60
Identity theft, 157
Illinois v. Allen, 89
Illinois v. Caballes, 51
Illinois v. Fisher, 93
Illinois v. Gates, 19
Illinois v. Lidster, 55
Illinois v. McArthur, 63
Illinois v. Perkins, 72
Inmate: control measures, 117–19; medical condition and record, 119–20; philosophy of rights, 112–13; prison regulations, 114–15; privacy rights, 113–14; private activities, 117; search of, 115–16
Intelligence Reform and Terrorism Prevention Act of 2004, 169–70

Inturri v. City of Hartford, 146
Investigative practices, 35–36

Jackson v. Howell, 140
Jaffe v. Redmond, 156
Jeffreys, Alec, xix, 176
Johnson v. Phelan, 117
Judicial analysis, 10–13
Judicial contact, 75; initial hearing, 76

Kansas v. Hendricks, 107
Katz v. United States, 1, 8, 165–66, 171
Kelley v. Johnson, 145
Kennedy, Anthony, 12, 141
Keylogger program, 180
Keystroke analysis, 178
Kilpatrick, Kwame, 77–78
Kohler v. Englade, 60
Kyllo v. United States, 17, 58

Lawrence v. Texas, 141–42
Lee, Rudolph, xiii
Lineup. *See* Pretrial identification
Los Angeles Police Department Rampart Division, 36, 94

MacWade v. Kelly, 172
Magic Lantern method, 180
Mapp, v. Ohio, 37
Marshall, Thurgood, xxi
Maryland v. Buie, 62
Maryland v. Craig, 90
Maryland v. Pringle, 11, 53
Massiah v. United States, 87–88
McClellan, Jack, xvi
Megan's Law, 108. *See also* Sex offender
Mercer v. City of Cedar Rapids, 139
Michigan Department of State Police v. Sitz, 53
Mincey v. Arizona, 28
Minnesota v. Dickerson, 45
Minnesota v. Murphy, 110
Miranda v. Arizona: exceptions to, 72–73; officer questioning, 42; suppressed evidence, 38; testimonial evidence, 71–72; warning, 49, 67, 71. *See also*

Fifth Amendment; *United States v. Patane*
Monroe v. Pape, 113
Moore v. Illinois, 96
Morrissey v. Brewer, 111
Motor vehicle: police traffic encounter, 45–47; search exception, 29; warrantless search of, 49–53. *See also* Search and seizure
Murphy v. Waterfront Comm'n, 85
Murray v. United States, 38

Narcoterrorism, 162
National Crime Victimization Survey (NCVS), 150–51, 157. *See also* Crime measurement
National Security Letter (NSL), 168
National Treasury Employees Union v. Von Raab, 12, 132–34
Net of suspicion, xxi, 159, 162, 183, 189–90, 192
New Jersey v. T.L.O., 25, 172
New privacy paradigm, xvii, xx, xxiv, 13, 185, 189, 192
New York v. Belton, 61
New York v. Burger, 22
New York v. Class, 50
New York v. Quarles, 72
Nifong, Mike, 94–95
9/11, xx, 12–13, 160–62, 167, 170, 172, 183, 187–89
Nontraditional suspect, 159–60

O'Brien v. DiGrazia, 137
O'Connor, Sandra Day, 11, 42, 54, 74, 97, 114, 126, 171
O'Connor v. Ortega, 11, 126–27, 132, 148
Oliver v. United States, 9
Olmstead v. United States, xiii, xxi, 4, 7
Omnibus Crime Control and Safe Streets Act of 1968, 165
Orwell, George, xviii, 39, 192; Orwellian effect, 160

Pappas v. Giuliani, 145
Parole. *See* Probation

Parrott v. District of Columbia, 147
Passenger name record, 174
Patriot Act of 2001, 167–69
Pedestrian: police contact of, 41–42, questioning of, 42–43; stop and detention of, 43–44; *Terry* frisk search, 44–45. *See also Terry v. Ohio*
Pen Register Act, 166; device, 164, 168, 180
People v. Bryant, 155–56
People v. Hall, 64
Personal data, 157
Personnel: appearance, 143–45; classification, 124–25; compulsory questioning of, 134–35; disclosure of personal matters, 135–37; drug testing of, 131–34; electronic surveillance, 128–31; fraternization, 140–41; intimate association and sexual conduct, 138–39, 141–42; political association, 142–43; polygraph, 134–35; regulation of, 125–26; religious practice, 147–48; search of, 126–28; speech and expression, 143–46
Pickering v. Board of Education, 144
Plain view, 29–30, 50
Plessy v. Ferguson, 11
Police detention, 43–44. *See also Terry v. Ohio*
Presentence investigation, 98–100
Pretrial identification, 65–68
Pretrial release: conditions of, 78–81; electronic supervision, 81–83; process, 76–78
Preventive law enforcement, 162, 172, 191
Prison. *See* Inmate
Privacy: American law, in, xiv, 3–5; boundaries of, xviii; concept of, 5–6; crime control, xvii; criminal justice, xvi; criminal law, in, 6–7; during adjudication, 88–89; inviolate personality, 5; 9/11, xx; right to, xv, 3, 5; tort law, 6. *See also* Expectation of privacy

Privacy Act of 1974, 158, 163–64
Privacy-criminal justice relationship,
  xx–xxi, xxiii, 185, 190
Privileged communication, 89; victim
  counseling, 156. *See also*
  Attorney-client privilege; Probation:
  self-incrimination privilege
Probable cause, 11, 19; *See also* Fourth
  Amendment
Probation: conditions of, 101–3; DNA
  collection, 105–6; drug testing, 105;
  electronic monitoring, 107;
  revocation of, 111–12; search, 103–4;
  self-incrimination privilege, 110–11
Protective sweep, 62
Public space: closed circuit television,
  171; public transportation search,
  172; regulating behavior in, 39–41;
  school monitoring, 172–73;
  suspicionless search in, 171–72;
  technology-assisted search in, 57–58.
  See also Airline passenger surveillance;
  Search and seizure

Quon v. Arch Wireless, 131

Radio Frequency Identification Device
  (RFID), 170
Rankin v. McPherson, 144
Rape shield law: counseling communica-
  tion privilege, 156–57; victim
  identity, 153–55; victim sexual
  history, 155–56
Rathert v. Village of Peotone, 146
REAL ID Act of 2005, 170, 179, 182
Reasonableness standard, 10–11
Recognition technology, 178–79
Rehnquist, William, 56, 109, 115
Ridgway, Gary, 31
Riggins v. Nevada, 97
Riggs v. City of Fort Worth, 146
Right to be let alone, xiii–xiv
Roadblock, police, 53
Roberts v. United States Jaycees, 137
Rochin v. California, 69
Rodriguez v. City of Chicago, 147

Rogers v. Richmond, 72
Roper v. Simmons, 39
Rousseau, Jean-Jacques, xxiii
Ruffin v. Commonwealth, 113
Ryan v. Department of Justice, 147

Samson v. California, 104
Scalia, Antonin, 39, 44, 46, 78
Schenck v. United States, 40
Schmerber v. California, 10, 49–50, 63–
  64, 68, 70
School search, 172–73. *See also New
  Jersey v. T.L.O.*
Search and seizure: administrative,
  21–23; computer search, 179–80;
  consent, 26; employee, 126–28;
  exigent, 27–28, 62–63; incident to
  arrest, 26–27; invasive, 63–65;
  inventory, 26–27; motor vehicle, 29,
  45–53; plain view, 29–30, 50; public
  transportation, 172; school, 172–73;
  sneak and peek, 168; stop and frisk,
  23–24; suspicionless, 171–72;
  technology-assisted, 57–58; warrant,
  18–21; warrantless, 21, 49–53
Secure flight program, 174
Security-surveillance complex, 190
See v. Seattle, 22
Self-incrimination. *See* Fifth Amend-
  ment
*Seling, Superintendent, Special
  Commitment Center v. Young,* 108
Sex offender: civil commitment of, 107–
  8; Megan's Law, 108; registration of,
  108–9. *See also* Adam Walsh Child
  Protection and Safety Act of 2006
Sherman v. Jones, 120
Simpson, O. J., 33–34
Sixth Amendment, 88
Sneak and peek warrant, 168, 180
Souter, David, 52–53
Speaker recognition, 177
Special needs beyond law enforcement,
  24–25, 163, 172–73, 190
Speiser v. Randall, 40
Stanley v. Georgia, 4

Stevens, John Paul, 10, 15, 17, 29
Stewart, Potter, 18, 87
Stop and frisk, 23, 43–44, 50. *See also* *Terry v. Ohio*
Stored Communications Act, 166
Stovall v. Denno, 66
Surreptitious recording, 73
Surveillance effects, 183

Technology: adaptation, 187–88; assisted search, 57–58; crime fighting, in, xviii–xx; crime transformation, 186; recognition, 178–79
Terrorism: laws, 167–70; 9/11, 161–63; privacy, xx; threat, 187–89
Terry v. Ohio, 11, 18, 23. *See also* Stop and frisk
Texas v. Brown, 17
Thornton v. United States, 62, 78
Threat adaptation, 188–89
Tort law, 2, 6
Total Information Awareness, 182
Totality of circumstances, 19–20
Transactional information, xxiv, 160, 163, 181, 190
Transnational crime, xvii, 160–61, 187–89
Trap and trace device, 164, 168, 180
Turner v. Safely, 114, 120

Überveillance, 192
Uniform Crime Reports (UCR), 150; case disposition, 73
Union Pacific Railway Company v. Botsford, 5
United Nations Convention against Organized Crime, 161
United States v. Agurs, 92
United States v. Banks, 20
United States v. Belton, 61
United States v. Biswell, 22
United States v. Brignoni-Ponce, 57
United States v. Dionisio, 68, 84
United States v. Flores-Montano, 57

United States v. Hunnicutt, 46
United States v. Kincade, 106
United States v. Knights, 103
United States v. Knotts, 46, 58
United States v. Lefkowitz, 3
United States v. Martinez-Fuente, 9, 54
United States v. Mendenhall, 42, 55
United States v. Montoya de Hernandez, 56
United States v. Patane, 38
United States v. Rabinowitz, 18
United States v. Ramsey, 56
United States v. Ross, 15
United States v. Scott, 80
United States v. Slanina, 130
United States v. Sokolow, 56
United States v. Taketa, 128
United States v. Tucker, 99
United States v. Waite, 126
United States v. White, 73
U.S. v. Edwards, 174
United States Visitor and Immigrant Status Indicator Technology (US-VISIT program), 175, 179, 182

Venters v. City of Delphi, 148
Violent Crime Control and Law Enforcement Act of 1994, 108
Virginia Tech shooting, 173

Warden v. Hayden, 28
Wardius v. Oregon, 94
Warren, Earl, 11, 24, 113
Warren, Samuel, xiv, 5
Washington v. Harper, 118
Weaver v. Henderson, 145
Weeks v. United States, 36
Whistleblowing, 144
White, Byron, 62
Whitley v. Albers, 117
Whren v. United States, 46
Williams v. New York, 99
Wilson v. Arkansas, 20
Winston v. Lee, 9, 63, 70

ABOUT THE AUTHOR

WILLIAM P. BLOSS is Professor of Criminal Justice and Director of the International Criminal Justice Studies Program at The Citadel in Charleston, South Carolina. Dr. Bloss has numerous academic and government publications on law and criminal justice topics including his latest book, *Transnational Crime and Terrorism in a Global Context* (2006). Dr. Bloss is actively involved in teaching, research, and consulting with government agencies. He is an advisor to international and U.S. academic publications and has been nationally recognized for teaching excellence. He regularly acts as a print and broadcast media source and public speaker on crime and criminal justice issues, both nationally and internationally.